sweet, sour : gū lōu yuhk gai
enoki mushroom gām gū
yím chāh
yím jau

Colloquial
Cantonese

The Colloquial Series

Series Adviser: Gary King

The following languages are available in the Colloquial series:

Afrikaans	Finnish	Portuguese of
Albanian	French	Brazil
Amharic	German	Romanian
* Arabic	Greek	Russian
(Levantine)	* Gujarati	Scottish Gaelic
Arabic of Egypt	Hebrew	Serbian
* Arabic of the	Hindi	Slovak
Gulf and Saudi	Hungarian	Slovene
Arabia	Icelandic	* Somali
* Basque	Indonesian	Spanish
Breton	Italian	Spanish of Latin
* Bulgarian	Japanese	America
Cambodian	Korean	Swahili
Cantonese	Latvian	Swedish
Catalan	Lithuanian	Tamil
Chinese	Malay	Thai
Croatian	Mongolian	Turkish
Czech	Norwegian	Ukrainian
Danish	* Panjabi	* Urdu
Dutch	Persian	Vietnamese
English	Polish	Welsh
Estonian	Portuguese	

Accompanying cassette(s) and CDs are available for all the above titles (cassettes only for the titles marked with *). They can be ordered through your bookseller, or send payment with order to Routledge Ltd, ITPS, Cheriton House, North Way, Andover, Hants SP10 5BE, or to Routledge Inc, 270 Madison Ave, New York, NY 10016, USA.

COLLOQUIAL CD-ROMs
Multimedia Language Courses
Available in: Chinese, French, Portuguese and Spanish

gwaan muhn deaih gāt 82 jō
dóu bai 114 gen
  136 btu douh
jāp jō lɛp 155 dogwo
ngàuh pā 177

hō jáau beer 139 shop

多行衣路以曲鬼
動行不義以自斃

selectronic
bookshop   go   个
supermarket   gān   catty   斤   about 500g
bakex
butcher/ticket jāun   bottle   樽
shoe shop   bāau   包
clothes shop
   hahp   盒
Amirtha   wūn   碗
Bhuvanendra   luhng   籠
Chris Neil   dihp   碟
Jonathan Kirby   zung   盅
   bohng   磅
   gūng gān   公斤
Filiberto
Perilli

Family   Present Past
Jobs   Past
Travel   Future
Holiday   Wh
Hotels Restaurant How
Shopping   How Many
Hobbies   How much
                classifier

Colloquial
Cantonese

The Complete Course
for Beginners

Keith S.T. Tong and Gregory James

Routledge
Taylor & Francis Group

LONDON AND NEW YORK

First published 1994
by Routledge
2 Park Square, Milton Park, Abingdon, Oxon, OX14 4RN

Simultaneously published in the USA and Canada
by Routledge
270 Madison Avenue, New York, NY 10016

Reprinted 1994, 1995, 1996 (with corrections), 1997, 1998, 1999, 2000
2003 (twice), 2005, 2006

Routledge is an imprint of the Taylor & Francis Group, an informa business

© 1994 Keith S. T. Tong and Gregory James

Typeset in Times by Florencetype Ltd, Stoodleigh, Devon

Printed and bound in Great Britain by Biddles Ltd, King's Lynn, Norfolk

British Library Cataloguing in Publication Data
A catalogue record for this book is available from the British Library

Library of Congress Cataloguing in Publication Data
A catalog record for this book has been requested

ISBN-10: 0-415-08202-1 (Book)
ISBN-10: 0-415-08203-X (Cassettes)
ISBN-10: 0-415-15532-0 (CDs)
ISBN-10: 0-415-08204-8 (Book, cassettes and CDs course)

ISBN-13: 978-0-415-08202-0 (Book)
ISBN-13: 978-0-415-08203-7 (Cassettes)
ISBN-13: 978-0-415-15532-8 (CDs)
ISBN-13: 978-0-415-08204-4 (Book, cassettes and CDs course)

Contents

Acknowledgements

We would like to thank our friends and colleagues for their help in the generation of this book: Elza Tsang Shuk-ching and Robert Davison for reading the proofs; Stephen Matthews and Virginia Yip for their comments on the content and presentation; Paul Best for his vivid illustrations; Wong Ping-kwong for his expert calligraphy; Amy Chi Man-lai, Tong Kin-kwok, Elza Tsang Shuk-ching and Kitty Wong Pui-yiu for their cassette-recording talents; Candice Poon Wai-yi for her patience; Shek Kin-shing for his technical expertise. We would also like to thank Simon Bell, Louisa Semlyen and Martin Barr of Routledge for their time and cooperation.

We are also indebted to several generations of students, whose inquisitiveness and percipience have provided invaluable insights into the structure of Cantonese and the way it is learned.

The preparation of any book entails an inevitable sacrifice of family life: we are grateful to our wives and families for their forbearance.

Introduction

Cantonese: language or dialect?

The 'Chinese language' is extremely diverse, yet the speakers of the different varieties of Chinese do not regard themselves as members of different linguistic communities. All the varieties of Chinese look towards a common 'standard' model, fundamentally the linguistic standards of the written language. In modern China, linguistic standards for speech have been based on the pronunciation of the capital, Beijing, and the national language of the People's Republic of China is called Putonghua, 'the common language', or Mandarin. Cantonese is that variety of Chinese which is spoken in wide areas of the southern coastal provinces of Guangdong (capital Guangzhou, or Canton) and Guangxi (capital Nanning), and in some neighboring places such as Hong Kong and Macao, as well as in numerous places in South-East Asia outside China proper, such as Cambodia, Indonesia, Malaysia, Singapore, Thailand and Vietnam. The latter half of the twentieth century has witnessed a great deal of accelerated emigration of Cantonese speakers, notably to Australia, Canada, New Zealand, the United Kingdom and the United States, and Cantonese is the dominant form of Chinese spoken in many families of the 'chinatowns' of the major cities in these countries. Indeed, in the United States, many of the early Chinese immigrants also trace their ancestry not only to Guangdong Province, but to one particular rural district, Taishan (about ninety kilometres southwest of Guangzhou), whose accessible harbor was used by American ships which came to recruit cheap labor along the Chinese coast in the middle of the nineteenth century.

Traditionally, Cantonese has been considered a 'dialect' of Chinese. However, this term is misleading, and tends to have more socio-political than linguistic significance. Over the four thousand and more years of the history of Chinese, the language has developed in different ways in the various regions of China. In particular, the regional varieties of the language that have emerged have been marked by their individual sound systems. Many of the varieties of modern Chinese are mutually incomprehensible when spoken, yet because of the uniformity of the written characters of the language, communication can often be effected successfully through the medium of writing. The situation, generalized throughout the language, is similar to, say, a Spanish speaker not understanding an English speaker saying the word 'five', yet comprehending fully the written figure '5'.

Some varieties of Chinese – like some varieties of English – enjoy more prestige in the language community than others. Ever since the Ming dynasty (1368–1644), by which time the Pearl River delta had become an important economic and cultural center, the Cantonese of Guangzhou has been an important variety of Chinese, and even the medium for an extensive vernacular literature, including ballads, epic poetry and some fiction writing. Although these styles are regarded as rustic by purists, their popularity has given rise to the generation of special written forms for Cantonese colloquialisms. Indeed, Cantonese is the only variety of Chinese (besides Mandarin) with widely recognized non-traditional written characters for such colloquial words and expressions. Such 'dialect writing' is disapproved of in the People's Republic of China, but is kept alive in the Cantonese press and other publications in Hong Kong and elsewhere. Many of the non-traditional characters of Cantonese are known throughout China – at least in the urban areas – and in the north the use of Cantonese colloquialisms, because of the association of this variety of Chinese with the West, through Hong Kong, adds a touch of exoticism or raciness to one's speech.

Cantonese is thus more than simply a dialect. It is a regional standard, with a national and an international prestige and currency not enjoyed by any other variety of Chinese, except Mandarin. In spite of the special written characters which have emerged, Cantonese remains essentially a spoken language, with no universally recognized written form. The language has several geographical dialects, distinguished largely by their phonological characteristics, but the 'Colloquial Cantonese' used in this book would be accepted by native speakers as a standard form of the language, as spoken in Hong Kong. Within this standard, there are levels of formality and informality in expression. We have aimed for a neutral style in speech, appropriate to a wide range of social and professional situations. In one or two instances, where the formal–informal distinction is significant, for example where the use of particular words in public broadcasting differs from the corresponding words that would be used in conversation, this has been pointed out.

Cantonese grammar

From several points of view, the grammar of Cantonese is extremely straightforward. Verbs do not conjugate for person or number, nor are there different forms for tense, mood or voice. Nouns and adjectives do not decline, and have no number, gender or case. There is no subject–verb or adjective–noun agreement. In short, Cantonese is refreshingly free of the bugbears that learners of European languages are so familiar with.

However, superficial simplicity of form does not mean that there is any less functional capability in the language. One can say in Cantonese anything that one would wish to say in English, or any other language; but the relationships between words and meanings which are made formally in English by, for example, inflection or agreements are expressed in different ways in Cantonese. Word order is important, and subject to more rigid regulation than English. Cantonese also possesses a series of 'classifiers' which identify objects largely by shape, and a rich repertoire of 'particles' which are used to express mood, emotion, attitude, etc. There are many multifunctional words, which can act as nouns, adjectives or verbs, depending upon the context (compare the various functions a word such as 'right' has in English); indeed, even the formal distinction between nouns, verbs and adjectives in Cantonese is often extremely blurred.

The varieties of Chinese show a great deal of syntactic uniformity. Yet, there do exist some significant differences amongst them. Cantonese and Mandarin, for example, differ in word order in certain constructions. In Cantonese the direct object precedes the indirect object, whereas the opposite obtains in Mandarin:

Cantonese:	**béi syū ngóh**
	give + book + (to) me
Mandarin:	**géi wǒ shū**
	give + (to) me + book.

Certain adverbs (such as **sīn** 'first') which precede the verb in Mandarin follow the verb in Cantonese (as in **heui sīn** 'go first' vs. Mandarin **xiān qù** 'first go'). Often the differences are more subtle: a Mandarin sentence pattern in Cantonese will sometimes be understood by native Cantonese speakers, but will nevertheless not be accepted as truly idiomatic. Conversely, colloquial Cantonese has a number of patterns that would not be linguistically acceptable in Mandarin.

Cantonese vocabulary

Cantonese, like all varieties of Chinese, is generally considered to be monosyllabic: almost every syllable carries meaning. Whilst there are many monosyllabic words (words of one syllable), it is by no means true, though, that every word is made up of one syllable: there are many words which are made up of two, or three, syllables, such as:

sáubīu	wristwatch
syutgwaih	refrigerator
fēigēichèuhng	airport
láahngheigēi	air conditioner

Whereas syllables in English are often individually meaningless, (e.g. '*syl-la-ble*', '*car-ries*'), syllables in Cantonese are largely individually meaningful:

sáubīu	**sáu** = 'hand' + **bīu** = 'watch'
syutgwaih	**syut** = 'snow' + **gwaih** = 'cupboard'

This is not always the case, and Cantonese has many examples of 'bound' syllables, which carry meaning only when they occur with other syllables:

bōlēi	glass
pùihwùih	to linger

Neither **bō** nor **lēi** nor **pùih** nor **wùih** carries any meaning apart from in these combinations. Similar examples in English are 'cranberry' or 'kith and kin'. The syllables 'cran-' and 'kith' have no individual meanings – that is, they cannot occur meaningfully alone – but they do have meaning when they occur with '-berry' and 'and kin' respectively.

Whilst most Cantonese vocabulary is the same as other varieties of Chinese, in some cases words which are common and everyday in Cantonese are seen as archaic and literary in Mandarin, for example:

mihn	face
hàahng	walk
sihk	eat
wah	say

At the same time, in recent history, Cantonese has, because of its socio-cultural contacts, borrowed a large number of words from other languages, especially English:

jyūgūlīk	chocolate
nèihlùhng	nylon
wàihtāmihng	vitamin
wāisihgéi	whisky

The sound system of Cantonese

The romanization adopted in this book, and in *Cantonese: A Comprehensive Grammar,* also published by Routledge, is the Yale system, which is a widely used and convenient learning tool. Note, however, that this is not the system generally found in official transliterations of personal and place names, where there has been little standardization over the centuries.

Below we list the various sounds of Cantonese, as they are transcribed in the Yale romanization. Two terms may need explanation: 'aspirated' and 'unreleased'. Aspirated consonants are pronounced with a puff of air, as in English 'p' in 'pan' and 'lip'. In some cases, such as, in English, after 's' ('span', 'spill'), the same consonants lose the puff of air and are unaspirated. At the end of a word they may not even be completed: the lips close to form the sound but do not open again to make the sound 'explode'; such sounds are termed 'unreleased'.

A more elaborate description of the Cantonese phonological system can be found in the *Comprehensive Grammar.*

Consonants

b   resembles the (unaspirated) 'p' in 'span', 'spill'; to an unaccustomed ear, an initial unaspirated *p* can often sound like 'b' in 'bill'.

d   resembles the (unaspirated) 't' in 'stand', 'still'.

g   resembles the (unaspirated) 'c' in 'scan', and 'k' 'skill'.

gw   resembles the 'qu' in 'squad', 'square'.
There is some evidence that this sound is becoming simplified over time, and words transcribed with **gw-** in this book may actually be heard, in the speech of some native-speakers, as beginning with **g-**. As a learner, you are advised to follow the pronunciation of the transcription.

j   an unaspirated sound something between 'ts' in 'cats' and 'tch' in 'catch'.

p   in initial position resembles the (aspirated) 'p' in 'pat', 'pin'; in final position, that is, at the end of a syllable, 'p' is unreleased.

t   in initial position resembles the (aspirated) 't' in 'top', 'tin'; in final position, 't' is unreleased.

k   in initial position resembles the 'k' in 'kick', 'kill'; in final position, 'k' is unreleased.

kw   a strongly aspirated plosive, resembles the 'qu' in 'quick', 'quill'.

ch   resembles the (aspirated) 'ch' in 'cheese', 'chill'.

f   resembles the 'f' in 'fan', 'scarf'.

s   resembles the 's' in 'sing', 'sit'.

h   (only in initial position in the syllable) resembles the 'h' in 'how', 'hand'. (Where it appears later in the syllable, 'h' is explained under Tone, below.)

l   resembles the 'l' in 'like', 'love'.

m   resembles the 'm' in 'man', 'stem'.

n   resembles the 'n' in 'now', 'nice'. There is a widespread tendency, particularly amongst the younger generation of Cantonese speakers, to replace an initial **n** by **l**, and there is consequently some variation in pronunciation: many words, which are transcribed with an initial letter *n* in this book may be heard as beginning with *l* for instance **néih** 'you', may be heard as **léih**. As a learner, you are advised to follow the pronunciation of the transcription.

ng   resembles the southern British English pronunciation of 'ng' as in 'sing' (that is, without pronouncing the 'g' separately). This sound occurs only after vowels in English, but in

Cantonese it can also occur at the beginning of syllables. However, many native speakers do not pronounce this sound initially. And, just as in English, a final **-ng**, particularly after the long vowel **aa**, is often replaced by **-n**, although this variation does not have the social connotation it has in British English (cf. runnin' and jumpin').

y   resembles the 'y' in 'yes', 'yellow'.
w   resembles the 'w' in 'wish', 'will'.

Vowels

a   resembles the 'u' in the southern British English pronunciation of 'but'.

aa   resembles the southern British English 'a' in 'father'. When this sound is not followed by a consonant in the same syllable, the second **a** of the **aa** is omitted in writing: **fā** is pronounced as if it were 'faa'.

e   resembles the 'e' of 'ten'.

eu   resembles the French 'eu' as in 'feu', or the German 'ö' as in 'schön'. It is pronounced like the 'e' of 'ten', but with rounded lips.

i   resembles the 'ee' of 'deep'.

o   resembles the 'aw' in 'saw'.

u   resembles the 'u' in the southern British English 'put'.

yu   resembles the French 'u' as in 'tu', or the German 'ü' as in 'Tür'. It is pronounced like the 'ee' of 'deep', but with the lips rounded instead of spread.

Diphthongs

The diphthongs consist of the vowels in different combinations:

ai   **a + i**, a combination of 'a' plus 'i', a very short diphthong, much shorter than the sound of 'y' in 'my'.

aai   **aa + i**, resembling the 'ie' in 'lie'.

au   **a + u**, resembling the 'ou' in 'out'.

aau   **aa + u**, resembling a long 'ou' in 'ouch!'

eui   **eu + i**, a combination of 'eu' plus 'i', something like the hesitation form 'er' in English (without the 'r' sound) followed by 'ee': 'e(r)-ee'.

iu   **i + u**, a combination of 'i' plus 'u', something like 'yew' in English.

oi   o + i, resembling the 'oy' in 'boy'.
ou   o + u, resembling the 'oe' in 'foe'.
ui   u + i, resembling the 'ooey' in 'phooey'.

Tone ▣

Cantonese is a *tone language*. This means that the same syllable pronounced on different pitches, or with different voice contours, carries different meanings. Consider first an example from English. To agree with someone, you might say simply, 'Yes.' The voice tends to fall, from a mid-level to a low pitch. If, however, the answer 'Yes' to a question is unexpected, you may repeat it as a question: 'Yes?' meaning: 'Did you really say "yes"?' The voice tends to rise from a mid-level to a high pitch, the span of the rise depending upon the amount of surprise you want to convey. A further example might be the answer 'Yes!' as an exclamation, to show surprise or amazement, with the voice tending to fall from a high to a mid-level pitch, again with the span of the fall depending on the intensity of the exclamation. These instances demonstrate that, in English, syllables can be pronounced on different pitches and with different voice contours to express different attitudes. The fundamental meaning of the syllable remains the same; 'yes' means 'yes' whatever the pitch. However, the variations in pitch indicate whether 'yes' is a statement 'yes', a questioning 'yes?', an exclamatory 'yes!' etc. In English the combinations of the sounds in individual words carry the formal meanings of the words, that is, what the words *denote*. The pitch, or intonation, variations, indicate the speaker's attitudes or emotions, that is, what the words *connote*.

Another example: if you asked, in English, 'What day is it today?' the answer might be 'Monday'. Normally, this would be said with the voice falling from mid-level to a lower level. Such an intonation contour indicates a plain statement of fact in English. If the answer were to be given with a rise at the end, it might be interpreted as insecurity on the part of the speaker ('[I'm not sure. Is it] Monday?'), or perhaps not even understood. On the other hand, a strongly stressed first syllable with a high pitch, followed by an unstressed second syllable on a lower pitch ('*Mon*day!') might indicate the speaker's surprise at being asked the question at all, perhaps expressing something like 'Don't you know it's Monday?' The differences in pitch contours indicate differences in the speaker's attitude, the *connotation* of the answer. However, in Cantonese, a similar question **Gāmyaht sīngkèih géi?** ('What day is it today?') might be answered **Sīngkèih yāt**, with the first syllable high, the second syllable a low fall and the third syllable high. This would mean, 'Monday'. With one change, from a relatively high pitch to a lower level pitch on the last syllable, **Sīngkèih yaht**, the meaning becomes 'Sunday'! The pitch, or tone, variation, indicates a change in the *denotation* of the word: it means something different – in this case, a different day of the week. Every syllable has to be said on a particular pitch for it to carry meaning, and the same syllable said on a different pitch has a different *denotational* meaning.

Connotation, which in English is conveyed by pitch variation in the voice, is often indicated in Cantonese by individual syllables, usually particles which occur at the end of the sentence, such as **gwa** or **lō**, as in the Cantonese equivalents to the answers discussed above:

> **Sīngkèih yāt gwa**   (= 'I'm not sure. Is it Monday?')
> **Sīngkèih yāt lō**   (= '*Mon*day! I'm surprised you asked me.')

How many tones are there in Cantonese? Analyses vary: some say six, some seven, some even nine. In this book, we distinguish six tones, not simply because this is the minimum with which to operate comprehensibly and successfully in Cantonese, but because further distinctions actually depend on fine theoretical linguistic arguments. Native Cantonese speakers appear nowadays to be confining themselves to these six definitive pitch differentiations in their speech, with any minor tonal variations beyond these certainly not being significant from the point of view of someone beginning an acquaintance with the language.

Actual pitch does not matter – everyone's voice is different in any case – but relative pitch is important. There are three levels of tones: *high*, *mid* and *low*, and as long as a distinction is made from one level to another, comprehensibility is enhanced.

The *mid* level is the normal level of one's voice in conversation, and is the point of reference for the other levels.

The *high* level is a pitch somewhat higher than the mid level.

The *low* level is a pitch somewhat lower than the mid level.

Cantonese has words which are distinguished by pitch at each level, such as:

(high)	**mā**	mother
(mid)	**ma**	*question particle*
(low)	**mah**	to scold

(high)	**sī**	poetry
(mid)	**si**	to try
(low)	**sih**	a matter

It is important to note the transcription adopted here. A macron (ˉ) is used to indicate a high-level tone (**mā, sī**). The absence of any such diacritic indicates a mid-level tone (**ma, si**) or a low-level tone (**mah, sih**), with the latter having an **h** following the vowel to indicate the low-level tone. The letter **h** is pronounced as in 'how' or 'hand' *only* when it occurs in initial position in the syllable; elsewhere it is merely a marker of low-level tone, and is not pronounced separately.

In addition to words said on a fixed level – high, mid or low – there are three tone combinations: two rising, and one falling.

The *high rising* tone is a rise from mid to high, rather like asking a question on one word in English: 'Monday?'

The *low rising* tone is a rise from low to mid, again like asking a question, but rather suspiciously.

The *low falling* tone is a fall from mid to low, somewhat like an ordinary statement in English.

Note the transcription: an acute accent mark (´) is used for a rising tone, and a grave accent mark (`) is used for a falling tone. Again, remember that the letter **h**, when not in initial position, indicates low level.

Look at the following lists of words, in which the pairs are contrasted by tone only. If you have the cassette tapes which accompany this book, listen to the pronunciations, and repeat what you hear. Try to ensure that you make the tonal distinctions between each pair of words. Return to this exercise often, so as to practice these differences – they *are* important!

High level		*Low falling*	
	tāu (to steal)		**tàuh** (head)
	sīng (star)		**sìhng** (city)
	tōng (soup)		**tòhng** (sugar)
	chīm (to sign)		**chìhm** (to dive under water)

High level		*Mid level*	
	dāng (lamp)		**dang** (chair)
	fān (to divide)		**fan** (to sleep)
	jēui (to chase)		**jeui** (drunk)
	gām (gold)		**gam** (to ban)

Mid level	**gin** (to see)	*Low level* clothes)	**gihn** (*classifier for*
	si (to try)		**sih** (a matter)
	seun (letter)		**seuhn** (smooth)
	yim (to loathe)		**yihm** (to test)
High rising	**séui** (water)	*Mid level*	**seui** (years of age)
	sáu (hand)		**sau** (thin)
	dím (a point)		**dim** (shop)
	séi (to die)		**sei** (four)

For further information on tone see Appendix, p. 247.

Using this book

This book is divided into fifteen Lessons. Each Lesson has a similar format. At the head of each Lesson, you will find a short list of the objectives which the lesson material aims to help you achieve.

The basic vocabulary of the Lesson is introduced in the *Vocabulary* sections. Look through the list of words. Read each item aloud, paying particular attention to the tone of every word. If you have the cassette tapes, you can model your pronunciation on the tape recording.

The *Dialogue* sections offer some short, realistic dialogues, preceded by questions. It is not necessary to understand every word of the dialogue to be able to answer these questions. At this stage, just concentrate on answering the questions, and do not worry about the rest. As the Lessons progress, material presented in earlier Lessons is recycled, for consolidation.

The *Idioms and structures* sections give explanations of the idiomatic expressions used in the dialogues, as well as comprchensive usage notes, covering all the grammatical constructions introduced. Review these sections carefully, referring to the dialogues for the examples of usages.

Next you will find a series of *Exercises* to give you practice in using the vocabulary and structures introduced in the Lesson.

Each Lesson ends with some Chinese characters. These are for recognition purposes only.

Special conventions of the Yale transcription

1 The tone mark on a diphthong always falls on the first written vowel, e.g. **yáuh**, **móuh**, but the tone is a characteristic of the diphthong as a whole.

2 In the syllable **ńgh**, which has no vowel letters, the tone mark is written over the **g**, but the tone is characteristic of the whole syllable.

3 When **aa** is *not* followed by a consonant in the same syllable, the second **a** is dropped from the written form. Thus, **fā**, for example, is pronounced as if it were **faa**.

Conventions used in this book

1 The apostrophe is used to indicate elision of numerals, as in **y'ah** (the elided form of **yih-sahp**), **sā'ah** (the elided form of **sāam-sahp**), etc. See Lesson 5.

2 The hyphen is used to indicate:

    (a) numbers above ten, e.g. **ńgh-sahp**, **sei-baak** (see Lesson 1);

    (b) verb-object constructions, e.g. **tái-syū**, **dá-dihnwá** (see Lesson 3);

    (c) reduplicated forms of nouns and adjectives, e.g. **fèih-féi-déi**, **gōu-gōu-sau-sau** (see Lesson 5);

    (d) comparative adjectives, e.g. **fèih-dī**, **gwai-dī** (see Lesson 6);

    (e) verbs with special markers, e.g. **sihk-jó faahn**, **cheung-gán gō** (see Lesson 6);

    (f) days of the week and months, e.g. **sīngkèih-yāt**, **gáu-yuht** (see Lesson 12).

3 The negative prefix for verbs, **m-**, becomes **-mh-** in choice-type questions (see Lesson 2), e.g. **mhaih/haih-mh-haih**, **msái/sái-mh-sái**. No tone mark is used on **m-** or **-mh-**, but the syllable is always pronounced on the low falling tone.

4 The asterisk is used to indicate sentence or structures which are not grammatically correct, but are for illustration only.

1 Máaih-yéh

Shopping

In Lesson 1 you will learn about:

- prices in shops
- buying goods by weight or item
- asking for goods and services, and thanking people for them
- terms for payment and change
- personal pronouns
- forming simple statements, and questions with question phrases

Vocabulary

Below is a list of the fruit most commonly found in a Hong Kong market. The list is followed by the cardinal numbers 1–100, and certain classifiers and numbers. Try reading out each item aloud, paying special attention to the tones. If you have the cassette tapes of this book with you, you can model your pronunciation on the tape recording.

Types of fruit

sāanggwó 生果	fruit
mōnggwó 芒果	mango
cháang 橙	orange
pìhnggwó 蘋果	apple
hēungjīu 香蕉	banana
tàihjí 提子	grape
boulām 布冧	plum
léi 梨	pear

sāigwā	water-melon
muhkgwā	papaya
bōlòh	pineapple
laihjī	lychee
kèihyihgwó	kiwifruit

Numbers

yāt	1	sahp-yāt	11
yih	2	sahp-yih	12
sāam	3	sahp-sāam	13
sei	4	sahp-sei	14
nǵh	5	sahp-nǵh	15
luhk	6	sahp-luhk	16
chāt	7	sahp-chāt	17
baat	8	sahp-baat	18
gáu	9	sahp-gáu	19
sahp	10	yih-sahp	20

yih-sahp yāt	21	sei-sahp	40
yih-sahp yih	22	nǵh-sahp	50
yih-sahp sāam	23	luhk-sahp	60
yih-sahp sei	24	chāt-sahp	70
yih-sahp nǵh	25	baat-sahp	80
yih-sahp luhk	26	gáu-sahp	90
yih-sahp chāt	27	yāt-baak	100
yih-sahp baat	28		
yih-sahp gáu	29		
sāam-sahp	30		

Note that there are two forms of the word 'two' in Cantonese. When 'two' is used as a nominal number, such as in a room number or telephone number, **yih** is used. But when it is used as a measure to indicate quantity, as in 'two times' or 'two pounds of bananas', then **léuhng** is used instead.

Classifiers and measures

yāt *go* cháang	an orange
yāt *dā* cháang	a dozen oranges

yāt *bohng* hēungjīu	a pound of bananas
yāt *mān*	one dollar

Classifiers

In Cantonese, a noun is always preceded by a classifier or a measure. For example, **bohng** is a measure meaning 'pound', so **yāt bohng hēungjīu** means 'one pound of bananas'. (This is the imperial pound, in other words 454g.) On the other hand, **go** is the classifier for oranges, so **yāt go cháang** means 'an orange'. There are many classifiers in Cantonese, the choice of which depends on the shape and size of the object referred to. For example, **go** is used for roundish objects such as oranges and apples, though its use also extends to other objects such as 'people' – thus **yāt go yàhn** is 'a person'.

Dialogues ▣

Below are three short dialogues, each preceded by a number of questions. Read the questions and then, bearing them in mind, read the dialogues to find the answers. If you have the cassette tapes, you may want to listen to the dialogues and answer the questions without reading the texts. You will not understand everything that is said, but you will be able to pick out the information needed to answer the questions.

1 Carmen is at a fruit-stall, asking the hawker about prices of fruit.

(a) What fruit did Carmen buy?
(b) How many did she buy?
(c) How much did she pay for them?

HAWKER:	Hóu leng sāanggwó. Máaih dī lā , síujé.
CARMEN:	Dī mōnggwó dím maaih a?
HAWKER:	Dī mōnggwó ńgh mān yāt go.
CARMEN:	Ngóh yiu sei go.
HAWKER:	Sei go mōnggwó, yih-sahp mān lā .
CARMEN:	Nīdouh yih-sahp mān.

HAWKER: Dōjeh.
CARMEN: Mgōi.

2 Carmen's partner, John, is at a fruit-stall, talking to the hawker.

(a) What fruit did John buy?
(b) How many did he buy?
(c) How much did he pay for them?

HAWKER: Sīnsāang, máaih dī sāanggwó lā.
JOHN: Dī cháang géidō chín yāt go a?
HAWKER: Sahp mān sei go.
JOHN: Mgōi béi luhk go ā.
HAWKER: Luhk go cháang, dōjeh sahp-ńgh mān.
JOHN: Nī douh yih-sahp mān.
HAWKER: Jáau fāan ńgh mān. Dōjeh.
JOHN: Mgōi.

3 Carmen is buying fruit from a hawker.

(a) What fruit did Carmen buy?
(b) How much did she buy?
(c) How much did she pay for it?

CARMEN: Tàihjí dím maaih a?
HAWKER: Sahp-yih mān yāt bohng.
CARMEN: Jauh yiu yāt bohng lā.
HAWKER: Yāt bohng tàihjí, dōjeh sahp-yih mān lā.
CARMEN: Nīdouh sahp-yih mān. Mgōi.

Idioms and structures

The items in the list below appear in the same order as they do in the dialogues above. The *italicized* items are *new* items. In the notes, numbers in brackets refer to the expressions listed below.

1 *hóu leng sāanggwó*   *very fresh fruit*
2 *máaih dī lā*   *please buy some*

3 *síujé*	*Miss* (a polite way of addressing a young lady)
4 *dī* **mōnggwó**	*the* mangoes
5 *dím maaih a?*	*what's the price?*
6 **ńgh mān yāt go**	five dollars each (lit. five dollars one)
7 *Ngóh yiu* **sei go.**	*I want* four.
8 **Sei go mōnggwó,** **yih-sahp mān** *lā*.	Four mangoes, *that's* twenty dollars.
9 *Nī douh* **yih-sahp mān**	*Here's* twenty dollars.
10 *Dōjeh.*	*Thank you* (for the money).
11 *Mgōi.*	*Thank you* (for the favor).
12 *sīnsāang*	*Mr* (a polite way of addressing a man)
13 *géidō chín* **yāt go a?**	*how much* each (lit. for one)?
14 *Mgōi béi* **luhk go** *ā*.	*Please give (me)* six.
15 *dōjeh* **sahp-ńgh mān**	fifteen dollars, *please*
16 *Jáau fāan* **ńgh mān.**	*Here's* five dollars *change.*
17 *Jauh* **yiu yāt** **bohng lā**.	*Then*, I'll have one pound.

Indefinite pronoun (2)

In this context **dī** functions as a pronoun referring to an unspecified number or amount of people or things. It is invariable, and is usually translated by 'some' in English.

Particles (2, 14; 5, 13)

Cantonese has a number of particles which speakers use to express moods and achieve certain rhetorical functions. The **lā** in the expression **máaih dī** *lā* is a particle which helps convey the mood of a cordial invitation. The **lā** on the other hand, in **Mgōi béi luhk go** *lā*, has a slightly different connotation of giving an affirmation rather than making a cordial invitation. Note that **lā** always occurs at the *end* of a sentence, so we refer to it as a sentence-final particle. Other particles are used, for example, in questions and polite requests (see below).

Definite determiner (4)

This **dī** functions as a *definite determiner* used before plural or uncountable nouns to specify people or objects. It translates into 'the' or 'those' (for plural countable nouns) or 'that' (for uncountable nouns) in English.

Questions (5, 13)

Dím maaih a? is a general question one would use to ask about prices that fluctuate, such as prices of fruit and vegetables in the market, which depend on the quantity and quality of supply and also vary with individual sellers. Another way to ask such a question is to say **Géidō chín yāt go a?**

Note that both questions contain a question phrase, namely, **dím maaih** (lit. how sold?) and **géidō chín** (lit. how much money?), and end with the interrogative, or question, particle **a**.

Personal pronouns (7)

ngóh	I, me	**ngóhdeih**	we, us
néih	you (singular)	**néihdeih**	you (plural)
kéuih	he, him, she, her, it	**kéuihdeih**	they, them

Topic–comment constructions (8)

In Cantonese, a sentence is often made up of a *topic* followed by a *comment*, the two of which are not joined by any grammatical parts, such as a verb. This sentence from Dialogue 1 is typical:

Sei go mōnggwó, yih-sahp mān lā.
(lit.) Four mangoes, twenty dollars.

In this case **sei go mōnggwó** is the topic, and **yih-sahp mān lā** is the comment about it. This construction is common among questions, too. The questions for asking for prices are good examples:

Dī mōnggwó dím maaih a?
(lit.) The mangoes, how (are they) sold?

Dī cháang géidō chín yāt go a?
(lit.) The oranges, how much money for one?

Expressing thanks (10, 11)

Cantonese distinguishes between two kinds of thanks. We say **dōjeh** to someone for a gift or a treat, but **mgōi** to someone for a favor or a service rendered. Thus, at the fruit-stall, the hawker will say **dōjeh** to thank the customer for the money paid for the fruit, while the customer will say **mgōi** to the hawker for his service.

Polite requests (14, 15)

The **mgōi** and **dōjeh** in these two cases are interjections used as a polite way of making a request. The **mgōi** in *Mgōi* **béi luhk go ā** is a request made by the customer for a service by the hawker, while the **dōjeh** in *dōjeh* **sahp-ńgh mān** is a request from the hawker for payment by the customer. (In a similar vein, in English a salesperson might say 'Five pounds, thank you' in order to solicit payment, that is, in anticipation of receipt, rather than in acknowledgement of it.)

The **ā** in **Mgōi béi luhk go** *ā* is a particle, conveying here the mood of a polite request.

Exercises

Exercise 1 Comprehension 🔲

Read the following questions. Then go back to the three dialogues and find the answers to the questions. You can, of course, listen to the dialogues if you have the cassette tapes with you.

(a) How much does the hawker say the fruit is in Dialogue 1?
  (i) $5 each
  (ii) $5 a pound
  (iii) $10 for two

(b) How much does the hawker say the fruit is in Dialogue 2?
  (i) $10 each
  (ii) $10 a pound
  (iii) $10 for four

(c) In Dialogue 2, how much change did the hawker give back to John?
  (i) $5
  (ii) $10
  (iii) $15

(d) How much does the hawker say the fruit is in Dialogue 3?
  (i) $12 each
  (ii) $12 a pound
  (iii) $12 for four

Exercise 2 Asking about prices

Imagine you are at a fruit-stall. Ask about the price of each kind of fruit with a **dím maaih a** question. Then guess whether the hawker will give the price for **yāt go** or **yāt bohng**.

(a) **léi:**
You: _____ dím maaih a?
Hawker: Sei mān _____

(b) **sāigwā:**
You: _____ dím maaih a?
Hawker: Sāam mān _____

(c) **muhkgwā:**
You: _____ dím maaih a?
Hawker: Sei mān _____

(d) **bōlòh:**
You: _____ dím maaih a?
Hawker: Sahp mān _____

(e) **laihjī:**
You: _____ dím maaih a?
Hawker: Sahp-yih mān _____

Exercise 3 Giving prices

Imagine you are a hawker selling fruit in the market. The table shows your prices.

Apples	Lychees	Papayas	Oranges	Water-melons	Pineapples	Pears
$10 for 3	$8/lb	$6/lb	$10 for 4	$4/lb	$9 each	$5 each

How would you answer the following enquiries about prices?

(a) Dī sāigwā dím maaih a?
(b) Dī léi dím maaih a?
(c) Dī muhkgwā dím maaih a?
(d) Dī cháang dím maaih a?
(e) Dī bōlòh dím maaih a?

Exercise 4 Making a sale 🔘

Now complete the following conversations, using the prices from Exercise 3.

(a) CUSTOMER 1:   Dī pìhnggwó dím maaih a?
    YOU:
    CUSTOMER 1:   Ngóh yiu yāt dā pìhnggwó.
    YOU:
    CUSTOMER 1:   Géidō chín a?
    YOU:
    CUSTOMER 1:   Nī douh sei-sahp mān. Mgōi.
    YOU:

(b) CUSTOMER 2:   Dī laihjī dím maaih a?
    YOU:
    CUSTOMER 2:   Ngóh yiu sāam bohng.
    YOU:
    CUSTOMER 2:   Géidō chín a?
    YOU:
    CUSTOMER 2:   Nī douh sāam-sahp mān.
    YOU:
    CUSTOMER 2:   Mgōi.
    YOU:

Exercise 5 Comparing prices 🔘

Mrs Wong is doing some shopping. She wants to buy two pounds of bananas, a dozen oranges and half a dozen apples, and she wants to buy all the fruit at one stall. She asks about the prices of bananas, oranges and apples at two different stalls. Read the two conversations she has at the two stalls and then decide at which one she gets the better deal. You can listen to the conversations if you have the cassette tapes.

At Stall A:
MRS WONG: Dī cháang dím maaih a?
HAWKER A: Sāam mān yāt go.

Mrs Wong:	Dī pìhnggwó nē ?
Hawker A:	Pìhnggwó sei mān yāt go.
Mrs Wong:	Hēungjīu yauh dím maaih a?
Hawker A:	Hēungjīu sahp-sāam mān yāt bohng.

At Stall B:

Mrs Wong:	Dī hēungjīu dím maaih a?
Hawker B:	Dī hēungjīu sahp-yāt mān yāt bohng.
Mrs Wong:	Dī pìhnggwzó nē?
Hawker B:	Pìhnggwó sāam mān yāt go.
Mrs Wong:	Dī cháang nē?
Hawker B:	Dī cháang sei mān yāt go.

(a) Which hawker offers a better deal to Mrs Wong?
(b) How much does she have to pay if she takes this deal?

Exercise 6 What are the prices?

Read the conversation and then fill in the prices in the picture of the fruit stall.

Customer:	Dī tàihjí dím maaih a?
Hawker:	Dī tàihjí sahp-ńgh mān yāt bohng.
Customer:	Gám, dī kèihyihgwó nē?
Hawker:	Dī kèihyihgwó sāam mān yāt go.

CUSTOMER:	Dī pìhnggwó nē?
HAWKER:	Pìhnggwó dōu haih sāam mān yāt go.
CUSTOMER:	Dī muhkgwā dím maaih a?
HAWKER:	Muhkgwā baat mān yāt bohng.
CUSTOMER:	Gám, sāigwā nē?
HAWKER:	Sāigwā léuhng mān yāt bohng.
CUSTOMER:	Dī cháang yauh dím maaih a?
HAWKER:	Dī cháang sahp mān sei go.
CUSTOMER:	Gám, dī léi nē?
HAWKER:	Dī léi dōu haih sahp mān sei go.

Recognizing Chinese characters

In the local market sometimes the prices are written in Arabic numerals, but often they are in Chinese characters. The Chinese characters for the numbers one to ten are as follows:

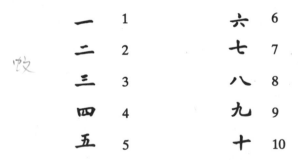

The Chinese character for 'dollar' is

元 .

Thus, one dollar is written as

一 元

This is pronounced as **yāt mān** in colloquial Cantonese.

The classifier for 'roundish' fruits is **go**, and is written as

個 or 个

in Chinese characters.

Thus, 'three dollars each' is written as

三元一个

and 'five dollars each' is written as

五元一个.

The Chinese character for the measure 'pound' is

磅.

'Eight dollars a pound' is thus

八元一磅

and 'ten dollars per pound' is

十元一磅.

2 Gāaujai 交陰

Meeting people

In Lesson 2 you will learn about:

- introducing yourself and others
- greeting people
- enquiring about someone
- the verbs 'to be' and 'can'
- forming negative statements
- forming choice-type questions and questions with question-words

---

Vocabulary 🔲

Countries

Below is a list of some of the countries in the world. Try reading out each item aloud. If you have the cassette tapes of this book with you, you can model your pronunciation on the recording on the tape.

Yìnggwok	Britain, the UK
Méihgwok	the USA
Gānàhdaaih	Canada
Oujāu	Australia
Náusāilàahn	New Zealand
Faatgwok	France
Dākgwok	Germany
Yidaaihleih	Italy
Sāibāanngàh	Spain
Fēileuhtbān	the Philippines
Yahtbún	Japan
Hòhngwok	Korea

Yandouh	India
Bāgēisītáan	Pakistan

Of course, we must not forget:

Hēunggóng	Hong Kong
Jūnggwok	China

Gwok literally means 'country'. Hence **Yīnggwok** is 'Britain', and **Faatgwok** is 'France', **Dākgwok** is 'Germany', etc. The Cantonese names for some other countries are apparently attempts at phonetic equivalents, for example: **Gānàhdaaih** for 'Canada', **Náusāilàahn** for 'New Zealand', **Yandouh** for 'India' and **Bāgēisītáan** for 'Pakistan'.

To refer to the inhabitants of different countries, the word **yàhn**, which literally means 'person(s)', is added to the name of a country. For example, a 'Briton' is **Yīnggwok yàhn**, an 'Australian' is **Oujāu yàhn**, 'Indians' are **Yandouh yàhn**, and 'Chinese' are **Jūnggwok yàhn**.

Now try reading out the list of countries again, but this time for each item add the word **yàhn** to the name of the country.

Languages

Yīngmán	English
Faatmán	French
Dākmán	German
Yidaaihleihmán	Italian
Yahtmán	Japanese
Hòhnmán	Korean

Mán and wá

Mán means 'language', which usually implies both the spoken and written forms. There is another word in Cantonese, **wá**, which refers only to the spoken form of a language. Thus, for the languages spoken by Filipinos, Indians and Pakistanis, which Cantonese-speaking people may hear being used but will probably never learn to read or write, **wá** is used instead. Hence, they use a vague term **Fēileuhtbānwá** for all languages spoken by Filipinos including Tagalog, **Yandouhwá** for all languages spoken by Indians, and **Bāgēisītáanwá** for all languages spoken by Pakistanis.

Jūngmán refers to Chinese in general, including written Chinese and a spoken form of it, while **wá** refers to individual varieties or dialects spoken in different parts of China. Hence:

Gwóngdūngwá/Gwóngjāuwá	Cantonese
Seuhnghóiwá	Shanghainese
Chìuhjāuwá	the Chiu Chow dialect
Póutūngwá	Putonghua (literally, 'the common dialect'), Mandarin

Dialogues

Read the questions, and then read or listen to each dialogue in order to find the answers to the questions. If you have the cassette tapes, you may want to listen to the dialogues and answer the questions without reading the texts.

1 John and Carmen are at a gathering of the Cantonese Students' Club, where foreigners learning Cantonese meet and practice their Cantonese. Carmen is talking to Richard.

(a) What country does Carmen come from?
(b) What country does Richard come from?

CARMEN:	Néih hóu, ngóh haih Carmen.
RICHARD:	Néih hóu, Carmen. Ngóh haih Richard. Carmen, néih haih bīndouh yàhn a?
CARMEN:	Ngóh haih Náusāilàahn yàhn.
RICHARD:	O, néih haih Náusāilàahn yàhn.
CARMEN:	Gám néih nē, Richard?
RICHARD:	Ngóh haih Méihgwok yàhn.

2 John is talking to Emily.

(a) Where does John come from?
(b) What languages does he speak?
(c) Where does Emily come from?
(d) What languages does she speak?

JOHN:	Néih hóu. Ngóh giujouh John. Néih giujouh mātyéh méng a?
EMILY:	Néih hóu. Ngóh giujouh Emily. Haih nē, John, néih haih-mh-haih Yīnggwok yàhn a?
JOHN:	Mhaih. Ngóh haih Oujāu yàhn. Ngóh sīk góng Yīngmán tùhng Dākmán.
EMILY:	Ngóh haih Gānàhdaaih yàhn. Ngóh sīk góng Yīngmán tùhng síusíu Faatmán.

3 Carmen is introducing her friend Grace to John.

(a) Where does Grace come from?
(b) What languages can she speak?

CARMEN:	Dáng ngóh lèih gaaisiuh. Nī wái haih Grace. Nī wái haih John.
GRACE:	Néih hóu, John.
JOHN:	Néih hóu, Grace.
CARMEN:	Grace haih Yahtbún yàhn. Kéuih sīk góng Yahtmán, Yīngmán tùhng Póutūngwá.
JOHN:	Ngóh tùhng Carmen sīk góng síusíu Gwóngjāuwá, bātgwo ngóhdeih msīk góng Póutūngwá. Haih nē, chíng mahn Grace néih gwai sing a?
GRACE:	Ngóh sing Sawada.

Idioms and structures

The items in the list below appear in the same order as they do in the dialogues above. The *italicized* items are *new* items. In the notes, numbers in brackets refer to the expressions listed below.

1 *Néih hóu*	*How are you?*
2 *Ngóh haih* **Carmen**	*I am* Carmen.
3 *Néih haih bīndouh yàhn a?*	*Where are you from?*
4 **Ngóh** *giujouh* **John.**	*My name is* John.
5 **Néih giujouh** *mātyéh méng* **a?**	*What is your name?*
6 *Gám, néih nē?*	*So, what about you?*
7 *Haih nē,*	*By the way,*
8 *Néih haih-mh-haih* **Yīnggwok yàhn a?**	*Are you* British?
9 *Mhaih.*	*No, I'm not.*

10 Ngóh *sīk góng* ...	I *can speak* ...
11 Yīngmán *tùhng* Dākmán	English *and* German
12 *síusíu* Faatmán	*a little* French
13 *Dáng ngóh lèih gaaisiuh.*	*Let me introduce you.*
14 *Nī wái haih* Grace.	*This is* Grace.
15 *bātgwo*	*but*
16 chíng mahn Grace néih *gwai sing a?*	Grace, may I know what your *surname* is?

Greeting (1)

Néih hóu is a slightly formal greeting expression which is used at all times of the day and which can be translated into 'How are you?' in English, except that it is not a question and the usual response is the same: **Néih hóu.**

Haih (2)

The verb **haih** is the Cantonese verb 'to be' and translates 'am', 'is', 'are' and so on.

Questions with question-words (3)

Like 'wh' questions in English (why, where, who, etc.), many questions in Cantonese are formed with a question-word. However, the question-word in Cantonese is not put at the beginning of the question like the question-word in English, but occupies the position taken by the required information in the answer. Thus, the word order in a Cantonese question is essentially the same as that of a statement. For example, to ask where someone is from you use the question-word **bīndouh** ('where') and say: **Néih haih bīndouh yàhn a?**, which literally means 'You are where person?' The answer **Ngóh haih Náusāilàahn yàhn** literally means 'I am New Zealand person'. To ask someone their name you use the question-word **mātyéh** (what) and say: **Néih giujouh mātyéh méng a?**, which literally means 'You are known as what name?', and the answer **Ngóh giujouh Emily** literally means 'I am known as Emily'.

Nē (6)

Nē is a particle used for addressing a question to a second person, in the same way as, for example, 'And you?' in English.

Negatives (9)

Negatives in Cantonese are often formed by inserting the negative prefix before a verb or an adjective. For example, **Ngóh haih Jūng-gwok yàhn** means 'I am Chinese' while **Ngoh *mhaih* Jūnggwok yàhn** means 'I am *not* Chinese'.

Choice-type questions (8)

Néih haih-mh-haih Yīnggwok yàhn a? is a 'choice-type' question, which is a very common structure in Cantonese for 'yes/no' questions. The question here literally means 'Are you or are you not British?' The positive answer to the question is **Ngóh haih Yīng-gwok yàhn** or **Haih** for short. The negative answer is **Ngóh mhaih Yīnggwok yàhn** or **Mhaih** for short.

Choice-type questions are formed by reduplicating the key word (putting it twice) and inserting the negative prefix **m-** in the middle. (In this system **m-** is written as **-mh-** in reduplicated structures.) In the choice-type question **Néih haih-mh-haih Yīnggwok yàhn a?**, the verb 'to be', **haih**, is reduplicated. In the choice-type question, **Néih sīk-mh-sīk góng Faatmán a?**, 'Can you speak French?', the modal verb **sīk**, 'can, know how to', is reduplicated.

Classifiers for people (14)

Nī wái is a polite way of referring to a person. Here **Nī go haih Grace** would also do, but **Nī wái** is more polite than **Nī go**. **Wái** is a classifier for persons and shows more respect than **go**. However, one normally never uses the classifier **wái** to refer to oneself, as it is a marker of respect to other people.

Introducing by surname (16)

To ask for someone's surname, the rather formal expression **néih gwai sing a?** is used. **Sing** is a verb which means 'to have the surname of', while **gwai** is an adverb meaning 'honorably'. So **néih gwai sing a?** translates into English as 'How are you honorably surnamed?' The respectful expression **chíng mahn** further heightens the degree of formality.

On formal occasions, it is very common for Chinese people to introduce themselves by surname:

Ngóh sing Léih. My (sur)name is Lee.

Similarly, when introducing somebody else on a formal occasion, one may choose to do so on a last-name basis. In such circumstances one does not use the verb **sing**, but instead introduces the person as Mr X or Miss X:

Nī wái haih Wòhng síujé. This is Miss Wong.

Chíng mahn (16)

Chíng mahn is a respectful way of beginning a question, which can be translated as 'Could I ask . . . please?' in English, with **chíng** meaning 'please' and **mahn** meaning 'ask' by themselves. The expression can be freely added to a question to raise the level of politeness. For example, you can say *Chíng mahn di pìhnggwó dím maaih a?* to ask the price of apples or *Chíng mahn néih giu mātyéh méng a?* to ask somebody's name.

Exercises

Exercise 1 Comprehension 🔲

Read the following questions. Then go back to the three dialogues and find the answers to the questions. You can, of course, choose to listen to the dialogues again for the answers if you have the cassette tapes with you.

(a) Who takes the initiative to greet the other person and then introduce himself or herself in Dialogue 1?

(i) Carmen
(ii) Richard

(b) What nationality does Emily presume John to be in Dialogue 2?
    (i) British
    (ii) Australian
    (iii) American

(c) How much French does Emily claim to speak in Dialogue 2?
    (i) A lot
    (ii) A little
    (iii) None

(d) According to Dialogue 3, do John and Carmen speak Putonghua?
    (i) Both John and Carmen
    (ii) Neither John nor Carmen
    (iii) Only John
    (iv) Only Carmen

Exercise 2 Introducing yourself

Imagine you are at a social gathering. Provide the information asked for by completing the following conversation.

STRANGER: Néih hóu. Ngóh giujouh Sam, néih nē?
YOU:
STRANGER: Néih haih bīndouh yàhn a?
YOU:
STRANGER: Ngóh haih Oujāu yàhn. Haih nē, néih sīk-mh-sīk góng Póutūngwá a?
YOU:

Exercise 3 Introducing others

Below is some information about six individuals. Imagine you have to introduce these people to some friends in Cantonese. Practice the language of introduction by yourself. The first one has been done for you. Then try introducing some of your real friends.

(a) *Name*: Jimmy Walkman
    Nationality: American
    Languages spoken: English, German

Kéuih giujouh Jimmy Walkman. Kéuih haih Méihgwok yàhn.
Kéuih sīk góng Yīngmán tùhng Dākmán.

(b) *Name*:   Pierre Gagnon
    Nationality: French
    Languages spoken: French, Spanish

Kéuih giujouh Pierre Gagnon . . .

(c) *Name*:   Paola Giannini
    Nationality: Italian
    Languages spoken: Italian, French, English

(d) *Name*:   Kim Yoo Sung
    Nationality: Korean
    Languages spoken: Korean, Japanese, English

Exercise 4 Information gathering

Read the two conversations in which four people introduce themselves saying where they come from and what languages they speak. Use the information you extract from the reading or listening to answer the questions that follow. You may find it useful to complete the table.

RAUL:	Néih hóu, ngóh haih Raul.
JANE:	Néih hóu, ngóh giujouh Jane.
RAUL:	Ngóh haih Fēileuhtbān yàhn. Néih nē?
JANE:	Ngóh haih Oujāu yàhn.
RAUL:	Ngóh sīk góng Yīngmán, Sāibāanngàhmán tùhng Fēileuhtbānwá. Néih nē?
JANE:	Ngóh sīk góng sāam júng wá, Yīngmán, Faatmán tùhng síusíu Yidaaihleihmán.

BRUCE:	Néih giujouh mātyéh méng a?
ANTONIA:	Ngóh giujouh Antonia. Néih nē?
BRUCE:	Ngóh giujouh Bruce. Ngóh haih Méihgwok yàhn.
ANTONIA:	Ngóh haih Gānàhdaaih yàhn. Ngóh sīk góng Yīngmán, Faatmán tùhng Yidaaihleihmán. Néih nē?
BRUCE:	Ngóh sīk góng Yīngmán, Dākmán, Faatmán tùhng Sāibāanngàhmán.

	Nationality	Languages spoken
Raul		
Jane		
Bruce		
Antonia		

(a) How many different countries do the four people come from?
(b) How many different languages do they speak altogether?
(c) Who speaks the most languages?
(d) Which language is spoken by all four people?
(e) Which languages are spoken by *two* of the four people?
(f) Which languages are spoken by only *one* of the four people?

Exercise 5 Ordering fruit

Imagine you are on the telephone ordering some fruit from a grocery store. Give your order in Cantonese, according to the information given in the table. The first item has been done for you as an example.

	Fruit	Place of origin	Quantity
(a)	apples	Australia	10
(b)	oranges	the USA	20
(c)	grapes	the USA	2 lb
(d)	pineapples	the Philippines	3
(e)	mangoes	the Philippines	8
(f)	pears	Australia	12

(a) **Ngóh yiu sahp go Oujāu pìhnggwó**.
(b)
(c)
(d)
(e)
(f)

Recognizing Chinese characters

英國人	Briton, British
美國人	American
法國人	French
德國人	German
韓國人	Korean
日本人	Japanese
卬度人	Indian
菲律賓人	Filipino
巴基斯坦人	Pakistani
意大利人	Italian
西班牙人	Spaniard, Spanish
加拿大人	Canadian
澳洲人	Australian
紐西蘭人	New Zealander

The character

人

which appears in each item is pronounced **yàhn** and means 'person', so a

英國人

(**Yīnggwok yàhn**) is a 'British person', and a

日本人

(**Yahtbún yàhn**) is a 'Japanese person'. The character

國

which appears in the first five items is pronounced **gwok** and means 'country', and so

法國

(**Faatgwok**) is 'the country of France' while

韓國

(**Hòhngwok**) is 'the country of Korea'. The character

洲

is pronounced **jāu** and means 'continent', and

澳洲

(**Oujāu**) means 'the continent of Australia'. The remaining ones are all straight transliterations of the countries' names read in English. For example,

意大利

is pronounced **Yidaaihleih** and represents 'Italy'.

3 Sihou

Interests and leisure activities

In Lesson 3 you will learn about:

- discussing interests and leisure activities
- more question words
- discussing how often you do things
- expressing likes and dislikes
- verb-object constructions
- the uses of **yáuh**, 'to have' and 'to exist'
- the uses of **hái** '(to be) in/at'

Vocabulary 🔘

Interests and leisure activities

Below is a list of some common interests. Try reading out each item aloud. If you have the cassette tapes of this book, you can model your pronunciation on the recording.

tái-dihnyíng/tái-hei	to watch a film
tái-dihnsih	to watch television
heui-léuihhàhng	to go traveling
yíng-séung	to take pictures
tēng-yāmngohk	to listen to music
tēng-sāuyāmgēi	to listen to the radio
dá-móhngkàuh	to play tennis
dá-làahmkàuh	to play basketball
tek-jūkkàuh	to play soccer
cháai-dāanchē	to ride a bicycle
yàuh-séui	to swim
páau-bouh	to run

cheung-gō	to sing
tái-syū	to read
tái-boují	to read the newspaper
hàahng-gāai	to go window-shopping
wáan-yàuhheigēi	to play electronic games

Verb-object constructions

The leisure activities given above are all expressed in *verb-object constructions*, and are thus hyphenated. The first four are straightforward, and easy for English speakers to understand, as the constructions and meanings correspond closely to English. For the rest, **tēng-yāmngohk** is 'listen-(to)-music', **tēng-sāuyāmgēi** is 'listen-(to the)-radio', **dá-móhngkàuh** is 'hit-(in)-tennis', **dá-làahmkàuh** is 'hit-(a)-basketball', and **tek-jūkkàuh** is literally 'kick-(a)-football'. And then **cháai-dāanchē** is 'pedal-(a)-bicycle', **yàuh-séui** is 'swim-(in)-water', and **páau-bouh** is 'run-paces'; **cheung-gō** is 'sing-(a)-song'; **tái-syū** is 'read-(a)-book', while **tái-boují** is 'read-(the)-newspaper'; **hàahng-gāai** is 'walk-(along the)-street'; **wáan-yàuhheigēi** is 'play-game-machine'.

Expressing likes

jūngyi	to like
héifūn	to like

Jūngyi and héifūn

The modal verbs **jūngyi** and **héifūn** are identical in meaning, but **héifūn** ranks higher on the level of formality and it is also used in Mandarin as well as in written Chinese, while **jūngyi** is only used in colloquial Cantonese. Of the two words **jūngyi** is more commonly used in daily conversations.

Thus, 'I like playing tennis' can be expressed as:

> **Ngóh jūngyi dá-móhngkàuh**
or > **Ngóh héifūn dá-móhngkàuh**.

Dialogues 🔲

Read the questions and then read or listen to each dialogue to find the answers.

1 John and Carmen are having tea with their two new friends at the Cantonese Students' Club.

Carmen is talking to Richard about her own interests and Richard's.

(a) What does Richard like to do in his spare time?
(b) What about Carmen?

CARMEN: Richard, néih yáuh dī mātyéh sihou a?
RICHARD: Ngóh yáuh hóu dō sihou. Ngóh jūngyi yàuh-séui tùhng
           dá-móhngkàuh. Hái ngūkkéi jauh jūngyi tēng-yām-
           ngohk. Gám, néih nē, Carmen?
CARMEN: Ngóh dōu jūngyi tēng-yāmngohk. Ngóh yauh jūngyi
           tái-syū tùhng tái-dihnsih.

2 John is talking to Emily.

(a) What does Emily like to do in her spare time?
(b) What about John? What does he say his likes and dislikes are?

JOHN: Emily, néih dākhàahn yáuh dī mātyéh jouh a?
EMILY: Ngóh héifūn hàahng-gāai tùhng tái-dihnyíng.
JOHN: Ngóh dōu héifūn tái-dihnyíng, bātgwo ngóh mjūngyi
         hàahng-gāai. Kèihsaht ngóh jeui jūngyi heui-léuihhàhng,
         yānwaih ngóh hóu jūngyi yíng-séung.

Idioms and structures

The items in the list below appear in the same order as they do in the dialogues above. The *italicized* items are *new* items. In the notes, numbers in brackets refer to the expressions listed below.

1 *sihou*	*hobbies/interests*
2 **Néih *yáuh* dī mātyéh sihou a?**	What hobbies do you *have*?

3 Ngóh yáuh hóu *dō* sihou.	I have very *many* hobbies.
4 *hái ngūkkéi* 社	*at home*
5 Ngóh hái ngūkkéi *jauh* jūngyi ...	(When I'm) at home *then* I like ...
6 Ngóh *dōu* jūngyi tēng-yāmngohk	I like listening to music *too*
7 Ngóh *yauh* jūngyi tái-syū	I *also* like reading
8 *dākhàahn*	*free, not busy*
9 néih dākhàahn yáuh dī mātyéh *jouh* a?	What do you *do* in your leisure time?
10 bātgwo ngóh *mjūngyi* hàahng-gāai	but I *don't like* window-shopping
11 *Kèihsaht*	*In fact*
12 ngóh *jeui* jūngyi heui-léuihhàhng	I like travelling *most*
13 *yānwaih*	*because*

Verbal *yáuh* (2, 3)

Yáuh is a verbal form which denotes both *possession* and *existence*. In Dialogue 1, **Ngóh *yáuh* hóu dō sihou** ('I have many hobbies') denotes possession; whereas a sentence like **Yáuh pìhnggwó** ('There are apples') denotes existence. The latter is very similar to 'il y a' in French, but notice that when **yáuh** is used to mean existence no subject noun or pronoun is mentioned.

Note that the negative of **yáuh** is **móuh**, not *myáuh. For example, **Ngóh móuh sihou** is 'I don't have any hobbies', while **Móuh pìhnggwó** is 'There are no apples'.

Indefinite pronoun (2, 9)

Dī here is used as an indefinite pronoun referring to an unspecified number of things. Used in this context it is usually translated as 'some' in English. (See Lesson 1.) Thus **Néih yáuh *dī* mātyeh sihou a?** more explicitly translates into 'What are some of the hobbies that you have?', while **Néih dākhàahn yáuh *dī* mātyeh jouh a?** more explicitly translates into 'What are some of the things you do in your leisure time?'

Locative marker (4)

Hái is a locative marker: it is used in statements about where things are. It can be either *verbal* or *prepositional*. When it is verbal, it means 'to be at/in'. For example, **Kéuih** *hái* **sāanggwódong** means 'He *is at* the fruit-stall.' But in another sentence, **Ngóh** *hái* **sāanggwódong maaih sāanggwó** ('I sell fruit *at* a fruit-stall'), **hái** is used as a preposition, denoting *where* I sell fruit. In the longer sentence **Ngóh** *hái* **ngūkkéi jauh jūngyi tēng-yāmngohk** ('When I am at home I like listening to music'), **hái** is verbal. The condition **ngóh** *hái* **ngūkkéi** ('when I am at home') specifies the location where the action denoted by the main verb **tēng-yāmngohk** takes place.

Conditional marker (5)

Jauh is a very common adverb used to state a condition. It is put before the main clause rather than the conditional clause, thus meaning 'then' rather than 'if'. For example, **Ngóh hái ngūkkéi** *jauh* **jūngyi tēng-yāmngohk** specifies that the preferred activity **tēng-yāmngohk** ('listening to music') takes place under the condition **ngóh hái ngūkkéih** ('I'm at home').

Dōu (6)

Dōu is an adverb used in a response to indicate a *shared* fact: in the context of this lesson, a *common hobby*. For example, to **Ngóh jūngyi dá-móhngkàuh** ('I like playing tennis') one says **Ngóh** *dōu* **jūngyi dá-móhngkàuh** ('I like playing tennis, too'). Here the adverb **dōu** qualifies the *subject* of the sentence, **ngóh**, and the use is similar to saying 'Me too' in response to 'I like playing tennis' in English.

Yauh (7)

Yauh is an adverb used to introduce a further item on a list (not to be confused with **dōu** above, which is used to respond to what somebody else has said). For example, one can say **Ngóh jūngyi dá-móhngkàuh. Ngóh** *yauh* **jūngyi tek-jūkkàuh.** ('I like playing tennis. I also like playing soccer.') Here the adverb **yauh** qualifies the *object* of the sentence, **tek-jūkkàuh**, and the use is similar to adding 'And soccer too' to 'I like playing tennis' in English.

Varying degrees of likes and dislikes

To express dislikes, the negative prefix **m-** is used before the modal verb. Thus, 'I don't like swimming' is **Ngóh mjūngyi yàuh-séui** or **Ngóh mhéifūn yàuh-séui.**

To express varying degrees of likes and dislikes, the following adverbs can be used *before* the modal:

hóu	very much
géi	quite (a lot)
màh-má-déi	not that much
mhaih géi	not that much

For example:

Kéuih hóu jūngyi tái-dihnyíng.	He likes watching films (*or* movies) very much.
Kéuih géi jūngyi tái-dihnyíng.	He quite likes watching films.
Kéuih màh-má-dei jūngyi tái-dihnyíng.	He doesn't like watching films that much.
Kéuih mhaih géi jūngyi tái-dihnyíng.	He doesn't like watching films that much.

Note that as both **màh-má-déi** and **mhaih géi** are already inherently negative in meaning, the modal remains *positive* to express a negative sentence meaning.

Vocabulary ▭

Days of the week

In Cantonese, a 'week' is known as either **sīngkèih** or **láihbaai**. Here are the seven days of the week in Cantonese:

sīngkèih-yāt	or	**láihbaai-yāt**	Monday
sīngkèih-yih	or	**láihbaai-yih**	Tuesday
sīngkèih-sāam	or	**láihbaai-sāam**	Wednesday
sīngkèih-sei	or	**láihbaai-sei**	Thursday

sīngkèih-ńgh	or	láihbaai-ńgh	Friday
sīngkèih-luhk	or	láihbaai-luhk	Saturday
sīngkèih-yaht	or	láihbaai-yaht	Sunday

Note that the pronunciation of 'Sunday' (sīngkèih-yaht/láihbaai-yaht) differs from that of 'Monday' (sīngkèih-yāt/láihbaai-yāt) *in tone only*. Remember that the tone for yaht (as in 'Sunday') is *low level*, and is much lower than that for yāt (as in 'Monday'), which is *high level*.

Time expressions

yāt yaht	a day
yāt go láihbaai	a week
yāt go yuht	a month
yāt nìhn	a year

Note that in Cantonese weeks and months take the classifier **go** (the same classifier as for apples, oranges and people), but days and years do not need any classifiers.

yāt chi	once
léuhng chi	twice
sāam chi	three times
sei chi	four times

Dialogues 🔲

Read the questions, and then try to find the answers in the dialogues either by reading the texts or by listening to the cassette recording.

3 Carmen is talking to Richard about his hobbies.

(a) How often does Richard play tennis?
(b) On what day(s) of the week does he play?

CARMEN: Richard, néih jūngyi dá-móhngkàuh. Gám, néih géi-noih dá yāt chi móhngkàuh a?

RICHARD: Ngóh yāt go láihbaai dá yāt chi móhngkàuh. Ngóh fùhng sīngkèih-luhk dá.

4 John is talking to Emily about hobbies.

(a) How often does Emily go to the cinema?
(b) How often does John go traveling?

JOHN: Emily, néih daaihyeuk géinoih tái yāt chi dihnyíng a?

EMILY: Ngóh hóu héifūn tái dihnyíng. Ngóh daaihyeuk yāt go láihbaai tái léuhng chi dihnyíng. Gám, John, néih géinoih heui yāt chi léuihhàhng a?

JOHN: Ngóh yáuh chèuhng gakèih jauh heui-léuihhàhng. Daaiyeuk yāt nìhn heui léuhng chi léuihhàhng.

Idioms and structures

The items in the list below appear in the same order as they do in the dialogues above. The *italicized* items are *new* items. In the notes, numbers in brackets refer to the expressions listed below.

1 **néih *géinoih* dá *yāt chi* móhngkàuh a?**   *How often* do you play tennis?

2 **Ngóh *yāt go láihbaai* dá *yāt chi* móhngkàuh.**   I play tennis *once a week*.

3 **Ngóh *fùhng sīngkèih-luhk* dá.**   I play (tennis) *every Saturday*.

4 *daaihyeuk*   *roughly, approximately*

5 *chèuhng gakèih*   *long holiday*

Asking about frequency   *(1)*

In a question about frequencies of activities, the question phrase **géinoih . . . yāt chi** is used. **Géinoih** is used to ask about the interval between occurrences, while **yāt chi** literally means 'one time'. Thus **géinoih . . . yāt chi?** is equivalent to asking 'how often?' in English. However, as most activities are expressed in verb-object constructions, always remember the special word order involved in such expressions of frequency, namely, the verb must be put *before* **yāt chi** while the object is put *after* it. For example, 'to go to the cinema once' is expressed as **tái *yāt chi* dihnyíng**, and 'how often do you go to the cinema' is **néih** *géinoih* **tái** *yāt chi* **dihnyíng a?** Similarly, 'how often do you play tennis' is **néih** *géinoih* **dá** *yāt chi* **móhngkàuh a?**

Expressing frequency (2)

To say how often an activity happens, an adverbial phrase of frequency is often used. This is typically formed by combining a phrase expressing a period of time and one expressing the number of occurrences in it.

yāt yaht yāt chi	once every day
yāt go láihbaai yāt chi	once a week
yāt go yuht léuhng chi	twice a month
yāt nìhn sāam chi	three times a year

Again, as leisure activities are often expressed in verb-object constructions (**tek-jūkkàuh**), the verb and object in the construction are *separated* in a sentence expressing frequency, and the following word order is used:

Subject	Period of time	Verb	Number of times	Object
Ngóh	**yāt go yuht**	**tek**	**léuhng chi**	**jūkkàuh.**
Ngóh	**yāt go láihbaai**	**dá**	**yāt chi**	**móhngkàuh.**

Regular activities (3)

For regular activities which take place on the same day every week, the word **fùhng** can be used. For example:

fùhng sīngkèih-yaht	every Sunday
fùhng sīngkèih-yih tùhng	every Tuesday and Thursday
(sīngkèih-)sei	

Thus, **Ngóh** *fùhng* **sīngkèih-yaht tek-jūkkàuh** is 'I play soccer every Sunday', while **Ngóh** *fùhng* **sīngkèih-luhk dá-móhngkàuh** is 'I play tennis every Saturday'.

Note that in Cantonese the time expression always *precedes* the verb.

Exercises

Exercise 1 Comprehension 🔊

Read the following questions. Then go back to the dialogues and find the answers to the questions. You may choose to listen to the dialogues on the cassette tape.

(a) According to Dialogue 1, what hobby do Richard and Carmen share?
   (i) swimming
   (ii) playing tennis
   (iii) listening to music
   (iv) reading
   (v) watching TV

(b) According to Dialogue 2, what is John's favorite hobby?
   (i) shopping
   (ii) going to the cinema
   (iii) traveling
   (iv) photography

(c) According to Dialogue 4, when does John go traveling?
   (i) whenever he has money
   (ii) whenever he has a long holiday

Exercise 2 Likes and dislikes

Translate the following English sentences into Cantonese. The first one has been done for you as an example.

(a) I like taking pictures very much.
   Ngóh hóu jūngyi yíng-séung.
(b) He doesn't like swimming.
   Kéuih mjūngyi . . .
(c) She quite likes reading.
(d) We don't enjoy watching television that much.
(e) They don't like singing.

Exercise 3 How often? 🔊

Translate the following English sentences into Cantonese. The first one has been done for you as an example.

(a) I play soccer once a week.
   Ngóh yāt go láihbaai tek yāt chi jūkkàuh.
(b) I go window-shopping twice a week.

Ngóh yāt go láihbaai . . .
(c) I go to the cinema twice a month.
(d) I go swimming three times a week.
(e) I go traveling four times a year.

Exercise 4 Your hobbies

At a social gathering with your Cantonese Club friends, someone asks you: **Néih yáuh dī mātyéh sihou a?** How would you answer?

Exercise 5 Common interests

The table summarizes the likes and dislikes of Richard, Carmen, Emily and John. Write in your own likes and dislikes in the fifth column. Then write some sentences to describe the common likes and dislikes. Then try reading the sentences aloud.

	Richard	Carmen	Emily	John	You
listening to music *tēng* ✔ *yām ngok* ✔					
watching movies *tái dihn yíng*			✔	✔	
watching TV *tái dihm sih*		✔			
traveling *léuih hàhng*				✔	
taking pictures *ying séung*				✔	
playing tennis *dá móhng* ✔ *kàuh*					
playing soccer *tek juk* ✗ *kàuh*	✗	✗	✗	✗	
swimming *yàuh séui* ✔					
singing *cheung gō* ✗	✗	✔	✔	✗	
reading *tái syū, boují jaahpji* ✔					
window-shopping *hàahng gāai*			✔	✗	

Example:
Richard tùhng Carmen dōu jūngyi tēng-yāmngohk.
Richard, Carmen, Emily tùhng John dōu mjūngyi tek-jūkkàuh.

Exercise 6 'Jack of All Sports'

Your friend Jack is a great sportsman. He likes many sports. Look at the picture and write about his interests and his busy schedule.

Example:

Jack yáuh hóu dō sihou. Kéuih jūngyi dá móhngkàuh. Kéuih fùhng sīngkèih-yāt dá móhngkàuh. Kéuih yauh jūngyi . . .

Recognizing Chinese characters

Of the two Cantonese words for 'week', **sīngkèih** and **láihbaai**, **sīngkèih** is much more commonly used in the written form, and is written as

星期

Thus, for Monday, which is the first day of the week, we write

星期一

and for Tuesday, the second day of the week, we write

星期二

and for Sunday, we write

星期日,

where

日

is the character for 'the sun'. Below is a full list of the seven days of the week written in Chinese characters.

星期一	Monday
星期二	Tuesday
星期三	Wednesday
星期四	Thursday
星期五	Friday
星期六	Saturday
星期日	Sunday

4 Sìhgaan

Telling the time

桌 cheuk

In Lesson 4 you will learn about:

- asking and telling the time
- discussing daily routines
- discussing what time things happen
- **ylu** as a modal verb, 'to have to'

Vocabulary

Reading the clock

Below is a list of the hours of the day. Try reading out each item aloud. If you have the cassette tapes of this book, you can model your pronunciation on the tape recording.

yāt dímjūng	1 o'clock
léuhng dímjūng	2 o'clock
sāam dímjūng	3 o'clock
sei dímjūng	4 o'clock
ngh dímjūng	5 o'clock
luhk dímjūng	6 o'clock
chāt dímjūng	7 o'clock
baat dímjūng	8 o'clock
gáu dímjūng	9 o'clock
sahp dímjūng	10 o'clock
sahp-yāt dímjūng	11 o'clock
sahp-yih dímjūng	12 o'clock

Note that in speech the **jūng** in **dímjūng** is often omitted, hence **yāt dím** is 1 o'clock and **léuhng dím** is 2 o'clock, etc. Notice that **léuhng** is used for 'two'.

To specify more precisely the time of day, one can add the following expressions:

seuhngjau	in the morning
hahjau	in the afternoon
yehmáahn	in the evening/at night
bunyeh	after midnight

Thus,

seuhngjau chāt dímjūng	7 a.m.
hahjau léuhng dímjūng	2 p.m.
yehmáahn gáu dímjūng	9 p.m.
bunyeh sāam dímjūng	3 a.m.

Note that in Cantonese, the expression for the 'time of day' always comes *before* the expression for the hour, e.g. **seuhngjau chāt dímjūng** and not *chāt dímjūng seuhngjau.

To indicate the minutes, one uses **fān**, as below:

léuhng dím sahp fān	ten minutes past two
sāam dím yih-sahp fān	twenty minutes past three
sei dím sei-sahp baat fān	forty-eight minutes past four

Note that when the minutes are indicated we only say **dím**, never **dímjūng**, thus **léuhng dím sahp fān** and never *léuhng dímjūng sahp fān.

Like English, Cantonese has special expressions for the half-hour and the quarter-hour, as below:

léuhng dím bun	half past two
sāam dím bun	half past three
sei dím yāt go gwāt	a quarter past four
ńgh dím sāam go gwāt	a quarter to six (lit. 'three quarters past five')

Note that **gwāt** (a quarter of an hour) must take the classifier **go**.

In Cantonese, there is one particular way of counting the minutes, not used in Mandarin Chinese. We divide up an hour into twelve five-minute units and we call each such unit a **jih**. **Jih**, like **gwāt**, must take the classifier **go**. Thus, **yāt go jih, léuhng go jih**. Below are some examples:

chāt dím yāt go jih	five past seven
chāt dím léuhng go jih	ten past seven
chāt dím sāam go jih	a quarter past seven
chāt dím sei go jih	twenty past seven

The **jih** in Cantonese refers to the numbers on the clock-face. Thus, if it is, say, twenty minutes past two o'clock, the minute-hand of the clock will be pointing at the *fourth* number on the clock, which is the figure *4*, and hence **léuhng dím** *sei* **go jih**.

Very often, in colloquial speech, **go jih** is omitted, and so:

baat dím chāt	eight thirty-five
baat dím baat	eight forty
baat dím gáu	a quarter to nine

Note that while **go jih** can be omitted, **fān** (for 'minutes') cannot. Consequently, **baat dím chāt** can only mean thirty-five minutes, *and not* seven minutes, past eight.

Quick practice 1
Match the times in the left-hand column below with the Cantonese phrases in the right-hand column.

(a) 9:50 a.m.   **seuhngjau sahp dím sei**   c
(b) 11:35 a.m.   **hahjau ńgh dím sahp-yāt**   d
(c) 10:20 a.m.   **hahjau sāam dím baat**   f
(d) 5:55 p.m.   **seuhngjau gáu dím sahp**   a
(e) 6:25 p.m.   **hahjau luhk dím ńgh**   e
(f) 3:40 p.m.   **seuhngjau chāt dím bun**   g
(g) 7:30 a.m.   **seuhngjau sahp-yāt dím chāt**   b

Quick practice 2
Look at the times on the digital clocks and then tell the time in '... **go jih**'. First write out the answer and then read it aloud. The first one has been done for you.

(a)

luhk dím chāt go jih

(b)

(c)

(d)

(e)

Dialogues

Read the questions, and then read or listen to each dialogue to find the answer.

1 John is talking to Emily at a Cantonese Students' Club gathering. Emily is about to leave.

(a) What time is it now?
(b) What time is Emily seeing a film?

EMILY: Yìhgā géidímjūng a, John?
JOHN: Yìhgā sei dím bun.
EMILY: Gám ngóh yiu jáu la. Ngóh yiu heui tái-dihnyíng a.
JOHN: Néih géidímjūng tái-dihnyíng a?
EMILY: Ngóh ńgh dím bun tái-díhnyíng.

2 Carmen is talking to Jack, the all-round sportsman.

(a) What time does Jack play tennis on Monday?
(b) What time does he go cycling on Saturday?
(c) What time does he play soccer on Sunday?

CARMEN: Jack, néih sīngkèih-yāt géidímjūng dá-móhngkàuh a?
JACK: Ngóh sīngkèih-yāt yehmáahn chāt dímjūng dá-móhngkàuh.
CARMEN: Gám, néih sīngkèih-luhk géidímjūng cháai-dāanchē a?

JACK: Ngóh sīngkèih-luhk hahjau sei dím bun cháai-dāanchē.
CARMEN: Sīngkèih-yaht nē? Sīngkèih-yaht néih géidímjūng tek-jūkkàuh a?
JACK: Sīngkèih-yaht ngóh seuhngjau gáu dím sāam go gwāt tek-jūkkàuh.

Idioms and structures

The items in the list below appear in the same order as they do in the dialogues above. The *italicized* items are *new* items. In the notes, numbers in brackets refer to the expressions listed below.

1 *yìhgā*   now
2 *géidímjūng a?*   *what time?*
3 *yiu*   *must/have to*
4 **ngóh yiu** *jáu la*   I have to *leave*
5 **heui**   go

Géi   *(2)*

Géi is an interrogative form in Cantonese which means 'what' or 'how'. In Lesson 1 we learnt that **géidō chín** is literally *and* functionally 'how much money?' Here, **géidímjūng** is literally 'what point of the clock?' and functionally means 'what time?'

Obligation   *(3)*

Yiu is used here as a modal to express obligation, as in **Ngóh** *yiu* **jáu la** ('I have to leave'). This is to be distinguished from the use of **yiu** as a main verb, which means 'want', as in Lesson 1: **Ngóh jauh** *yiu* **yāt bohng lā** ('Then I want one pound').

La   *(4)*

La is a sentence-final particle in Cantonese to indicate changed status. In Dialogue 1 above, Emily uses **la** with **Ngóh yiu jáu** to indicate she is leaving instead of staying.

Vocabulary ▣

Daily routine

Below are some vocabulary items referring to daily routine. Try reading out each item aloud. If you have the cassette tapes of this book, you can model your pronunciation on the tape recording.

héi-sān 起身	to get up
sihk-jóuchāan 食早餐	to have breakfast
fāan-gūng 返工	to go to work
sihk-ngaan 食晏	to have lunch
fong-gūng 放工	to go off work
sihk-máahnfaahn	to have dinner 食晚飯
fan-gaau	to sleep 瞓覺

Note that **sihk-jóuchāan**, **sihk-ngaan** and **sihk-máahnfaahn** are verb-object constructions formed with the verb **sihk** ('to eat') and an object denoting a meal, **jóuchāan** for 'breakfast', **ngaan** for 'lunch' and **máahnfaahn** for 'dinner'.

More time expressions

gāmyaht 今日	today
tīngyaht 聽日	tomorrow
chàhmyaht 尋日	yesterday
gāmmáahn 今晚	this evening/tonight
tīngmáahn 聽晚	tomorrow evening/tomorrow night
chàhmmáahn 尋晚	yesterday evening/last night

Note that many Cantonese speakers say **kàhmmáahn** instead of **chàhmmáahn**. This is a case of free variation where neither pronunciation is more correct than the other.

Types of television program

sānmán 新聞	news
tīnhei bougou 天氣報告	weather report
dihnsihkehk	TV drama 電視劇
dihnyíng 電影	film
géiluhkpín 記錄片	documentary

táiyuhk sports
choimáh horse-racing

Dialogues

Read the questions, and then try to find the answers in the dialogues either by reading the texts or by listening to the cassette recording. (Dialogue 5 is not included on the cassette.)

3 John is talking to Richard about their daily routine.

(a) What time does Richard get up in the morning?
(b) What time does Richard go to bed?
(c) What about John?

JOHN: Richard, néih tūngsèuhng géidímjūng héi-sān a?
RICHARD: Ngóh tūngsèuhng seuhngjau chāt dím sāam héi-sān.
JOHN: Gám néih yehmáahn géidímjūng fan-gaau a?
RICHARD: Ngóh yehmáahn tūngsèuhng sahp-yāt dím bun fan-gaau. Néih nē, John?
JOHN: Ngóh seuhngjau baat dímjūng héi-sān. Yehmáahn daaihyeuk sahp-yih dím fan-gaau.

4 Carmen is talking to her friend Mary on the phone. Mary has a TV guide and Carmen is asking her about tonight's programs.

(a) What time is the evening TV film?
(b) What times is the daily news on?
(c) What time is the weather report?

CARMEN: Mary, dihnsih gāmmáahn géidímjūng yáuh dihnyíng tái a?
MARY: Gāmmáahn gáu dím bun yáuh dihnyíng tái.
CARMEN: Gám, géidímjūng yáuh sānmán tái a?
MARY: Gāmmáahn chāt dímjūng tùhng sahp-yāt dím bun dōu yáuh sānmán tái.
CARMEN: Gám, tīnhei bougou nē? Géidímjūng yáuh dāk tái a?
MARY: Tīnhei bougou hái chāt dím bun jouh.

5 John is talking to Jack on the phone. Jack is telling him about the sports programs being shown on TV over the next two evenings.

(a) When is tennis shown on TV?
(b) When is soccer shown?
(c) What about horse-racing?

JOHN: Jack, gāmmáahn tùhng tīngmáahn dihnsih yáuh mātyeh hóutái a?

JACK: Gāmmáahn luhk dím yáuh móhngkàuh tái. Yìhnhauh baat dím bun yáuh jūkkàuh tái.

JOHN: Ngóh mjūngyi tái móhngkàuh tùhng jūkkàuh. Gāmmáahn yáuh móuh choimáh tái a?

JACK: Gāmmáahn dihnsih móuh choimáh tái. Bātgwo tīngmáahn yáuh.

JOHN: Tīngmáahn géidímjūng yáuh choimáh tái a?

JACK: Tīngmáahn gáu dím chāt yáuh choimáh tái.

Idioms and structures

The items in the list below appear in the same order as they do in the dialogues above. The *italicized* items are *new* items. In the notes, numbers in brackets refer to the expressions listed below.

1 *tūngsèuhng* — usually
2 **gāmmáahn géidímjūng yáuh dihnyíng tái a?** — At what time is the film on tonight?
3 **Géidímjūng yáuh *dāk* tái a?** — At what time *can* it be seen?
4 *hái* chāt dím bun *jouh* — *shows at* half past seven
5 *hóutái* — interesting (literally, good to watch)
6 *yìhnhauh* — *then, later on*
7 **Gāmmáahn *yáuh móuh* choimáh tái a?** — *Is there any* horse-racing on tonight?

Existential *yáuh* (2)

Yáuh is used existentially here (see Lesson 3 for the uses of **yáuh**). *Yáuh* dihnyíng tái means literally 'There is a film to see'.

Possibility (3)

Dāk is a verbal particle which is used to indicate possibility or permission. For example, in Dialogue 4, in **Géidímjūng yáuh _dāk_ tái a?**, **dāk** follows the existential verb **yáuh** and precedes the main verb **tái**, and the consequent expression **yáuh _dāk_ tái** means 'can be seen'.

Point of time (4)

Here **hái** is a time marker used prepositionally, meaning 'at (a certain time)'. Thus, **Tīnhei bougou _hái_ chāt dím bun jouh** means 'The weather report is shown at half past seven'.

Jouh 做 (4)

天気 報告

Jouh is a verb with a wide range of meanings. Here it is not used in its most common meaning, 'to do'. Instead it refers to a TV program or a film being on. Thus, **Tīnhei bougou hái chāt dím bun _jouh_** means 'The weather report is shown at half past seven', while **Nī chēut dihnyíng hái Palace Theatre _jouh_** means 'This film is on at the Palace Theatre' (**chēut** being the classifier for **dihnyíng**). Note that the word order of such sentences differs in Cantonese from English. In Cantonese, the time expression comes _before_ the verb, hence **Tīnhei bougou hái chāt dímjūng _jouh_**. In English, the time expression comes _after_ the verb, as in 'The weather report is (shown) at 7 o'clock'.

Yáuh móuh (7)

A choice-type question with the existential verb **yáuh** is formed from the positive verb **yáuh** and its negative counterpart **móuh**. This choice-interrogative, **yáuh móuh**, is complemented by the particle **a**, in the function of sentence-interrogative. Hence the question **Gāmmáahn _yáuh móuh_ choimáh tái a?**

Exercises

Exercise 1 Comprehension
Read the following questions. Then go back to Dialogues 3, 4 and 5 and find the answers to the questions.

(a) According to Dialogue 3, who sleeps longer every night?
/ (i) John
(ii) Richard
(b) According to Dialogue 4, how many times is the TV news shown in the evening?
(i) once
/ (ii) twice
(iii) three times
(c) According to Dialogue 5, what kind of program does John like watching?
(i) news
(ii) soccer
(iii) tennis
/ (iv) horse-racing
(d) According to Dialogue 5, what kinds of program does Jack enjoy watching?
(i) news and weather
/ (ii) tennis and soccer
(iii) horse-racing

Exercise 2 Telling the time
You are in the street. Someone comes up to you and asks, 'Yìhgā géidímjūng a?' Reply according to the times given below. Remember you have several options as to how to tell the time. Write out your answers first and then try reading out the answers aloud. (The first one has been done for you as an example.)

(a) 12:45 p.m. Yìhgā (haih) sahp-yih dím gáu.
Yìhgā (haih) sahp-yih dím sei-sahp ńgh fān.
Yìhgā (haih) sahp-yih dím sāam go gwāt.
(b) 3:35 p.m.
(c) 9:18 a.m.
(d) 11:52 a.m.
(e) 5:15 p.m.

Exercise 3 Daily routine

The table shows the daily routines of John, Carmen and Richard. Write your own routine in the fourth column. Then write sentences to describe each person's routine, including your own. After that, read the sentences aloud. (A few sentences have been written for you as examples.)

	John	Carmen	Richard	You
héi-sān	8:00	7:30	7:15	
fāan-gūng	9:30	9:00	9:00	
sihk-ngaan	1:00	12:30	1:00	
fong-gūng	6:00	5:15	5:30	
sihk-máahnfaahn	8:00	8:00	7:00	
fan-gaau	12:00	1:00	11:30	

(a) *John*
   John seuhngjau baat dímjūng héi-sān, gáu dím bun fāan-gūng. Kéuih hahjau yāt dímjūng sihk-ngaan, yìhnhauh luhk dím fong-gūng. . . .
(b) *Carmen*
(c) *Richard*
(d) *You*
   Ngóh . . . héi-sān . . .

Exercise 4 What's on TV tonight?

Referring to the TV guide here, answer all the questions by first writing out the answers and then reading them aloud.

7:05 p.m.	News
7:25 p.m.	Weather Report
7:30 p.m.	TV Drama
8:30 p.m.	Documentary
9:30 p.m.	TV Film
11:45 p.m.	Late News
12:10 a.m.	Weather Report
12:15 a.m.	Soccer

(a) **Gāmmáahn géidímjūng yáuh sānmán tái a?** 7.05 pm 11.45 pm
(b) **Gāmmáahn géidímjūng yáuh tīnhéi bougou tái a?** 1.25 pm 12.10 am
(c) **Ngóh jūngyi tái géiluhkpín. Gāmmáahn yáuh móuh géiluhkpín**
   tái a? Géidímjūng yáuh dāk tái a? 8.30 pm
(d) **Gāmmáahn gáu dím bun yáuh mātyéh tái a?** dihn yíng
(e) **Gāmmáahn géidímjūng yáuh móhngkàuh tái a?**
                                      Móuh

Recognizing Chinese characters

When telling the time in colloquial Cantonese, the expression
dímjūng is used to refer to 'o'clock'. However, in written Chinese,
a different expression

時

(pronounced as **sìh** in Cantonese) is used instead. Thus,

一時   dim

is 'one o'clock',

二時

is 'two o'clock', and

三時

is 'three o'clock'. The Chinese word for 'minute', namely,

分

(**fān**), on the other hand, is shared by spoken Mandarin and
colloquial Cantonese, and so is the word for the 'half-hour',

半

(**bun**). The written Chinese word for the 'quarter-hour',

刻

(pronounced **hāak** in Cantonese), however, is also a completely
different expression from **gwāt** used exclusively in colloquial
Cantonese.

一刻

is 'a quarter of an hour' and

三刻

is 'three quarters of an hour'. Below are some examples of times written in Chinese characters:

四 時   4 o'clock

五 時 十 分   5:10

六 時 半   6:30

七 時 一 刻   7:15

八 時 三 刻   8:45

The Chinese word for 'morning' is written as

上午

(pronounced **seuhngngh** in Cantonese), and is different from the most common colloquial Cantonese term of **seuhngjau**, though both share **seuhng**, which means 'the upper part'. Similarly, the Chinese word for 'afternoon' is written as

下午

(pronounced **hahngh** in Cantonese), as opposed to **hahjau** in colloquial Cantonese, **hah** meaning 'the lower part'.

踢足球 tek juk kau

戲院 hei yún

游泳池 yau wing chi

網球場 Nóng kau cheung

羽毛球場 yú mou kau cheung

唱K cheung K

游水 yau seui

打排球 da paai kau

打藍球 laam

田徑 tin ging

賽跑 chói paau

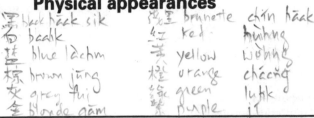

金 gold gām   chek 尺
銀 silver ngán   chyun 吋
銅 copper tùng   bohng 磅

5 Ngoihbíu 外表

Physical appearances

黑 black hāak sik   啡 brunette chín hāak
白 baahk   紅 red hùhng
藍 blue làahm   黃 yellow wòhng
棕 brown jūng   橙 orange cháaang
灰 grey fūi   綠 green luhk
金 blonde gām   紫 purple jí

In Lesson 5 you will learn about: 對手

- describing people's age and physical appearance
- pointing out people and objects
- terms for family members
- possessive forms

Vocabulary

眼睛 ngáan jīng
大細 daaihsai

Physical appearances

Below are some words and expressions for describing people's physical appearances. Try reading out each item aloud. If you have the cassette tapes of this book with you, you can model your pronunciation on the recording.

gōu	tall height sān gōu
ngái	short foot chek
gōudaaih	big weight tái chúhng
ngáisai	small 磅 pound bohng
fèih	fat
sau	thin
chèuhng tàuhfaat	long-haired curly lyūn dyed yím tàufaat
dyún tàuhfaat	short-haired permed din
leng	pretty
lengjái	handsome boy
lóuh	old
hauhsāang	young
daai ngáahngéng	wears glasses
móuh daai ngáahngéng	does not wear glasses

yáuh wùhsōu	has a moustache/beard
móuh wùhsōu	does not have a moustache/beard

This list gives the adjectives or adjective phrases in pairs of opposite meanings. However, words such as **gōu** (tall) and **ngái** (short) represent two poles between which are intermediate points for various degrees of height. Below is a list of expressions for expressing different perceptions of height:

hóu gōu	very tall
géi gōu/gōu-gōu-déi	quite tall
mhaih géi gōu/màh-má-déi gōu	not too tall
géi ngái/ngái-ngái-déi	quite short
hóu ngái	very short

Reduplicated adjective + **déi**

The pattern 'adjective + reduplicated adjective + **déi**', such as **gōu-gōu-déi**, is very common in colloquial Cantonese. However, there is a rule to observe when forming such a pattern. The reduplicated adjective always undergoes a tone change and takes on the *high rising tone*. Thus, **géi sau** can be expressed as **sau-*sáu*-déi**, **géi fèih** as **fèih-*féi*-déi**, and **géi lóuh** as **lóuh-*lóu*-déi**. However, when the adjective is on a high level tone (e.g. **gōu**) or high rising tone (e.g. **ngái**), the tone of the reduplicated adjective remains unchanged, e.g. **gōu-gōu-déi**, **ngái-ngái-déi**.

Adjective phrases such as **daai ngáahngéng** vs. **móuh daai ngáahngéng** and **yáuh wùhsōu** vs. **móuh wùhsōu** belong to another category in that they represent 'either-or' situations without any intermediate possibilities. Thus someone can only be **daai ngáahngéng** or **móuh daai ngáahngéng** but never *****géi daai ngáahngéng.**

Dialogues

Read the questions, and then read or listen to each dialogue to find the answers. If you have the cassette tapes, you may wish to listen to the dialogues and answer the questions without reading the texts.

1 John is on the phone arranging to meet Susan, whom he has never met before. They need to find out about each other's appearance so that they can recognize each other when they meet.

(a) What does John look like? *wear glasses not fat not thin*

(b) What does Susan look like? *hair short hair ; a bit thin not very tall, not wearing glasses*

SUSAN: Chíng mahn néih haih dímyéung ga?

JOHN: Ngóh daai ngáahngéng, géi gōu.

SUSAN: Gám, néih fèih dihng sau a?

JOHN: Ngóh mhaih hóu fèih, mhaih hóu sau. Gám, néih nē? Néih haih dímyéung ga?

SUSAN: Ngóh haih yāt go dyún tàuhfaat ge néuihjái, sau-sáu-déi, mhaih géi gōu.

JOHN: Gám néih yáuh móuh daai ngáahngéng a?

SUSAN: Móuh, ngóh móuh daai ngáahngéng.

How old is Mrs Lam?

2 John and Carmen are at a gathering of the Cantonese Students' Club. Carmen is pointing out to John which is Mr Tong, her Cantonese teacher.

Very tall quite thin wear glasses short hair quite good looking

(a) What does Mr Tong, Carmen's Cantonese teacher, look like?

(b) What does Mrs Lam, John's Cantonese teacher, look like?

long hair not wear glasses quite good looking rather short very young

JOHN: Carmen, bīngo haih Tòhng lóuhsī a?

CARMEN: Nē! Gó bīn hóu gōu, sau-sáu-déi, daai ngáahngéng gó go jauh haih Tòhng lóuhsī laak.

JOHN: Gó bīn gōu-gōu-sau-sau, daai ngáahngéng, dyún tàuhfaat, géi lengjái gó go jauh haih Tòhng lóuhsī àh?

CARMEN: Haih laak. Gám, néih go Gwóngdūngwá lóuhsī Làhm táai nē? Kéuih hái bīndouh a?

JOHN: Nē! Gó bīn chèuhng tàuhfaat, móuh daai ngáahngéng, géi leng gó go jauh haih Làhm táai laak.

CARMEN: Haih-mh-haih ngái-ngái-déi gó go a?

JOHN: Haih laak.

CARMEN: Kéuih hóu hauhsāang wo.

JOHN: Haih a. Kéuih yih-sahp chāt seui ja. *only 二十七歲咋*

Idioms and structures

The items in the list below appear in the same order as they do in the dialogue above. The *italicized* items are *new* items. In the notes, numbers in brackets refer to the expressions listed below.

1	*néih haih dímyéung ga?*	*What do you look like?*
2	néih fèih dihng sau a?	Are you fat or thin?
3	*Ngóh haih yāt go dyún* *tàuhfaat ge néuihjái.*	*I am a short-haired girl.*
4	néih yáuh móuh daai ngáahngéng a?	Do you wear glasses?
5	*Nē!*	*Look over there!*
6	*gó bīn*	*over there*
7	*gó go*	*that person*
8	*Tòhng lóuhsī*	*my teacher Mr Tong*
9	gó go *jauh haih* Tòhng lóuhsī *laak*	*that is* my teacher Mr Tong
10	gó bīn . . . gó go *jauh haih* Tòhng lóuhsī *àh?*	*so*, the . . . one over there *is* Mr Tong
11	*Haih laak.*	*That's right.*
12	*néih go* Gwóngdūngwá lóuhsī	*your* Cantonese teacher
13	*Làhm táai*	*Mrs Lam*
14	Kéuih hóu hauhsāang *wo*.	She looks very young.
15	Kéuih *yih-sahp chāt seui ja.*	She's *only 27 years old.*

Asking about physical appearance (1, 2, 4)

There are several ways to ask about somebody's appearance. The first way is to ask a general question:

Kéuih (haih) dímyéung ga? What does he/she look like?

Note that to ask what somebody looks like, the particle **ga**, and not **a**, is used. The question **Kéuih dímyéung a?** has a different meaning, that of 'How is he/she?', asking about feelings rather than appearance.

Instead of asking a general question, you can ask about a particular physical feature. There are two ways of doing this. The first way is to use the *unmarked* form of a pair of opposite attributes (for instance, 'tall' is used in the pair of 'tall vs. short') and form a choice-type question:

Kéuih gōu-mh-gōu a?	Is he/she tall?
Kéuih fèih-mh-fèih a?	Is he/she fat?

The second way is to form an 'either/or' question with the two opposing attributes by using the word **dihng** (or) in between:

Kéuih gōu dihng ngái a?	Is he/she tall or short?
Kéuih fèih dihng sau a?	Is he/she fat or thin?

To ask about 'glasses vs. no glasses' or 'moustache/beard vs. no moustache/beard', a choice-type question using the existential verbs **yáuh** and **móuh** is used:

Kéuih yáuh móuh daai ngáahngéng a?	Does he/she wear glasses?
Kéuih yáuh móuh wùhsōu a?	Does he have a beard/moustache?

Describing physical appearance (3)

There are two ways to form sentences to describe somebody's physical appearance. The first way is to use the adjectives *predicatively*, i.e. without a noun:

Kéuih hóu gōu.	He is very tall.
Kéuih gōu-gōu-sau-sau.	He is tall and thin.
Kéuih màh-má-déi gōu.	He's not very tall.

The second way is to use the adjectives *attributively*, that is, before the nouns they modify:

Kéuih haih yāt go hóu gōu ge nàahmjái.	He is a very tall boy.
Kéuih haih yāt go gōu-gōu-sau-sau ge nàahmjái.	He is a tall, thin boy.
Kéuih haih yāt go màh-má-déi gōu ge nàahmjái.	He is not a very tall boy.

There are several things to bear in mind when using the adjectives *attributively*. First of all, the verb **haih** is needed. Secondly, a noun phrase is formed with a numeral (in this case, **yāt**), a classifier (in this case, **go**), and a noun (in this case, **nàahmjái**). Lastly, there is a special particle **ge** which must be used after the adjective, hence **hóu gōu ge**, **gōu-gōu-sau-sau ge** and **màh-má-déi gōu ge**.

Nàahmjái can be translated into English as either 'man' or 'boy', depending on the context. It is used to refer to boys in their teens or young men in their twenties or thirties. The female counterpart of this is **néuihjái**. To refer to a more mature-looking man, the word **nàahmyán** is used. The female counterpart for **nàahmyán** is **néuih-yán**.

Interjective *nē* (5)

Nē is used here as an interjection to indicate to someone to look in a particular direction for a particular target. It is totally different in meaning from the **nē** used as a final particle.

Adverbial phrase of place (6)

Gó bīn is an adverbial phrase of place to refer to people or objects not immediately by the speaker, and can be translated into English as 'over there'. The corresponding adverbial phrase of place for referring to people or objects who are close to the speaker is **nī bīn**, which means 'over here'.

Demonstrative pronoun (7)

Gó go is a demonstrative pronoun used to refer to a person or object not near to the speaker, and can be translated into English as 'that'. **Gó go** is made up of two parts, namely, the determiner **gó** and the classifier **go**. Hence, it can only refer to nouns which take the classifier **go**. For example, *gó go* **yàhn** ('that person') and *gó go* **cháang** ('that orange') are fine but not **gó go* **dihnyíng**. The corresponding demonstrative pronoun for referring to people or objects close to the speaker is **nī go**, which has the specifier **nī** and means 'this'.

Addressing people by title (8)

Lóuhsī is a respectful word meaning 'teacher'. In Cantonese it can be used as a title after the surname of the teacher. Thus, a teacher whose surname is **Tòhng** would be addressed as **Tòhng lóuhsī**. The same applies to some professions which enjoy a high social status.

For example, 醫生 the word for 'lawyer' is **leuhtsī**, and the word for 律師 'doctor' is **yīsāng**; thus a lawyer whose surname is **Tòhng** is addressed as **Tòhng leuhtsī**, and a doctor named **Tòhng** is addressed as **Tòhng yīsāng**.

Emphasis *exactly* (9)

In **gó go jauh haih Tòhng lóuhsī laak**, both the adverb **jauh**, which means 'precisely' and the final particle **laak**, which is often used to indicate changed status, are used to give emphasis to **gó go haih Tòhng lóuhsī** ('That is Mr Tong').

Question with **àh** 呀 (10)

Gó go jauh haih Tòhng lóuhsī àh? is a question which is not asking for new information, but simply acknowledges what has been said and asks for confirmation. **Gó go jauh haih Tòhng lóuhsī** is a repetition of the original statement and the final particle **àh** turns it into a question.

Genitive pronoun *give me example* (12)

你个 Here **néih go** is used as a genitive (possessive) phrase to mean 'your' and so **néih go Gwóngdūngwá lóuhsī** means 'your Cantonese teacher'. Notice that the genitive phrase **néih go** is made up of the pronoun **néih** (you) and the classifier **go**. By the same token, 'my mango' would be **ngóh go mōnggwó**, and 'his book' would be **kéuih bún syū**, **bún** being the classifier for books.

Addressing married women (13)

In Cantonese, we address a married woman by using the word **taai-táai** *after* her husband's surname. Thus, 'Mrs Lam' is **Làhm taai-táai**, which in colloquial speech is often shortened into **Làhm táai**.

Final particle *wo* (14)

Wo is a final particle to express emphatic recognition of a mildly surprising fact; in the case of the sentence **Kéuih hóu hauhsāang** *wo* the unexpected observation is how young Mrs Lam looks.

Expressing age (15)

Seui means 'years of age', and so **yih-sahp chāt seui** is 'twenty-seven years old'. Below are some examples of different ages:

yāt seui	one year old
léuhng seui	two years old
sāam seui	three years old
sahp seui	ten years old
yih-sahp seui	twenty years old
yih-sahp ńgh seui	twenty-five years old
sāam-sahp seui	thirty years old

As the numbers under a hundred are so commonly used in colloquial speech, the two-syllable words such as **yih-sahp**, **sāam-sahp**, **sei-sahp** are often elided in natural speech to form new shorter sounds. For example, **yih-sahp** is elided into the single syllable **y'ah** (the apostrophe denotes the elision); thus, **y'ah seui** is '20 years old' and **y'ah yāt seui** is '21 years old'. **Sāam-sahp** is elided into **sā'ah** and so **sā'ah seui** is '30 years old' and **sā'ah chāt seui** is '37 years old'. Here is a list of such elided forms:

y'ah mān	**yih-sahp mān**	$20
sā'ah mān	**sāam-sahp mān**	$30
sei'ah mān	**sei-sahp mān**	$40
ńgh'ah mān	**ńgh-sahp mān**	$50
luhk'ah mān	**luhk-sahp mān**	$60
chāt'ah mān	**chāt-sahp mān**	$70
baat'ah mān	**baat-sahp mān**	$80
gáu'ah mān	**gáu-sahp mān**	$90

To ask somebody's age, you say: **Néih géidō seui a?** (lit. 'You how many years old?').

*Final particle **ja*** (15)

Ja is a final particle which adds the meaning of 'only'. For example, **Kéuih yih-sahp chāt seui** *ja* means 'She's *only* 27', while **Ngóh yáuh sahp mān** *ja* means 'I have *only* ten dollars'.

Vocabulary 🔲

Kinship terms

Chinese kinship terms are much more specific and complex than English ones. Below is a list of the most common ones. Try reading out each aloud, and listen to them if you have the cassette tapes.

bàh-bā	father
màh-mā	mother
gòh-gō/daaihlóu	elder brother
dàih-dái/sailóu	younger brother
jèh-jé/gājē	elder sister
(mùih-)múi	younger sister
jái	son
néui	daughter

Notice that the first six are all reduplicated words, but the same character is pronounced on two different tones, though all six terms begin with a *low falling tone*. The alternatives for 'elder brother', 'younger brother', and 'elder sister' do not follow the same pattern. **Daaihlóu** literally means 'big boy', **daaih** meaning 'big', **sailóu** literally means 'small boy', **sai** meaning 'small', and **gājē** literally means 'big sister at home', as **gā** by itself means 'home'.

Dialogue 🔲

Read the questions, and then read or listen to the dialogue to find the answers.

3 John is looking at Emily's family photo. Emily is telling him about the members of her family.

(a) How old are Emily's parents? both 49

(b) How old is Emily's brother?
(c) How old is Emily's sister?

EMILY: Nī sei go jauh haih ngóh dī ngūkkéiyàhn laak.
JOHN: Nī go haih-mh-haih néih bàh-bā a?
EMILY: Haih laak. Nī go jauh haih ngóh bàh-bā laak. Gaaklèih nī go haih ngóh màh-mā. Ngóh bàh-bā tùhng ngóh màh-mā dōu haih sei-sahp gáu seui.
JOHN: Kéuihdeih sei-sahp gáu seui làh? Kéuihdeih go yéung hóu hauhsāang wo.
EMILY: Haih a. Nē! Gaaklèih gó léuhng go jauh haih ngóh go sailóu tùhng ngóh go mùih-múi laak. Ngóh sailóu gāmnín sahp-yih seui. Ngóh go múi gāmnín sahp-yāt seui.

Idioms and structures

The items in the list below appear in the same order as they do in the dialogue above. The *italicized* items are *new* items. In the notes, numbers in brackets refer to the expressions listed below.

1 *Nī géi go* — these (several people)
2 ngūkkéiyàhn — family members
3 ngóh *dī* ngūkkéiyàhn — *my* family members
4 *Jóbīn* nī go — the one *on the left*
5 *ngóh* bàh-bā — *my* father
6 *gaaklèih* — *by the side*
7 Kéuihdeih sei-sahp gáu seui *làh?* — So they are forty-nine? (showing surprise)
8 Kéuihdeih go *yéung* — Their *appearance*
9 *Yauhbīn* nī léuhng go — the two *on the right*
10 *gāmnìhn* — *this year*

Demonstrative pronoun with classifier (1)

Nī **géi go** is the demonstrative pronoun **nī go** with the numeral **géi** (several) in between, meaning 'these (several people)'. Remember that **go** is a classifier for some nouns only, and other demonstrative pronouns with different classifiers are needed for certain nouns. In **Nī géi go jauh haih ngóh dī ngūkkéiyàhn laak** the noun that **nī géi go** refers to is **yàhn** (people), which takes the classifier **go**.

my

néih dī

Modification of plurals (3)

ngóh

The **dī** in **ngóh dī ngūkkéiyàhn** is a marker of modification for plural nouns. It combines with **ngóh** to form the modifier **ngóh dī** to indicate possession. (Remember **néih go Gwóngdūngwá lóuhsī**, above.) Thus, **ngóh dī ngūkkéiyàhn** means 'my family members'. Similarly, **ngóh dī syū** means 'my books'.

Possession with family members (6)

Ngóh bàh-bā means 'my father'. It is a shortened form of **ngóh go bàh-bā**, where the classifier **go** is used. This kind of ellipsis can only take place with nouns pertaining to close family relationships, such as **néih màh-mā**, and not with other nouns, hence **ngóh bún syū** cannot be replaced by *ngóh syū**.

Final particle **làh** (8)

Làh is a final particle used to form questions showing surprise. Here, the question **Kéuihdeih sei-sahp gáu seui làh?** is a response to **Ngóh bàh-bā tùhng ngóh màh-mā dōu haih sei-sahp gáu seui**. The proposition that both parents are forty-nine is repeated and the anticipated answer is a confirmatory **Haih a**.

Exercises

Exercise 1 John's college friends

The dialogue below is between John and Carmen. They are looking at a picture taken of John's college friends. John is telling Carmen his friends' names. Read the dialogue or, preferably, listen to the recording on the cassette tape, and then label the picture with the correct names. Also, write their nationalities under the names in brackets.

CARMEN: John, nī go yáuh wùhsōu ge haih bīngo a?
JOHN: Nī go yáuh wùhsōu, daai ngáahngéng ge haih Michael. Kéuih haih Méihgwok yàhn.
CARMEN: Gám, nī go gōu-gōu-sau-sau, chèuhng tàuhfaat ge néuihjái nē? Kéuih giu mātyeh méng a?

JOHN: Nī go gōu-gōu-sau-sau ge néuihjái haih Christine. Kéuih haih Faatgwok yàhn.

CARMEN: Gaaklèih nī go daai ngáahngéng ge néuihjái yauh haih bīngo a? Kéuih hóu leng wo.

JOHN: Haih a. Judy géi leng ga. Judy haih Yīnggwok yàhn.

CARMEN: Nī go ngái-ngái-déi, móuh daai ngáahngéng ge nàahmjái haih bīngo a? Kéuih haih-mh-haih Jūng gwok yàhn a?

JOHN: Haih a. Kéuih haih Jūnggwok yàhn. Kéuih giujouh Li Ming.

Exercise 2 Elided forms of numbers

Read the following elided forms of numbers and then write out the correct numbers. The first one has been done for you as an example. (A more fruitful way of doing this exercise is to listen to the cassette tape and write down the numbers.)

(a) **y'ah sei seui** — 24 years old
(b) **ńgh'ah yih seui** — 52
(c) **sā'ah baat seui** — 38
(d) **chāt'ah yāt seui** — 71
(e) **gáu'ah luhk seui** — 96
(f) **sei'ah gáu seui** — 49

Mon wùcòu

Exercise 3 Teddy's family *b Martin gamnín ngh saph yih seui*

Refer to the picture of Teddy's family and answer the questions.
The first answer has been given for you as an example.

b Kéuih feifei dei mhaih gei hóu daaih, ngaan géng dyún tsubfaat
c Pam gamnin sei saph géi seui Keui ngái ngái dei, mhaih hou fei
mhaih hóu sau daai ngaan géng chèung tàuh faat

CLARA 17   MARTIN 52   PAM 49   JIMMY 13

d) Clara gamnín saph chat seui. Kéuih góu góu sau sau
mouh dai ngaan géng, chèung tàuh faat, kéuih dei long ga
e) Jimmy gamnín saph saam seui. Keui hou ngái géi sau ga
daai ngaangéng dyún tàuh faat

(a) **Teddy yáuh géidō go ngūkkéiyàhn a?**
  Teddy yáuh sei go ngūkkéiyàhn. Kéuih bàh-bā giu Martin.
  Kéuih màh-mā giu Pam. Kéuih yáuh yāt go gājē, giujouh
  Clara. Kéuih yáuh yāt go sailóu, giujouh Jimmy.
(b) **Martin gāmnín géidō seui a? Kéuih dímyéung ga?**
  Martin gāmnín . . . seui. Kéuih daai ngáahngéng . . .
(c) **Pam géidō seui a? Kéuih gōu dihng ngái, fèih dihng sau a?**
(d) **Clara nē? Kéuih dímyéung ga? Kéuih leng-mh-leng ga?**
(e) **Jimmy gāmnín géidō seui a? Kéuih dímyéung ga?**

Exercise 4 Your family members

Now introduce your own family by first saying how many family
members you have, and then describing what each of them looks
like.

  Ngóh yáuh . . . go ngūkkéiyàhn. Kéuihdeih haih . . .

Recognizing Chinese characters

Below are the kinship terms relating to members of the family, written in Chinese characters.

爸爸　　father

媽媽　　mother

哥哥　　elder brother

弟弟　　younger brother

姐姐　　elder sister

妹妹　　younger sister

z 0.65 } lùhk saph ngh bin sí
₣1.50 bohng hon
z 2.78 léuhng bohng chāt saph heat
₣14.30 saph sei bohng saam

6 Gachìhn

Prices *Where do they buy furniture?*

In Lesson 6 you will learn about:

- larger numbers
- comparing
- using -jó for completion of action
- how to indicate the superlative

Vocabulary 📼

Furniture

Below is a list of some items of furniture. The Cantonese word for 'furniture', namely, **gāsī**, is, like its English counterpart, a collective and 'a piece of furniture' needs the classifier **gihn**, hence **yāt gihn gāsī**. The classifier for specific furniture items such as tables and chairs is **jēung**, hence **yāt jēung sōfá, yāt jēung chāantói**. The classifier for other furniture items is often **go**, as in **yāt go syūgá**.

yāt jēung sōfá	a sofa	梳化
yāt jēung chāantói	a dining table	餐枱
yāt jēung chāanyí	a dining chair	餐椅
yāt jēung chàhgēi	a coffee table	茶几
yāt jēung ōnlohkyí	an easy chair	安樂椅
yāt go syūgá	a bookcase	書架

Dining chair and coffee table

Chāandang is sometimes used instead of **chāanyí** to refer to 'dining chairs'. To refer to an ordinary chair, probably **dang** is more commonly used in colloquial speech than **yí**, which is used in spoken Mandarin and written Chinese.

A coffee table is referred to as **chàhgēi** (lit. 'tea table') in Cantonese, as Chinese people drink *tea* at the same kind of short, four-legged table usually put in front of a sofa which Westerners drink *coffee* at and call a 'coffee table'.

Amounts of money

In Lesson 1 we introduced the numbers 1 to 100 and we noted that 'dollar' is **mān** in Cantonese. In this lesson we shall talk about larger amounts of money, up to one million. Below is a list of expressions for stating different amounts of money. Try reading out each item aloud. If you have the cassette tapes of this book with you, you can model your pronunciation on the recording.

yāt mān	$1
sahp mān	$10
yāt-baak mān	$100
yāt-chīn mān	$1,000
yāt-maahn mān	$10,000
sahp-maahn mān	$100,000
yāt-baakmaahn mān	$1,000,000

The table shows the Cantonese terms and English terms assigned to the digits up to a million.

baakmaahn	sahpmaahn	maahn	chīn	baak	sahp	go
million	hundred thousand	ten thousand	thousand	hundred	ten	unit

To state a particular number, one reads from the leftmost digit to the right, as in English. The figures in the second table are spelt out below.

baakmaahn	sahpmaahn	maahn	chīn	baak	sahp	go
					8	9
				1	2	3
			6	5	4	3
		5	6	7	8	9
	3	3	0	0	0	0
2	7	0	0	0	0	0

baat-sahp gáu
yāt-baak yih-sahp sāam
luhk-chīn ńgh-baak sei-sahp sāam
ńgh-maahn luhk-chīn chāt-baak baat-sahp gáu
sāam-sahp sāam maahn
yih-baak chāt-sahp maahn

Quick practice 1

Translate the sums of money into Cantonese. The first one has been done for you as an example.

(a) $147   **yāt-baak sei-sahp chāt mān**
(b) $256   *yih baak ńgh saph luhk mān*
(c) $1,789   *yāt chīn chāt baak baat saph gáu mān*
(d) $5,620   *ńgh chīn luhk baak yih saph mān*
(e) $15,000   *yāt maahn ńgh chīn mān*
(f) $37,500   *sāam maahn chāt chīn ńgh baak mān*
(g) $937,000   *gáu saph sāam maahn chāt chīn mān*
(h) $562,100   *ńgh saph luhk maahn yih chīn yāt baak mān*
(i) $1,520,000   *yāt baak ńgh saph yih maahn mān*
(j) $4,689,000   *sei baak luhk saph baat maahn gáu chīn mān*

Note that when there are zeros in the middle of a figure, like $194,022, the word **lìhng** is used to link up the two parts. Thus, $194,022 is read as **sahp-gáu maahn sei chīn lìhng yih-sahp yih mān**.

Quick practice 2

Translate the following figures into Cantonese. The first one has been done for you as an example.

(a) $203   **yih-baak lìhng sāam mān**
(b) $1,030   *yāt chīn lìhng sāam saph mān*
(c) $27,005   *yih* ~~sahp~~ *maahn chāt chīn lìhng ńgh mān*
(d) $500,400   *ńgh saph maahn lìhng sei baak mān*
(e) $1,900,800   *yāt baak gáu saph maahn lìhng baat baak mān*

Uncertain amounts of money

Sometimes when the speaker is not certain about the exact amount of money, then the Cantonese word **géi** is used as a 'wild card' to refer to the uncertain part. For example, *géi* **mān** is 'several dollars', and *géi*-**baak mān** is 'a few hundred dollars'. On the other hand, **sahp**-*géi* **mān** means 'ten dollars odd', while **baak**-*géi* **mān** means 'a hundred dollars odd'. Below is a list of how the word *géi* functions in such uncertain contexts:

géi mān	$?
sahp-géi mān	$1?
géi-sahp mān	$?0
baak-géi mān	$1??
géi-baak mān	$?00
chīn-géi mān	$1,???
géi-chīn mān	$?,000
maahn-géi mān	$1?,???
géi-maahn mān	$?0,000
sahp-géi maahn mān	$1??,???
géi-sahp maahn mān	$?00,000
baak-géi maahn mān	$1,???,???
géi-baak maahn mān	$?,000,000

> *Several*
>
> While the Cantonese word **géi** can be translated into either 'several', as in *géi***chīn mān** ('several thousand dollars'), or 'odd', as in **baak***géi* **mān** ('a hundred dollars odd'), there is apparently no equivalent in English for *géi***sahp mān**, which literally means 'several ten dollars'.

Quick practice 3
Translate each of the 'uncertain' figures below into Cantonese, using the word **géi**. The first one has been done for you as an example.

(a) $32?   **sāam-baak yih-sahp géi mān**
(b) $5??   *ńgh baak géi sahp mān*
(c) $4,2??   *sei chīn yih baak géi sahp mān*
(d) $36,???   *sāam màahn luhk chīn géi baak*
(e) $1??,???   *sahp géi màahn*

(f) $92?,??? _gáu seph yih lnechn géi man_
(g) $1,2??,??? _yāt baak yih seph gáet maahn nen_
(h) $4,???,??? _sei baak géi meahn nen_

Dialogues

Read the questions, and then read or listen to each dialogue to find the answers.

1 John and Carmen have been invited to dinner at Mrs Lam's home. They are admiring the furniture in Mrs Lam's flat.

(a) How much did Mrs Lam's sofa cost?
(b) How much did Mrs Lam's dining table and dining chairs cost?
(c) How much did Mrs Lam's coffee table cost?

CARMEN: Làhmtáai, néih ngūkkéi dī gāsī hóu leng wo.
MRS LAM: Dōjeh. Ngóh dōu hóu jūngyi ngóh ngūkkéi dī gāsī ga.
CARMEN: Nī jēung sōfá yiu géidō chín a?
MRS LAM: Nī jēung sōfá máaih-jó yāt-maahn yih-chīn ńgh-baak mān.
CARMEN: Gám, nī jēung chāantói nē?
MRS LAM: Nī jēung chāantói máaih-jó chāt-chīn mān. Dī chāanyí jauh baat-baak mān yāt jēung.
JOHN: Ngóh jeui jūngyi nī jēung chàhgēi. Yiu géidō chín a?
MRS LAM: Nī jēung chàhgēi yiu sei-chīn luhk-baak mān.

2 John and Carmen are chatting to Jack, the sportsman.

(a) According to Jack, about how much does a decent tennis racket cost?
(b) About how much does a good pair of running shoes cost?
(c) About how much does a good bicycle cost?

JOHN: Jack, ngóh séung máaih yāt go hóu ge móhngkàuh-páak. Daaihyeuk yiu géidō chín a?

JACK:	Yāt go géi hóu ge móhngkàuhpáak daaihyeuk yiu yāt-chīn mān lā.
JOHN:	Gám, yāt deui hóu ge páaubouhhàaih nē? Yiu géidō chín a?
JACK:	Yāt deui páaubouhhàaih daaihyeuk yiu ńgh-baak mān.
CARMEN:	Ngóh séung máaih yāt ga dāanchē. Yiu géidō chín a?
JACK:	Yāt ga hóu ge dāanchē daaihyeuk yiu baat-chīn mān.

Idioms and structures

The items in the list below appear in the same order as they do in the dialogues above. The *italicized* items are *new* items. In the notes, numbers in brackets refer to the expressions listed below.

1 **Nī jēung sōfá yiu géidō chín a?**	How much did this sofa cost?
2 *máaih-jó*	*bought*
3 **Nī jēung sōfá máaih-jó yāt-maahn yih-chīn ńgh-baak mān**	I bought this sofa for $12,500.
4 **baat-baak mān yāt jēung**	$800 each
5 **yāt go hóu ge móhngkàuhpáak**	a decent tennis racket
6 **yāt *deui* páaubouhhàaih**	a *pair* of *running shoes*
7 **yāt *ga* dāanchē**	a bicycle (**ga** is the classifier for vehicles)

The verb **yiu** *(1)*

The verb **yiu** by itself means 'need' or 'require'. For example, **Dá móhngkàuh *yiu* géidō go yàhn a?** is 'How many people does it take to play a game of tennis?' In the context of prices, **géidō chín** is used. For example, **Dá yāt chi móhngkàuh *yiu* géidō chín a?** is 'How much does it cost to play a game of tennis?'

The aspect marker **-jó** *for completion of action (2)*

Cantonese verbs do not change in the way English verbs do ('buys, bought, buying') to show past, present, future and so on. However, certain aspects of the verb – whether it is a completed action or an action in progress, for example – are shown by attaching a particle (an aspect marker) to the end of the verb.

Máaih is a verb which means 'buy', and **-jó** is an aspect marker which indicates completion of an action. Thus, **Nī jēung sōfá ngóh máaih-*jó* yāt-maahn yih-chīn ńgh-baak mān** translates into 'This sofa was bought for $12,500.' Similarly, **Ngóh máaih-*jó* yāt dā pìhng-gwó** translates into 'I have bought a dozen apples'.

The aspect marker **-jó** is a bound form: it cannot exist by itself or be separated from the verb, hence the hyphen before **jó**. In the case of a verb-object construction, **-jó** will come between the verb and the object, as in **Kéuih heui-*jó* léuihhàhng** (he/she has gone traveling).

Vocabulary

Small units of money

In Cantonese, a smaller unit of money than the dollar (**mān**) is **hòuhjí**, which is a 'ten-cent unit'. Thus, 'ten cents' is **yāt hòuhjí**, 'twenty cents' is **léuhng hòuhjí**, and 'ninety cents' is **gáu hòuhjí**. When both dollars and cents are mentioned, we put the dollars before the cents. For example, 'three dollars and forty cents' is **sāam mān sei hòuhjí**, and 'five dollars and seventy cents' is **ńgh mān chāt hòuhjí**. However, in colloquial speech, most people would use a shorter form by dropping the **hòuhjí** at the end and using **go** instead of **mān** in between the two numbers. In this way, 'three dollars forty' becomes **sāam go sei**, and 'five dollars seventy' becomes **ńgh go chāt**. Below are a few more examples:

chāt go luhk	$7.60
baat go yāt	$8.10
gáu go sei	$9.40
sahp-yih go sāam	$12.30
sāam go yih	$3.20
sei go bun	$4.50
go chāt	$1.70

Note that $3.20 can be read as **sāam mān léuhng hòuhjí** or **sāam go yih,** but not *sāam go léuhng. (This is because when we say **léuhng hòuhjí** we are counting the number of **hòuhjí**'s there are, hence we use **léuhng**; but when we say **sāam go yih** we are reading out the number 2 from the figure $3.20, and hence **yih** is used.) However, $4.50 is read as **sei mān nǵh hòuhjí** or **sei go bun**, **bun** meaning 'half (a dollar)', but not as *sei go nǵh. $1.70 can be read as **yāt mān chāt hòuhjí** or **go chāt**, the **yāt** being dropped for the latter. Similarly, $1.80 is read as **go baat**.

Quick practice 4

Translate each of the following amounts into Cantonese, using the short colloquial form. The first one has been done for you as an example.

(a) $5.90   **nǵh go gáu**
(b) $9.10   *gáu go yat*
(c) $5.50   *ńgh go bun*
(d) $8.20   *baat go yih*
(e) $1.40   *go sei*
(f) $0.60   *luhk hòuhjí*

Postage   🔲

Below is a list of different mail items. Pay special attention to the classifiers used – **fūng** for letters, **go** for aerograms and **jēung** for postcards. 本港

yāt fūng seun 信	a letter
yāt fūng búngóng seun	a local letter
yāt fūng hòhnghūng seun	an air-mail letter
yāt fūng pìhngyàuh seun	a surface mail letter
yāt go yàuhgáan 郵柬	an aerogram
yāt jēung mìhngseunpín	a postcard

航空
平郵

明 信 片

Búngóng   *bún deih* 本地
本 港

The Cantonese word in Hong Kong for 'local letter', **búngóng**, is made up of two forms, **bún**, which means 'local', and **góng**, which is the second half of the name **Heūnggóng** (Hong Kong).

Dialogue 🔲

Read the questions, and then read or listen to the dialogue to find the answers.

3 John is talking to his colleague Kathy, who has recently arrived in Hong Kong from the USA and wants to find out about the postal rates in Hong Kong.

(a) How much does it cost to post a local letter?
(b) How much does it cost to send a postcard or an air-mail letter to the USA?
(c) How much does it cost to send a letter to the USA by surface mail?
(d) How much does it cost to send an aerogram?

KATHY: John, hái Hēunggóng gei-seun pèhng-mh-pèhng a?
JOHN: Hái Hēunggóng gei-seun hóu pèhng.
KATHY: Gám, gei yāt fūng seun yiu géidō chín a?
JOHN: Gei yāt fūng búngóng seun yiu yāt mān jēk.
KATHY: Hóu pèhng wo. Gám, gei yāt jēung mìhngseunpín heui Méihgwok yiu géidō chín a?
JOHN: Gei mìhngseunpín heui Méihgwok yiu léuhng go sei. Gei hòhnghūng seun heui Méihgwok dōu haih léuhng go sei.
KATHY: Gám, gei pìhngyàuh seun nē? Gei pìhngyàuh seun géidō chín a?
JOHN: Gei pìhngyàuh seun pèhng-dī, léuhng mān jēk.
KATHY: Gám, gei-seun heui Méihgwok dímyéung jeui pèhng a?
JOHN: Gei yàuhgāan jeui pèhng. Gei yāt go yàuhgáan heui Méihgwok yiu go gáu jēk.

Idioms and structures

The items in the list below appear in the same order as they do in the dialogues above. The *italicized* items are *new* items. In the notes, numbers in brackets refer to the expressions listed below.

1 **gei-seun**   *to send something by post*
2 **yiu baat hòuhjí jēk**   *it costs no more than 80 cents*

3 *gei ... heui Méihgwok*   *to send ... to the USA*
4 **gei-seun heui Méihgwok**   What is *the cheapest* way to send
     dímyéung *jeui pèhng* **a?**   letters to the USA?

The verb-object construction **gei-seun**   (1)

寄 信

Gei-seun is a verb-object construction in which **gei** means 'to send by post', while **seun** refers to any postal item(s). Thus, **Ngóh yiu** *gei-seun* means 'I have to get something posted' while **Ngóh yiu** *gei* **yāt fūng** *seun* means 'I have to post a letter', with **seun** meaning literally 'a letter'.

Jēk

Jēk is a sentence-final particle which indicates 'no more than' or 'only', here emphasizing the cheapness of the rate.

Adjectives for comparing prices   (4)

The following three adjectives are probably the most commonly used in comparing prices:

pèhng 平	cheap
gwai 貴	expensive
dái 抵	good value

When we compare the prices of two items, we use one of the two bound particles of comparison, namely, **-gwo** and **-dī,** depending on the structure.

-gwo is used when both items for comparison are mentioned:

Nī go móhngkàuhpáak gwai-*gwo* **gó go (móhngkàuhpáak).**
This tennis racket is more expensive than that (tennis racket).
Nī ga dāanchē dái-*gwo* **gó ga (dāanchē).**
This bicycle is better value than that (bicycle).

However, when only one item is mentioned, **-di** is used:

Nī go móhngkàuhpáak gwai-*dī.*
This tennis racket is more expensive.
Nī ga dāanchē dái-*dī.*
This bicycle is better value.

When three or more items are compared, the superlative **jeui** is often used, as follows:

Nī deui páaubouhhàaih *jeui* pèhng. *jeui most*
This pair of running shoes is the cheapest.

Nī jēung chāantói *jeui* gwai.
This dining table is the most expensive.

Exercises *Role play.*

Exercise 1 At the travel agent's 📼

John and Carmen plan to go for a ten-day holiday, but have not decided where to go. They are now at the travel agent's, asking the prices of holidays to different destinations. Grace is the travel agent.

Read the dialogue or, preferably, listen to the recording, and then complete the table that follows.

GRACE: Néihdeih séung heui bīndouh léuihhàhng a?
CARMEN: Ngóhdeih séung heui Yahtbún léuihhàhng. Heui Yahtbún yiu géidō chín a?
GRACE: Heui Yahtbún sahp yaht daaihyeuk yiu yāt-maahn yih-chīn mān.
CARMEN: Gam gwai àh? Gám, heui Hahwāiyìh nē? Heui Hahwāiyìh yiu géidō chín a?
GRACE: Heui Hahwāiyìh dōu haih yiu yāt-maahn yih-chīn mān.
JOHN: Hóu gwai wo. Gám, heui bīndouh pèhng-dī a?
GRACE: Heui Hòhngwok lā. Heui Hòhngwok daaihyeuk baat-chīn ńgh-baak mān jēk.
JOHN: Baat-chīn ńgh-baak mān dōu haih gwai wo. Gám, heui bīndouh jeui pèhng a?
GRACE: Heui Fēileùhtbān lā. Heui Fēileuhtbān yiu sei-chīn mān jēk.

Destination	Price of holiday
Japan	12,000
Hawaii	12,000
Korea	8,500
the Philippines	4,000

Exercise 2 Buying fruit 📼

Carmen is buying some fruit at Ah Wong's fruit-stall. Read the dialogue between Carmen and Ah Wong or, preferably, listen to the recording, and then complete the table with the information about how much of each fruit Carmen has bought and how much she has paid.

CARMEN:	Dī cháang dím maaih a?
AH WONG:	Dī cháang léuhng go bun yāt go.
CARMEN:	Ngóh yiu ńgh go cháang.
AH WONG:	Ńgh go cháang, sahp-yih go bun lā.
CARMEN:	Ngóh juhng yiu dī pìhnggwó.
AH WONG:	Pìhnggwó go chāt yāt go.
CARMEN:	Ngóh yiu sei go.
AH WONG:	Sei go pìhnggwó, luhk go baat lā.
CARMEN:	Yáuh móuh sāigwā a?
AH WONG:	Yáuh a. Dī sāigwā hóu leng a.
CARMEN:	Sāigwā géidō chín yāt bohng a?
AH WONG:	Sāigwā go sei yāt bohng . . . Nī go jeui leng laak . . . sahp bohng . . . sahp-sei mān lā.
CARMEN:	Júngguhng géidō chín a?
AH WONG:	Dī cháang sahp-yih go bun, pìhnggwó luhk go baat, sāigwā sahp-sei mān. Júngguhng sāam-sahp sāam go sāam lā.
CARMEN:	Nīdouh sāam-sahp sāam go sāam. Mgōi.
AH WONG:	Dōjeh.

Fruit	Amount	Price
Orange		
apple		
water melon		
		Total: 33.30

Exercise 3 At the furniture shop

You are a salesperson in a furniture shop. A customer comes in and asks for the prices of various pieces of furniture. Answer the questions by referring to the price-list. The first item has been done for you as an example.

sofa	$7,800
coffee table	$1,400
easy chair	$1,050

dining table b	$8,250
dining chair c	$910
bookcase h	$2,100

(a) **Nī go syūgá géidō chín a?** 亮要
   Nī go syūgá yih-chīn yāt-baak mān. 2100
(b) **Gám, nī jēung chāantói nē? Maaih géidō chín a?** beat chin yih baak ńgh
(c) **Dī chāanyí géidō chín yāt jēung a?** ǵui beak yāt saph man : saph men
(d) **Gó jēung sōfá yauh géidō chín a?** chāt chīn beat baak men
(e) **Nī jēung ōnlohkyí yauh géidō chín a?** yāt chīn ling ńgh saph man

Exercise 4 *Carmen's classmates*

Refer to the picture of Carmen's classmates, and answer the
questions about their physical appearance. The first one has been
done for you as an example.

(a) **Bīngo néuihjái jeui gōu a?**
   Diana jeui gōu.
(b) **Bīngo nàahmjái jeui ngái a?** Chris
(c) **Bīngo néuihjái jeui sau a?** Elsie °Diana°
(d) **Bīngo nàahmjái jeui fèih a?** chris

(e) **Sally dihng Elsie fèih-dī a?** Sally
(f) **William dihng Raul sau-dī a?** Raul
(g) **Bīngo néuihjái yáuh daai ngáahngéng a?** Elsie
(h) **Bīngo nàahmjái yáuh wùhsōu a?** Terry

Exercise 5 Which apples?

Four kinds of apples are sold in the supermarket. (See the picture.)
They come from four different countries, namely, Australia, the
USA, Japan and China. Compare their prices and then answer the
questions. The first has been done for you as an example.

(a) **Oujāu pìhnggwó dím maaih a?**
 Oujāu pìhnggwó sahp mān sāam go.
(b) **Méihgwok pìhnggwó géidō chín yāt go a?** sāam mān yāt go
(c) **Jūnggwok pìhnggwó dím maaih a?** léuhng mān yāt go
(d) **Yahtbún pìhnggwó nē? Géidō chín yāt go a?** yah ngh mān
(e) **Bīndī pìhnggwó jeui pèhng a?** jūng guok   yih sahp ngh
(f) **Bīndī pìhnggwó jeui gwai a?** yaht bún
(g) **Oujāu pìhnggwó tùhng Méihgwok pìhnggwó bīndī pèhng-dī a?**
(h) **Bīndī pìhnggwó jeui dái a?**   Méihgwok

Exercise 6 Comparisons

Translate the following sentences into Cantonese, using the com-
parative particles **-gwo** and **dī** and the superlative **jeui** as appropriate. The first has been done for you as an example.

(a) John is taller than Carmen. *gó jēung chāentói leng dī*
   John gōu-gwo Carmen.
(b) Carmen is thinner than Emily. *C sau gwo E*
(c) This coffee table is better value than that one. *nī jēung chàh gei dái*
(d) That dining chair is prettier. *gwo gó jēung*
(e) My tennis racket is more expensive. *ngóh jek Mòhng kàuh paak hai hóu gwai dī*
(f) This sofa is the cheapest. *nī jēung sōfá hai jeui pèhng*
(g) Carmen's bicycle is the best value. *C ga dāan chē hai jeui dái*

Recognizing Chinese characters

十 ten *sahp*

百 hundred *baak*

千 thousand *chīn*

萬 ten thousand *maahn*

十萬 hundred thousand *sahp maahp*

百萬 million *baak maahn*

Thus, 'twenty dollars' is

二十元, 元

being the Chinese character for 'dollars', 'three hundred dollars' is

三百元,

'four thousand dollars' is

四千元,

'fifty thousand dollars' is

五萬元,

and 'sixty-seven thousand dollars' is

六萬七千元.

7 Fāan-gūng

Commuting

In Lesson 7 you will learn about:

- describing means of transportation
- discussing how long journeys take
- expressing necessity

Vocabulary 🔲

Means of transportation

Below is a list of expressions about taking different means of transportation. Note that each of them is a verb-object construction, composed of the verb **daap**, which means 'to take a ride on', and a particular means of transportation. Try reading out each item aloud. If you have the cassette tapes of this book, you can model your pronunciation on the tape recording.

daap-deihtit 搭地鐵		to take the underground (in Hong Kong, MTR or Mass Transit Railway)
daap-fóchē 搭火車		to take a train
daap-bāsí 搭巴士		to take a bus
daap-síubā 搭小巴		to take a minibus
daap-dihnchē 搭電車		to take a tram
daap-dīksí 搭的士		to take a taxi
daap-syùhn 搭船		to take a ferry
daap-fēigēi 搭飛機		to take a plane

'To drive', on the other hand, is **jā-chē**, which literally means 'drive-(a)-car'. 'To walk' is **hàahng-louh**, which literally means 'walk-(along the)-road'.

Duration of time

Below are ways in which duration of time is expressed in Cantonese. Some items require the classifier **go** while others do not. Try reading out each item aloud, or model your pronunciation on the cassette tape.

yāt fānjūng	1 minute
yāt go jūngtàuh	1 hour
yāt yaht	1 day
yāt go láihbaai/sīngkèih	1 week
yāt go yuht	1 month
yāt nìhn	1 year

Note that special attention needs to be paid to the pronunciation of **yāt yaht** (one day) as there is only *tonal difference* between **yāt** and **yaht**.

As discussed in Lesson 4, **jih** is used to refer to five-minute spans, and it takes the classifier **go**. For example:

yāt go jih	5 minutes
léuhng go jih	10 minutes
sāam go jih	15 minutes

Dialogues 📼

Read the questions, and then read or listen to the dialogues to find the answers.

1 John and Carmen are chatting to Emily.

(a) How does Carmen go to work? And how long does it take?
(b) How does John go to work? How long does it take?
(c) How about Emily? What means of transportation does she use to go to work? And how long does it take her?

EMILY: Carmen, néih jīujóu dímyéung fāan-gūng a?
CARMEN: Ngóh jīujóu dōsou daap-deihtit fāan-gūng.
EMILY: Gám, daap-deihtit yiu géinoih a?
CARMEN: Yiu daaihyeuk gáu go jih.
EMILY: Yiu gáu go jih gam noih àh?
CARMEN: Haih a.

EMILY: Gám, néih nē, John? Néih daap mātyéh chē fāan-gūng a?
JOHN: Ngóh jā-chē fāan-gūng.
EMILY: Gám, yiu jā géinoih chē a?
JOHN: Yiu jā daaihyeuk y'ah ńgh fānjūng chē. Gám, néih nē, Emily? Néih yauh dímyéung fāan-gūng a?
EMILY: Ngóh msái daap-chē. Ngóh hàahng-louh fāan-gūng. Daaihyeuk hàahng bun go jūngtàuh jauh dāk laak.
CARMEN: Gám, dōu géi faai wo!

2 Mary and Jack are talking about how each of them goes to work.

(a) How does Jack go to work? How long does it take?
(b) How does Mary go to work? How long does it take?

MARY: Jack, néih jyuh hái bīndouh a?
JACK: Ngóh jyuh hái lèihdóu. 荔島
MARY: Gám, néih haih-mh-haih yiu daap-syùhn fāan-gūng a?
JACK: Haih a.
MARY: Gám, yiu daap géinoih syùhn a?
JACK: Yiu daap yāt go jūngtàuh léuhng go jih. Gám, néih nē, Mary? Néih dím fāan-gūng a?
MARY: Ngóh dōsou daap-dīksí fāan-gūng. Daaihyeuk daap léuhng go jih dīksí jauh dāk laak.

Idioms and structures

The items in the list below appear in the same order as they do in the dialogue above. The *italicized* items are *new* items. In the notes, numbers in brackets refer to the expressions listed below.

1 *jīujóu*	*in the early morning*
2 **néih jīujóu *dímyéung* fāan-gūng a?**	*how do you go to work* in the morning?
3 *dōsou*	*mostly*
4 **daap-deihtit *yiu géinoih* a?**	*How long does it take* to go by MTR?
5 **Yiu gáu go jih *gam noih* àh?**	Does it really take *as long* as 45 minutes?
6 **gam noih**	so long (time)

7 Néih *daap mātyéh* *chē* fāan-gūng a?	*What means of transportation* do you take to go to work?
8 *yiu* jā *géinoih* chē *a?*	*How long* is the drive?
9 Ngóh *msái* daap-chē	I *don't need to* take any means of transportation.
10 Daaihyeuk hàahng bun go jūngtàuh jauh *dāk* laak.	I walk for half an hour and that's all it takes.
11 Gám, dōu géi *faai* wo!	That's pretty *quick!*
12 Néih *jyuh* hái bīndouh a?	Where do you *live?*
13 Ngóh jyuh hái *lèihdóu.*	I live on an *outlying island.*
14 Yiu daap yāt go jūngtàuh léuhng go jih.	It takes one hour ten minutes.

Means of transportation (2, 7)

There are two ways of asking somebody what means of transportation they use, say, to commute to work. The first way is to use the question word **dímyéung**, sometimes reduced to **dìm**:

Néih dímyéung fāan-gūng a?   How do you go to work?

Another way is to form a question with the question word **mātyéh**:

Néih daap mātyéh chē **fāan-gūng a?**

What means of transportation do you take to go to work?

NB The word **chē** in the expression **daap mātyéh chē** does not mean 'private car', but refers to all kinds of vehicles, including buses, trams, etc.

To say what means of transportation you use to commute to work, you mention the means of transportation *before* the verb **fāan-gūng**:

Ngóh daap-dihnchē fāan-gūng. I go to work by tram.
Ngóh gòh-gō daap-syùhn **fāan-gūng.**

My elder brother goes to work by ferry.

Ngóh mùih-múi hàahng-louh fāan-gūng.

My younger sister walks to work.

Asking and saying how long (4, 8)

To ask about the time taken to do something, say, to go to work, the question word **géinoih** (how long?) is used. Two kinds of structure are possible. The first uses the verb **yiu** (require) immediately before **géinoih**:

> **Néih jā-chē fāan-gūng** *yiu géinoih* **a?**
> How long does it take you to drive to work?
> **Néih hàahng-louh fāan-gūng** *yiu géinoih* **a?**
> How long does it take you to walk to work?

In the second structure, **yiu** is used as a modal preceding the verb, while the question word **géinoih** is inserted between the verb and the object in the verb-object construction:

> **Néih fāan-gūng** *yiu* **jā** *géinoih* **chē a?**
> How long do you have to drive to go to work?
> **Néih fāan-gūng** *yiu* **hàahng** *géinoih* **louh a?**
> How long do you have to walk to go to work?

Similarly, two kinds of structure are employed in saying how long it takes to commute to work. The first structure is to use **yiu** as the main verb as follows:

> **Ngóh jā-chē fāan-gūng yiu ńgh go jih.**
> It takes me 25 minutes to drive to work.
> **Ngóh hàahng-louh fāan-gūng yiu bun go jūngtàuh.**
> It takes me half an hour to go to work on foot.

The second structure uses **yiu** as a modal, followed by a *split verb-object construction*:

> **Ngóh fāan-gūng yiu jā ńgh go jih chē.**
> I have to drive for 25 minutes to go to work.
> **Ngóh fāan-gūng yiu hàahng bun go jūngtàuh louh.**
> I have to walk for half an hour to go to work.

Question with *àh* to express surprise   (5)

Here the question with **àh** expresses surprise, or in this case, Emily's shock at hearing how long it takes Carmen to commute to work, hence the comment **gam noih** *àh*?

Msái (9)

Msái, which means 'do(es) not need to', is the opposite of **yiu**, which means 'need(s) to'. It is important to remember that **sái** is always used with **m-** to mean the negative while **yiu** ('need') is always used in the positive. Hence, **Ngóh sái daap-chē is wrong and so, in this context, is **Ngóh myiu daap-chē**. To form a choice-type question to ask about necessity, **sái**, rather than **yiu**, is used, hence **Néih *sái-mh-sái* daap-chē fāan-gūng a?** but not **Néih yiu-mh-yiu daap-chē fāan-gūng a?**

Halves (5)

Bun is used to refer to 'halves' of time units, as follows:

bun fānjūng	half a minute
bun go jūngtàuh	half an hour
bun yaht	half a day
bun go láihbaai/sīngkèih	half a week
bun go yuht	half a month
bun nìhn	half a year

Special attention has to be paid to the position of **bun** in expressions involving a whole number plus a half. For time durations which do not take the classifier **go**, **bun** comes right after the time unit, for example, 'five and a half days' is **ńgh yaht *bun***. For time durations which do require the classifier **go**, **bun** comes after **go** rather than the time unit. Thus, 'three and a half hours' is **sāam go *bun* jūngtàuh**, and not **sāam go jūngtàuh bun. Below is a list of how the 'halves' are expressed:

yāt fān bun jūng	1½ minutes
yāt go bun jūngtàuh	1½ hours
yāt yaht bun	1½ days
yāt go bun láihbaai/sīngkèih	1½ weeks
yāt go bun yuht	1½ months
yāt nìhn bun	1½ years

Note that when the figure is 1½, the word **yāt** is often omitted. Thus 1½ minutes can become **fān bun jūng**, 1½ hours can become **go bun jūngtàuh**, and 1½ days can become **yaht bun**, and so on. Another possible omission is the **tàuh** in **jūngtàuh**, and so 1½ hours can simply be expressed as **go bun jūng**.

Dāk 得 *(10)*

Dāk is an adjective which means 'OK' or 'all right', indicating successful achievement of a goal. When the expression **jauh *dāk laak** is used as the comment of a topic-comment construction it emphasizes the relative ease with which something is done.

Faai 快 *(11)*

The adjective **faai** has two meanings. The first meaning is 'at a *fast* speed', and the opposite is **maahn**, which means 'slow'. But in this context **faai** refers to the '*short time* it takes', and is the opposite of **noih**, as in the expression **géinoih**, discussed above.

Lèihdóu *(13)*

In Hong Kong, there are a number of outlying islands which are linked to Hong Kong Island, the commercial center of the territory, by ferry, the most important being Lantau Island, Cheung Chau, Peng Chau and Lamma Island.

Durations of time *(14)*

When a duration consists of both hours and minutes, the hours (the larger unit) come before the minutes (the smaller unit), as in English:

léuhng go jūngtàuh sei go jih	2 hours 20 minutes
sei go jūngtàuh ńgh-sahp fānjūng	4 hours 50 minutes

With units of time larger than the hour, the word **lìhng**, which can be translated as 'and', is used to join the larger unit and the smaller one. For example:

sei go láihbaai lìhng sāam yaht	4 weeks and 3 days
sāam nìhn lìhng baat go yuht	3 years and 8 months

Vocabulary

Stations, terminals and stops

Cantonese does not distinguish between stations, terminals and stops, and we call all of them **jaahm**. Sometimes we do use **júng-jaahm** though to refer to bus terminals and tram terminals when precise specification is called for. Below is a list of places where one boards vehicles and ferries.

deihtitjaahm	underground (MTR) station
fóchējaahm	railway station
bāsí júngjaahm	bus terminal
bāsíjaahm	bus stop
dihnchē júngjaahm	tram terminal
dihnchējaahm	tram stop
máhtàuh	ferry pier

Describing a sequence of actions

Very often we take more than one means of transport in a journey. When we want to give a detailed step-by-step description of the journey, we may wish to use the following expressions to organize our description.

sáusīn 跎佢	first of all
yìhnhauh/gānjyuh	and then, later on
joi 再	and again
jeui hauh 長佢	finally

Dialogues 🔈

Read the questions, and then read or listen to the dialogues to find the answers.

3 Richard is telling John how he goes to work.

(a) How many kinds of transport does Richard have to take to commute to work?

(b) How long is his walk to the MTR station?
(c) How long is his MTR ride?
(d) How long is his bus ride?
(e) How long does it take Richard to go from home to work?

JOHN: Richard, néih fāan-gūng sái-mh-sái daap-chē a?
RICHARD: Yiu a. Ngóh fāan-gūng yiu daap deihtit tùhng bāsí.
JOHN: Gám, yiu géinoih a?
RICHARD: Ngóh jīujóu baat dímjūng chēut-mùhnháu, sáusīn
            hàahng léuhng go jih louh heui deihtitjaahm,
            yìhnhauh daap bun go jūngtàuh deihtit, gānjyuh daap
            sei go jih bāsí, daaihyeuk gáu dímjūng jauh fāan dou
            gūngsī laak.
JOHN: Gám, júngguhng yiu géinoih a?
RICHARD: Yàuh ngūkkéi fāan dou gūngsī júngguhng yiu
            daaihyeuk yāt go jūngtàuh lā.

4 Mrs Wong teaches in the same school as Mrs Lam. She is asking Mrs Lam how she travels to work in the morning.

(a) Altogether how long does it take Mrs Lam to go to her school?
(b) How long is her walk to the railway station?
(c) How long is her train ride?
(d) How long is her MTR ride?
(e) How long is her walk to the school?

MRS WONG: Làhm táai, néih jīujóu dímyéung fāan-hohk a?
MRS LAM: Ngóh jyuh dāk yúhn, yiu yāt go jūngtàuh sīnji
             fāan dou hohkhaauh. Ngóh sáusīn hàahng léuhng
             go jih louh heui fóchējaahm, yìhnhauh daap ńgh go
             jih fóchē, yìhnhauh jyun deihtit, daap sei go jih
             deihtit, joi hàahng léuhng go jih louh sīnji fāan dou
             hohkhaauh.
MRS WONG: Gám jān haih yiu sèhng go jūngtàuh wo!

Idioms and structures

The items in the list below appear in the same order as they do in the dialogue above. The *italicized* items are *new* items. In the notes, numbers in brackets refer to the expressions listed below.

1 **Yìu a.**	Yes, I do (need to).
2 **chēut-mùhnháu**	*leave home*
3 **hàahng léuhng go jih louh**	(I) walk for 10 minutes *to the*
heui deihtitjaahm	*underground station*
4 **daaihyeuk gáu dímjūng**	I *arrive* in my office at about
jauh *fāan dou* **gūngsī laak**	9 o'clock
5 **jūngguhng**	altogether
6 *yàuh* **ngūkkéi fāan dou gūngsī**	*from* home to the office
7 *fāan-hohk*	*go to school*
8 **Ngóh** *jyuh dāk yúhn.*	I *live far (from school).*
9 **yìhnhauh** *jyun* **deihtit**	and then I *change for* the
	underground
10 **joi hàahng léuhng go jih**	and (I) walk for ten more
louh *sīnji* **fāan dou**	minutes *and only then* do I
hohkhaauh	arrive at the school
11 *sèhng* **go jūngtàuh**	a *whole* hour
12 **Gám,** *jān haih* **yiu sèhng go**	So it *really does* take one whole
jūngtàuh wo!	hour!

Expressing necessity (1)

Here **Yiu a** is a short response to the question **néih fāan-gūng sái-mh-sái daap-chē a?**, meaning 'Yes, I have to (commute to work).' A long response would be **Ngóh fāan-gūng yiu daap-chē a.** Once again, note that a negative response would be **Msái**, which means 'No, I don't need to (commute to work)', and not **Myiu,** in which **yiu** is not used as a modal of necessity but as a verb meaning 'want to'.

Destinations (3, 4)

In a sentence which describes action or motion, the destination always comes at the end, introduced by the word **heui**:

Ngóh hàahng yih-sahp fāanjūng louh *heui deihtitjaahm.*
I walk for twenty minutes to the MTR station.

Heui is the word used to introduce a destination, for example, **Ngóh séung gei-seun** *heui* **Méihgwok** (I want to send some mail to the USA). However, for 'going to the office' and 'going to school' we use **fāan**, which literally means 'return', instead; hence **fāan**

gūngsī and **fāan hohkhaauh**. A more predictable use is, of course, **fāan ngūkkéi** (to go home).

> **Ngóh jā baat go jih chē** *fāan gūngsī*.
> I drive for 40 minutes to go to my office.
> **Ngóh daap yāt go jūngtàuh syùhn** *fāan hohkhaauh*.
> I take a one-hour ferry ride to go to my school.

Dou (4, 6, 10)

Dou is a particle used between a verb of motion and a noun denoting a destination. **Fāan** *dou* **gūngsī** indicates the 'successful' arrival at the office. Similar expressions are **fāan** *dou* **hohkhaauh** (arrive at the school), **fāan** *dou* **ngūkkéi** (arrive home) and **heui** *dou* **deihtitjaahm** (arrive at the underground station) and **heui** *dou* **máhtàuh** (arrive at the pier).

Fāan-hohk 返學 (7)

Fāan-gūng is a verb-object construction which means 'to go to work'. **Fāan-hohk**, on the other hand, means 'to go to school', but it applies to both students, who 'go to school to learn', and teachers, who 'go to school to teach'.

Dāk 搭 (8)

The particle **dāk** is used between a verb and an adjective to indicate the result of an action. **Ngóh jyuh** *dāk* **yuhn** is 'I live far away', while **Ngóh jyuh dāk káhn** means 'I live near'. Similar expressions are **Kéuih páau dāk faai** (He/She runs fast) and **Néih jouh dāk hóu hóu** (You've done a good job).

Sīnji 先至 (10)

Sīnji is an adverb often used with the modal **yiu** to emphasize the fact that a condition has to be satisfied to accomplish something. When used in a question, it stresses the 'How long does it take you?' part of the question. When used in a statement, it stresses the effort made to accomplish something, and bears the opposite connotation to that of **jauh dāk laak** discussed earlier in this lesson. A comparison of the sentences below will illustrate the contrast.

Ngóh *yiu* jā yāt go jūngtàuh chē *sīnji* fāan dou gūngsī.
It takes me a whole hour to drive to work.
Ngóh jā-chē fāan-gūng ńgh go jih *jauh dāk laak*.
It takes me *only* 25 minutes to drive to work.

Sèhng 成 *(11)*

Sèhng go jūngtàuh is an emphatic way of saying 'an hour', and goes together well with the word **sīnji**, as the sentence **yiu *sèhng* go jūngtàuh sīnji fāandou hohkhaauh** (it takes a whole hour to get to my school) shows. Similar expressions are ***sèhng* yaht** (a whole day), ***sèhng* go láihbaai** (a whole week), ***sèhng* go yuht** (a whole month) and ***sèhng* nìhn** (a whole year).

Exercises

Exercise 1 Traveling to work

Three people are describing their journeys to work. Read the texts and then use the information to draw a diagram. Jane's part has been done for you as an example.

JANE: **Ngóh jīujóu chāt dímjūng chēut-mùhnháu, sáusīn hàahng léuhng go jih louh heui fóchējaahm, yìhnhauh daap sei-sahp fānjūng fóchē, gānjyuh hàahng yāt go jih louh jauh fāan dou gūngsī laak.**

JANE: HOME → walk (10 minutes) → train (40 minutes) → walk (5 minutes) → OFFICE

JIM: **Ngóh yiu daap-syùhn fāan-gūng. Ngóh chāt dímjūng chēut-mùhnháu, hàahng sahp-ńgh fānjūng louh heui máhtàuh, gānjyuh daap ńgh-sahp fānjūng syùhn, joi hàahng sahp fānjūng louh jauh fāan dou gūngsī laak. Júngguhng yiu yāt go jūngtàuh sāam go jih.**

JIM: HOME → . . . OFFICE

BILL: **Ngóh jīujóu baat dím bun chēut-mùhnháu, hàahng yāt go jih louh heui bāsíjaahm, yìhnhauh daap sāam go jih bāsí heui deihtitjaahm, gānjyuh daap bun go jūngtàuh deihtit**

> **jauh fāan dou gūngsī laak. Júngguhng daaihyeuk ńgh-sahp fānjūng lā.**

Bill: HOME → . . . OFFICE

Exercise 2 Durations of time

Translate the following time expressions into Cantonese, paying special attention to instances where the word **lìhng** has to be used. The first one has been done for you as an example.

(a) 38 minutes   **sāam-sahp baat fānjūng**
(b) 5 hours 55 minutes
(c) 6 days
(d) 1 week and 4 days
(e) 3 months
(f) 2 years and 11 months

Exercise 3 Durations of time

Translate the following time durations into Cantonese, using the word **bun** if applicable, and paying special attention to its position. The first one has been done for you as an example.

(a) 30 minutes   **bun go jūngtàuh**
(b) 2 hours 30 minutes
(c) 4½ hours
(d) 5½ days
(e) 9½ weeks
(f) 7½ months
(g) 5 years and 6 months

Exercise 4 Durations of time

Translate the following times into Cantonese. Some can have more than one possible answer. The first one is done for you as an example.

(a) 20 minutes   **yih-sahp fānjūng** or **sei go jih**
(b) 36 minutes
(c) 45 minutes
(d) 55 minutes
(e) 1 hour 50 minutes
(f) 2 hours 7 minutes

Exercise 5 How you go to work
Now describe how you travel to work and then write out the description in Cantonese.

HOME → ... OFFICE
Description:
Ngóh ... chēut-mùhnháu ...

Exercise 6 The optimist and the moaner ▢▢
Some people take a long time to commute to work, depending on where they live and where their office is, while others take much shorter times. At the same time, some people are born optimists and accept things cheerfully while others moan about everything. In this exercise, each item provides information about how two people commute to work in exactly the same way and take the same amount of time but describe their journeys in different styles.

Follow the example and write out what each person says.

(a) A ½-hour bus ride, the optimist:

Ngóh daap bun go jūngtàuh bāsí *jauh* fāan dou gūngsī *laak*.

(b) A ½-hour bus ride, the moaner:

Ngóh yiu daap bun go jūngtàuh bāsí *sīnji* fāan dou gūngsī *a*.

(c) A 20-minute walk, the optimist.

(d) A 20-minute walk, the moaner

(e) A 50-minute train ride and a 15-minute walk, the optimist.

(f) A 50-minute train ride and a 15-minute walk, the moaner.

Exercise 7 Going to Guangzhou
Imagine you work for a travel agency, and specialize in organizing trips between Hong Kong and Guangzhou. Some potential customers are at your office asking for information. Answer their questions by referring to the price-list. The first one is done for you as an example.

Price-list of trips between Hong Kong and Guangzhou for the year 1993		
	Price	Duration
by air	$410	30 minutes
by train	$183	2 hrs 45 minutes
by ferry	$223	8 hrs
by bus	$145	6 hrs

NB: Prices and time durations are the same for both HK → GZ and GZ → HK

Conversation 1:

CUSTOMER: Chíng mahn yàuh Hēunggóng heui Gwóngjāu dímyéung jeui faai a?

YOU: Yàuh Hēunggóng heui Gwóngjāu daap-fēigēi jeui faai.

CUSTOMER: Gám, daap-fēigēi yiu géidō chín a?

YOU: (i)

CUSTOMER: Gám, yiu daap géinoih a?

YOU: (ii)

CUSTOMER: Gám, daap-syùhn nē? Daap-syùhn yauh géidō chín a?

YOU: (iii)

CUSTOMER: Daap-syùhn yiu daap géinoih a?

YOU: (iv)

CUSTOMER: Hóu, mgōi saai.

Conversation 2:

CUSTOMER: Chíng mahn Hēunggóng heui Gwóngjāu daap-fóchē dihng daap-bāsí pèhng-dī a?

YOU: (i)

CUSTOMER: Gám, daap-fóchē yiu géinoih a? Daap-bāsí yauh yiu géinoih a?

YOU: (ii)

CUSTOMER: Gám, daap-syùhn nē? Daap-syùhn yauh dím a?

YOU: (iii)

CUSTOMER: Hóu, mgōi saai néih.

Conversation 3:

CUSTOMER: Chíng mahn heui Gwóngjāu dímyéung jeui dái a?

YOU:

Recognizing Chinese characters

地鐵站   underground station

火車站   railway station

巴士站   bus-stop

的士站   taxi rank

飛機場   airport

This list of Chinese characters shows places where different means of public transport can be taken. The word

站

(**jaahm**) is used in all items except the airport (**fēigēichèuhng**), with

場

(**chèuhng**) meaning literally 'field', though sometimes the word **fēi** is omitted and **fēigēichèuhng** becomes **gēichèuhng**.

8 Kéuihdeih jouh-gán mātyéh?

What are they doing?

In Lesson 8 you will learn about:

- discussing what people are doing and where
- using **-gán** to show action in progress
- more uses of **-jó** for completed actions

Vocabulary 🔲

In Hong Kong most people live in rather small flats in high-rise residential blocks. Only the wealthy can afford to live in detached houses or mansions. However, we do not distinguish between flats, houses and mansions in Cantonese. We call all of them **ngūk**, which takes the classifier **gāan**, hence 'a flat' is **yāt gāan ngūk**, 'my flat' is **ngóh gāan ngūk**, and 'your flat' is **néih gāan ngūk**.

The typical Hong Kong flat consists of a sitting room, a dining room, two to three bedrooms, a kitchen and toilet/bathroom. Gardens and garages are luxuries found only in the houses of the wealthy, though a servant's room is not uncommon in some of the bigger flats. Below is a list of Cantonese words related to different parts of a flat. All of these take **go** as the classifier, though the items ending in **fóng** can also take **gāan** as their classifier. Try reading out each item aloud. If you have the cassette tapes of this book with you, you can model your pronunciation on the recording.

yāt go haaktēng	a sitting room
yāt go faahntēng	a dining room
yāt go chisó	a toilet
yāt go fāyún	a garden
yāt go chēfòhng	a garage
yāt go/gāan seuihfóng	a bedroom

yāt go/gāan syūfóng	a study
yāt go/gāan haakfóng	a guest room
yāt go/gāan chyùhfóng	a kitchen
yāt go/gāan chūnglèuhngfóng	a bathroom
yāt go/gāan gūngyàhnfóng	a servant's room

Rooms

Most of the words end in **fóng,** which translates satisfactorily into the English word 'room'. But Cantonese distinguishes between **tēng** and **fóng,** in that **tēng** refers to bigger rooms often used for entertaining guests. This is a function of the sitting room and the dining room, hence the terms **haaktēng** (literally 'guest room') and **faahntēng** (literally 'meal room'). Also, the word **chyùhfóng** ('kitchen') has the alternative pronunciation of **chèuihfóng.** In fact, the two pronunciations are equally common, and can be regarded as free variations. The **fòhng** in **chēfòhng** (garage) refers to the same Chinese word as the **fóng** in **seuihfóng** or **syūfóng,** but it takes the *low falling tone* when combined with **chē,** hence **chēfòhng.**

Dialogue 🔲

Read the questions, and then read or listen to the dialogue to find the answers.

1 John and Carmen have been invited to Mrs Lam's home for dinner. They are having a chat in her sitting room before dinner.

(a) How many rooms are there in Mrs Lam's flat? What are they?
(b) How many people live in the flat? Who are they?
(c) How old are Mrs Lam's two children?

JOHN:	Làhm táai, néih gāan ngúk hóu daaih wo.
MRS LAM:	Haih a. Nī gāan ngúk syun géi daaih ga la.
JOHN:	Gám, júngguhng yáuh géidō gāan fóng a?
MRS LAM:	Júngguhng yáuh léuhng go tēng tùhng sei gāan fóng:

yāt go haaktēng, yāt go faahntēng, sāam gāan
seuihfóng, tùhng yāt gāan syūfóng. Lihngngoih yáuh
yāt go chyùhfóng, léuhng go chisó, tùhng yāt go
gūngyàhnfóng.

CARMEN: Gám, néihdeih ngūkkéi júngguhng yáuh géidō yàhn
a?

MRS LAM: Júngguhng luhk go yàhn. Ngóh tùhng ngóh sīnsāang
lā, ngóh bàh-bā tùhng ngóh màh-mā lā, juhng yáuh
ngóh go jái Kenny tùhng ngóh go néui Angel.

CARMEN: Kenny tùhng Angel yáuh géi daaih a?

MRS LAM: Kenny gāmnín baat seui, Angel jauh chāt seui.

Idioms and structures

The items in the list below appear in the same order as they do in
the dialogues above. The *italicized* items are *new* items. In the
notes, numbers in brackets refer to the expressions listed below.

1 **Nī gāan ngūk *syun* géi daaih**   *I suppose* it's quite a large flat.
  ga la.
2 ***Lihngngoih* . . .**   *In addition,* . . .
3 ***néihdeih ngūkkéi***   *your family*
4 ***ngóh sīnsāang***   *my husband*
5 **Ngóh tùhng ngóh sīnsāang**   *There's* me and my husband
  lā . . .   . . .
6 **Kenny tùhng Angel *yáuh géi***   *How old* are Kenny and
  ***daaih* a?**   Angel?

Syun 算   *(1)*

Syun is a word used before the comment in a topic-comment
sentence to indicate concession, as if saying in English: 'Well, I
suppose you can say that.' A more literal translation is '. . . can
be regarded as . . . '. The mood is often reinforced by the use of the
double particle **ga la** at the end of the sentence, as in **Kéuih *syun* géi
gōu ga la**, which translates into 'He can be regarded as tall' or 'You
can say he's rather tall'.

The possessive *néihdeih* (3)

Here **néihdeih** is used as a possessive adjective, and so *néihdeih* **ngūkkéi** is 'your family'. Again, the classifier **go** is omitted because close family relationships are being referred to. (See Lesson 5.)

Sīnsāang (4)

The noun **sīnsāang** has several meanings. It is a polite way of addressing a man (see Lesson 1). It also means 'teacher' (both male and female) as well as 'husband'. The distinction between **sīnsāang** meaning 'teacher' and meaning 'husband' lies in the presence of the classifier **go**. In the former use this noun is most likely to be qualified by the subject taught and the classifier **go** is used, as in **Kéuih haih ngóh** *go* **Yīngmán** *sīnsāang* (He is my English teacher). In the latter, as with all intimate family relationships, **go** is omitted and so **Kéuih haih ngóh** *sīnsāang* has to be 'He is my husband'. The Cantonese word for 'wife' is **taai-táai**, and 'my wife' is **ngóh taai-táai**.

The particle *lā* (5)

One function of the particle **lā** is listing a number of items of the same nature. In Dialogue 1, Mrs Lam is listing the people in her family. Another example would be: **Ngóh yáuh hóu dō sihou: yàuh-séui** *lā*, **dá-móhngkàuh** *lā*, **tek-jūkkàuh** *lā*, **tùhng cháai-dāanchē** (I have many hobbies: swimming, playing tennis, playing soccer and cycling).

Asking about age (6)

In Lesson 5 we introduced the question **Kéuih géidō seui a?** to ask somebody's age. Another way of asking someone's age is **Kéuih yáuh géi daaih a?**, which literally means 'How big is he/she?'

Vocabulary

Completed actions

In Lesson 6, we learned that the bound particle **-jó** is used with a verb to indicate the completion of an action. For example, **Kéuih máaih-jó yāt ga chē** is 'He has bought a car'. Below are some more expressions, all beginning with **heui-jó**, some followed by a word denoting a place and some by a word denoting an action. The first expression **heui-jó gāai**, however, means simply 'has gone out' but does not specify where or why.

heui-jó gāai	has/have gone out
heui-jó tòuhsyūgún	has/have gone to the library
heui-jó gāaisíh	has/have gone to the market
heui-jó hóitāan	has/have gone to the beach
heui-jó wihngchìh	has/have gone to the swimming pool
heui-jó tái-dihnyíng	has/have gone to the cinema
heui-jó yám-bējáu	has/have gone for a beer
heui-jó dá-móhngkàuh	has/have gone to play tennis
heui-jó yàuh-séui	has/have gone swimming
heui-jó tái-jūkkàuh	has/have gone to watch football
heui-jó tēng-yāmngohk	has/have gone to a concert

Very often both the 'where' and the 'why' are mentioned in a statement. In such a case the 'where' always comes before the 'why':

Ngóh taai-táai heui-jó gāaisíh máaih sāanggwó.
My wife has gone to the market to buy fruit.
Kéuih gòh-gō heui-jó hóitāan yàuh-séui.
His brother has gone to the beach to swim.

In certain instances the word **fāan**, which literally means 'return', is used instead of **heui**. The best examples are **fāan ngūkkéi** (to go home), **fāan hohkhaauh** (to go to school) and **fāan gūngsī** (to go to the office). (See Lesson 7.) They are fixed expressions and it would be wrong to replace **fāan** by **heui**, regardless of where the speaker is. In other words, both 'He has gone home' (said by, say, a colleague in the office on the phone) and 'He has come home' (said by, say, one member of the family to another at home) would translate into **Kéuih fāan-jó ngūkkéi**. Below are two more examples:

Kéuih fāan-jó hohkhaauh dá-móhngkàuh.
He/She has gone to his/her school to play tennis.
Kéuih fāan-jó gūngsī hōi-wúi.
He/She has gone to the office for a meeting.

To ask where somebody has gone, however, **heui-jó** is used (and never **fāan-jó**), together with the question word **bīndouh**, as follows:

Kéuih heui-jó bīndouh a?
Where has he/she gone?

Dialogue 🔳

Read the questions, and then read or listen to the dialogue to find the answers.

2 John and Carmen are still chatting with Mrs Lam in the sitting room before dinner.

(a) Where is Mrs Lam's husband?
(b) Where is Mrs Lam's father?
(c) Where is Mrs Lam's mother?
(d) Where has Kenny gone?
(e) Where has Angel gone?

JOHN:	Làhm táai, néih sīnsāang hái bīndouh a?
MRS LAM:	Ngóh sīnsāang juhng hái gūngsī. Kéuih yìhgā hōi-gán wúi. Kéuih daaihyeuk chāt dímjūng jauh fāan lèih ga laak.
JOHN:	Gám, néih bàh-bā tùhng màh-mā nē?
MRS LAM:	Ngóh màh-mā hái chyùhfóng jyū-gán faahn. Ngóh bàh-bā jauh hái kéuih gāan fóng tái-gán dihnsih.
CARMEN:	Gám, Kenny tùhng Angel nē?
MRS LAM:	Kenny heui-jó yàuh-séui. Angel fāan-jó hohkhaauh.
CARMEN:	Kenny heui-jó bīndouh yàuh-séui a?
MRS LAM:	Kéuih heui-jó wihngchìh yàuh-séui.
JOHN:	Gám, Angel fāan hohkhaauh jouh mātyéh a?
MRS LAM:	Angel fāan-jó hohkhaauh cheung-gō. Kéuihdeih daaihyeuk luhk dím bun jauh fāan lèih ga laak.

Idioms and structures

The items in the list below appear in the same order as they do in the dialogues above. The *italicized* items are *new* items. In the notes, numbers in brackets refer to the expressions listed below.

1 *néih sīnsāang hái bīndouh a?*   Where is your husband?
2 **Ngóh sīnsāang** *juhng* **hái gūngsī.**   My husband is *still* in his office.
3 **Kéuih yìhgā** *hōi-gán wúi.*   He is *having a meeting*.
4 **Keuih daaihyeuk chāt dímjūng**   *I'm sure* (he) will be back at
   jauh fāan lèih *ga laak.*   seven.
5 **Ngóh màh-mā hái chyùhfóng**   My mother is cooking in the
   jyú-gán faahn.   kitchen.

Asking and stating where somebody is   (1)

As discussed in Lesson 3, **hái** is a locative marker which can be either *verbal* or *prepositional*. In the question **Néih sīnsāang hái bīndouh a?** (Where is your husband?), **hái** is used as a verb and the enquiry is about a *state* rather than an action.

/Progressive action   (3)

In Cantonese, we use the aspect marker **-gán** with a verb to describe an action which is in the process of taking place. Thus, **Kéuih dá-***gán* **móhngkàuh** is 'He/She is playing tennis', and **Ngóh tēng-***gán* **yāmngohk** is 'I am listening to music'. Below are some more examples of 'actions in progress'.

tái-gán dihnsih	watching television
jyú-gán faahn	cooking
chūng-gán lèuhng	taking a bath/shower
dūhk-gán syū	studying
fan-gán gaau	sleeping
góng-gán dihnwá	talking on the phone

To ask what somebody is doing at a particular time, we use the verb **jouh** with the aspect marker **-gán**, as follows:

   Kéuih (yìhgā) jouh-gán mātyéh a?
   What is he/she doing (now)?

Ga laak (4)

Ga laak is a combination of two sentence-final particles used to express *reassurance.*

Stating whereabouts and action (5)

Very often, in a statement information is given about both where somebody is and what he or she is doing there:

Ngóh mùih-múi hái syūfóng tái-gán syū.
My younger sister is reading in the study.

There are two ways of interpreting the statement, depending on the emphasis. If it is a response to the question **Néih mùih-múi hái bīndouh a?** (Where is your younger sister?), then the emphasis of the statement is on **hái syūfóng,** while **tái-gán syū** provides supplementary information about what she is doing, and in such cases the function of **hái** remains that of a verb.

On the other hand, if **hái syūfóng** is *known* information and the statement is a response to the question **Néih mùih-múi hái syūfóng jouh-gán mātyéh a?** (What is your younger sister doing in the study?), then the emphasis is shifted from the state of where someone is to the *action* that is taking place, such as **tái-gán syū,** and at the same time the function of **hái** changes from that of a verb to that of a preposition. Bear in mind, though, that regardless of where the emphasis of the statement lies, the prepositional phrase indicating location, such as **hái syūfóng,** *always precedes* the verb phrase (**tái-gán syū**).

Exercises

Exercise 1 Comprehension ▉▉

Read Dialogue 2 again, or if you have the cassette tapes of this book with you, listen to the recording again, and then answer the following questions.

During Mrs Lam's conversation with John and Carmen,

(a) What is Mr Lam doing?
(b) What is Mrs Lam's father doing?
(c) What is Mrs Lam's mother doing?

(d) What is Kenny doing?
(e) What is Angel doing?

Exercise 2 Action in progress

Answer the questions with the cue word provided, using **-gán** for action in progress. The first one has been done for you as an example.

(a) **John jouh-gán mātyéh a?**   yàuh-séui
     Answer: John yàuh-gán seui.

(b) **Mary jouh-gán mātyéh a?**   jyú-faahn
(c) **Susan jouh-gán mātyéh a?**   cheung-gō
(d) **Jimmy jouh-gán mātyéh a?**   dá-làahmkàuh
(e) **Wendy jouh-gán mātyéh a?**   tái-dihnsih

Exercise 3 Actions in progress vs. habitual actions

Remember that **-gán** is used *only when* referring to actions currently taking place, *not* when referring to habitual actions or likes and dislikes. Translate the English sentences into Cantonese, focusing on the use of the verb. The first one has been done for you as an example.

(a) He is reading in his study.
    Answer: **Kéuih hái syūfóng tái-gán syū.**
(b) I go to work by MTR.
(c) She enjoys watching films.
(d) I play tennis every Tuesday.
(e) My mother is sleeping.
(f) My father likes listening to music.
(g) My wife enjoys cooking.

Exercise 4 My house

(a) The Chans live in a flat on the sixth floor of a residential block. Referring to the picture below, complete Mr Chan's description of his flat.

MR CHAN: **Ngóhdeih gāan ngūk yáuh yāt go haaktēng, yāt go faahntēng, . . .**

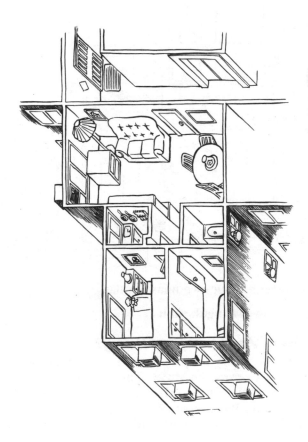

(b) The Poons are one of the few rich families in Hong Kong who can afford to live in a garden house. Referring to the picture below, complete Mr Poon's description of his house.

MR POON: **Ngóhdeih gāan ngūk yáuh yāt go haaktēng . . .**

FIG 9

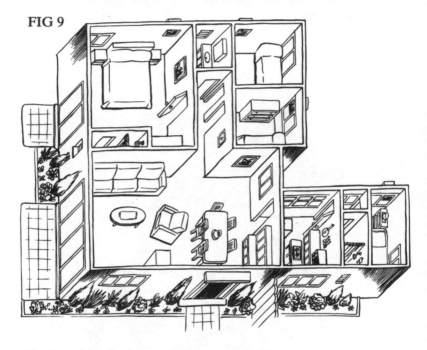

(c) Now describe your own house or flat.

YOU: **Ngóh gāan ngūk yáuh . . .**

Exercise 5 *What are they doing?*

The Wongs are a nosy couple. They like watching the activities of their neighbors across the street. This evening they are watching the activities of the Chans. Mr Wong, who has poor eyesight, is asking what Mrs Wong sees. Referring to the picture on p. 119, complete the conversation between Mr Wong and Mrs Wong.

MR WONG: Chàhn táai jouh-gán mātyéh a?
MRS WONG: Chàhn táai hái chyùhfóng sái-gán wún.
MR WONG: Gám, Chàhn sīnsāang nē?
MRS WONG: (a) Chàhn sīnsāang hái faahntēng . . .
MR WONG: Gám, kéuihdeih go jái jouh-gán mātyéh a?

Mrs Wong:	(b) Kéuih hái haaktēng . . .
Mr Wong:	Kéuihdeih go néui nē?
Mrs Wong:	(c) Kéuih . . .

Exercise 6 Where have they gone?

It is Sunday. John rings Mrs Lam, and her father answers the phone. He tells John that the whole family have gone out for different activities, and patiently tells John where each one has gone. Referring to the information below, complete the conversation between John and Mrs Lam's father.

Mr Lam:	to watch a football match
Mrs Lam:	shopping
Kenny:	to play tennis
Angel:	to a concert

| John: | Làhm táai heui-jó bīndouh a? |
| Mrs Lam's father: | (a) Kéuih heui-jó . . . |

JOHN:	Gám, Làhm sīnsāang nē?
MRS LAM'S FATHER:	(b) Kéuih . . .
JOHN:	Kenny yauh heui-jó bīndouh a?
MRS LAM'S FATHER:	(c) Kenny . . .
JOHN:	Gám, Angel nē?
MRS LAM'S FATHER:	(d)

Recognizing Chinese characters

客廳	sitting room
飯廳	dining room
睡房	bedroom
書房	study
客房	guest room
厨房	kitchen
厠所	toilet
浴室	bathroom
工人房	servant's room

9 Bōng ngóh jouh dī yéh   *Chores*

Do me a favor

In Lesson 9 you will learn about:

- asking people to do things
- responding to requests
- using **meih** for actions still to be taken
- using **yùhn** to discuss when actions are completed

Vocabulary 🔲

Housework

Below is a list of household tasks. Try reading out each item aloud.
If you have the cassette tapes of this book, you can model your pronunciation on the tape recording.

jāp-chòhng	to make the bed
jyú-faahn	to cook
jāp-tói	to clear the table
sái-wún	to wash up
dóu-laahpsaap	to empty the rubbish bin
máaih-yéh	to go shopping
máaih-sung	to buy food (for meals)
sái-sāam	to wash the clothes
lohng-sāam	to hang the clothes
tong-sāam	to iron the clothes
sou-deih	to sweep the floor
kāp-chàhn	to vacuum-clean
maat-chēung	to clean the windows

The examples of housework in the list above are all expressed in *verb-object constructions*, and are thus hyphenated. Most of the translations in the right-hand column are literal translations of the verb and the object. Exceptions include **jyú-faahn**, which literally means 'cook-rice', **dóu-laahpsaap**, which literally means 'pour-rubbish', **máaih-yéh**, which literally means 'buy-things', and **kāp-chàhn**, which literally means 'suck-dust'. **Jyú-faahn** is used when it is assumed that a Chinese meal is being prepared, but if the cooking is apparently not Chinese, the more general term of **jyú-yéhsihk** (literally 'cook-food') can be used. Similarly, **sái-wún** (literally 'wash-bowls') is used if the meal is Chinese, and bowls are used instead of plates; another expression, **sái-díp** (literally 'wash-plates'), can be used if the meal is apparently Western.

Máaih-sung

In the construction **máaih-sung**, the object **sung** refers specifically to raw food (meat and vegetables) which one buys in the traditional Chinese wet market to cook for lunch or dinner. It does not include food one usually buys in a supermarket such as cereals, cheese, cake, ice-cream, etc. It has no exact equivalent in English.

Dialogues 🔾🔾

Read the questions, and then read or listen to each dialogue to find the answers.

1 Mrs Lam is busy with housework, and wants her children to help.

(a) What does Mrs Lam want help with?
(b) Which of her two children is able to help?

MRS LAM: Angel, dī sāam meih sái. Néih hó-mh-hóyíh tùhng ngóh sái-sāam a?

ANGEL: Mdāk a, māmìh. Ngóh yiu heui yàuh-séui a.

MRS LAM: Gám, Kenny nē? Néih tùhng ngóh sái-sāam dāk-mh-dāk a?

KENNY: Dāk, móuh mahntàih.

2 It is eight in the evening. The Lams have just finished dinner. Mrs Lam is distributing the housework to the members of her family.

(a) Who is going to clear the table?
(b) Who is going to wash up?
(c) Who is going to empty the rubbish bin?

MRS LAM:	Kenny, néih bōngsáu jāp-tói dāk-mh-dāk?
KENNY:	Háu ak.
MRS LAM:	Gám, Angel, mgōi néih sái-wún ā.
ANGEL:	Dāk, ngóh sái-wún lā.
MRS LAM:	Gám, George, néih hó-mh-hóyíh dóu-laahpsaap a?
MR LAM:	Hóyíh.

Idioms and structures

The items in the list below appear in the same order as they do in the dialogues above. The *italicized* items are *new* items. In the notes, numbers in brackets refer to the expressions listed below.

1 **dī sāam** *meih sái*	the clothes *have yet to be washed*
2 *Néih hó-mh-hóyíh tùhng ngóh sái-sāam a?*	*Can you wash the clothes for me?*
3 *māmìh*	*Mummy*
4 *Néih tùhng ngóh sái-sāam dāk-mh-dāk a?*	*Is it all right if I ask you to wash the clothes for me?*
5 néih *bōngsáu* jāp-tói dāk-mh-dāk a?	Can you *help* to clear the table?
6 **Dāk, ngóh sái-wún** *lā.*	OK, I'll do the washing up.

Meih to refer to action not yet taken (1)

Here **meih** indicates action which is not yet taken. Thus, **dī sāam** *meih* **sái** means 'the clothes have yet to be washed'. Similarly, **dī chēung** *meih* **maat** means 'the windows have yet to be cleaned', and **dī laapsaap** *meih* **dóu** means 'the bin is yet to be emptied'.

Asking a favor and responding to the request
(2, 4, 5, 6)

There are four ways of asking a favor, as follows:

(a) By using the modal **hóyíh** in a choice-type question:

Néih hó-mh-hóyíh tùhng ngóh sái-wún a?
Can you wash the bowls up for me?

Note that in a choice-type question, only the first syllable of a two-syllable word is repeated, thus **hó-mh-hóyíh** but not *****hóyíh-mh-hóyíh**. **Tùhng ngóh** means 'for me' but note that, unlike English 'for me', it comes *before* the verb.

(b) By using the question phrase **dāk-mh-dāk**, plus the particle **a** at the end of the sentence:

Néih tùhng ngóh sái-wún dāk-mh-dāk a?
Is it all right if I ask you to wash the bowls for me?

(c) By using **Mgōi néih** ('Please') at the beginning of a sentence with an optional **ā** at the end:

Mgōi néih tùhng ngóh sái-wún (ā).
Please wash up for me.

(d) An alternative to using **Mgōi** is to use **Màhfàahn**:

Màhfàahn néih tùhng ngóh sái-wún ā.
Can I trouble you to wash up for me?

The most direct responses to the question in (a) are:

Hóyíh.	Yes, I can.
or **Mhóyíh.**	No, I can't.

The most direct responses to the question in (b) are:

Dāk.	Yes, it's all right.
or **Mdāk.**	No, it's not all right.

Two universal positive responses to (a), (b), (c) and (d) are:

Dāk, móuh mahntàih.	Yes, no problem.
Hóu aak.	OK.

A universal negative response to (a), (b), (c) and (d) is:

Mdāk a.	I'm afraid I can't help.

Note that the sentence-final particle **a** in **Mdāk a** helps express regret at not being able to help. You can use the expression **Deui mjyuh** to complement **Mdāk a** to sound more apologetic, for instance, *Mdāk a, deui mjyuh*, **ngóh mhóyíh tùhng néih sái-wún a.**

Lā (6)

The sentence-final particle **lā** used here helps to convey cheerful acceptance of the task.

Vocabulary 🔛

Office jobs

Below are a few small jobs one might ask junior staff in an office to do:

gei-seun	to mail letters
dá(-jih)	to type
yíngyan	to make photocopies
yíngyan géi fūng seun	to photocopy several letters
je-syū	to borrow books
je géi bún syū	to borrow several books
máaih-fēi	to buy tickets
máaih jēung fóchē fēi	to buy a train ticket

Dialogues 🔛

Read the questions, and then read or listen to each dialogue to find the answers.

3 Mr Lam is having a busy day in the office. He is looking for someone to help him with typing and photocopying.

(a) Who volunteers to help with the typing?
(b) Who volunteers to help with the photocopying?

MR LAM:	Ngóh séung wán yàhn tùhng ngóh dá géi fūng seun. Bīngo dākhàahn a?
VICKY:	Ngóh dākhàahn. Ngóh tùhng néih dá lā, lahm sīnsaang.
MR LAM:	Mgōi néih, Vicky. Gám, yáuh móuh yàhn hóyíh tùhng ngóh yíngyan a?
MARY:	Ngóh bōng néih yíngyan lā, Làhm sīnsāang.
MR LAM:	Mgōi saai, Mary.
MARY:	Msái mgōi.

4 It's Sunday and Mrs Lam is organizing some housework.

(a) Who agrees to do the ironing?
(b) Who volunteers to sweep the floor?
(c) Who will clean the windows?

MRS LAM:	Yáuh hóu dō sāam meih tong. Bīngo hóyíh tùhng ngóh tong-jó dī sāam a? Kenny, néih dāk-mh-dāk a?
KENNY:	Mdāk a. Ngóh tái-gán jūkkàuh a. Angel nē?
ANGEL:	Hóu lā. Ngóh tùhng néih tong lā.
MRS LAM:	Mgōi, Angel. Juhng yáuh, deihhá hóu wūjōu, bīngo hóyíh tùhng ngóh sou-deih a?
MR LAM:	Ngóh tùhng néih sou-deih lā.
MRS LAM:	Mgōi saai, George. Gám, Kenny, néih géidímjūng tái yùhn jūkkàuh a?
KENNY:	Juhng yáuh sāam go jih jauh tái yùhn la.
MRS LAM:	Gám, néih tái yùhn jūkkàuh tùhng ngóh maat-jó dī chēung dāk-mh-dāk a?
KENNY:	Dāk, móuh mahntàih.

Idioms and structures

The items in the list below appear in the same order as they do in the dialogues above. The *italicized* items are *new* items. In the notes, numbers in brackets refer to the expressions listed below.

1 **Ngóh séung wán yàhn tùhng ngóh dá géi fūng seun. *Bīngo dākhàahn a?*** I want to find someone to type several letters for me. *Who is free?*

2 *Yáuh móuh yàhn hóyíh tùhng ngóh yíngyan a?*	*Is there anyone who can help me do some photocopying?*
3 **Ngóh** *bōng* **néih yíngyan lā.**	I'll *help* you to do the photo-copying.
4 *Mgōi saai.*	*Thank you so much.*
5 *Msái mgōi.*	*Not at all* (a conventional response to **mgōi** which literally means 'There's no need to thank me').
6 **Bīngo hóyíh tùhng ngóh** *tong-jó dī sāam* **a?**	Who can help me *get the clothes ironed*?
7 **Juhng yáuh . . .**	And also . . .
8 *deihhá* **hóu** *wūjōu*	*the floor* is *dirty*
9 **Néih géidímjūng** *tái yùhn* **jūkkàuh a?**	When will you *finish watching* soccer?
10 *Juhng yáuh* **sāam go jih** *jauh* **tái yùhn laak.**	Fifteen more minutes to go, and then I'll finish watching (soccer).

Asking for a volunteer to help (1, 2)

One way to ask for a volunteer to help get something done is to say what you want done and then ask who is free:

> **Ngóh séung wán yàhn tùhng ngóh dá géi fūng seun. Bīngo dākhàahn a?**
> I want someone to type several letters for me. Who is free?

Wán in the phrase **wán yàhn** is a verb which means 'to look for'. **Yàhn**, on the other hand, is a noun of an indefinite nature in this context, and can thus be translated into either 'someone' or 'people'. The modal verb **séung** used before the phrase can be translated into 'want to' or 'wish to'.

Another way to ask around for a volunteer is to use the question word **bīngo** (who) with the modal **hóyíh**, as below:

> **Bīngo hóyíh tùhng ngóh dá géi fūng seun a?**
> Who can help me type a few letters?

A third way to make an open request for a favor is to use the question phrase **Yáuh móuh yàhn** (Is there anybody?) with the modal **hóyíh** to form a question, as follows:

> **Yáuh móuh yàhn hóyíh tùhng ngóh dá-jih a?**
> Is there anyone who can do some typing for me?

The verbal particle *saai* (2)

The particle **saai** is used with a verb and conveys the meaning of 'completely'. Thus, **mgōi** *saai* is an emphatic form of 'thank you' for a favor, while **dōjeh** *saai* is an emphatic form of 'thank you' for a gift.

Anticipating completion of action (6)

Lesson 6 introduced the use of the aspect marker **-jó** to refer to completed action. Sometimes when we ask people to do a favor we can use the aspect marker **-jó** with the verb to indicate anticipation of some action being completed soon. This use is not unlike the notion of 'getting something done' in English. Below are two examples:

> **Néih hó-mh-hóyíh tùhng ngóh dóu-jó dī laahpsaap a?**
> Could you get the rubbish bin emptied for me, please?
> **Bīngo hóyíh tùhng ngóh gei-jó dī seun a?**
> Can somebody get these letters posted for me, please?

Hóu

Hóu in **deihhà** *hóu* **wūjōu** functions as an adverb meaning 'very', to qualify the adjective **wūjōu** when it is stressed. But when it is *not* stressed, **hóu** in colloquial Cantonese does not carry the meaning of 'very'. So *hóu* **wūjōu** simply means 'dirty' rather than 'very dirty'.

The verbal particle *yùhn* (9)

Yùhn is a particle used after a verb to indicate finishing an action. It is different from the aspect marker -jó in that it is used to specify the finishing time of an action in progress. The question in Dialogue 4: **néih géidímjūng tái** *yùhn* **jūkkàuh a?** asks when Kenny will finish watching soccer, as he is watching while his mother is talking to him. Similarly, if you rang up your friend and found that he was having dinner, then you could ask: **Néih géidímjūng sihk** *yùhn* **faahn a?** (When will you finish eating your dinner?). If you rang up your friend for a chat in the evening, you might start the conversation by asking: **Néih sihk-jó faahn meih a?** (Have you eaten your dinner?) This habit of asking whether somebody has had a meal, by the way, is a social norm among Cantonese-speakers, and can be compared to English people talking about the weather as an opener to a conversation.

重 存

Juhng yáuh . . . jauh (10)

Juhng yáuh in this context means 'there is still', with **yáuh** in its existential use, while **jauh** is used to mean 'and then', leading on to the consequence of a condition. Thus, *juhng yáuh* **sāam go jih** *jauh* **tái yùhn jūkkàuh laak** literally means 'There are fifteen more minutes to go and then I'll finish watching soccer'.

Exercises 🔘

Exercise 1 What's to be done?

Dora is a part-time domestic helper for the Chans. Today when she arrives at the flat she finds that Mrs Chan has forgotten to leave her instructions about what work to do. But then the phone rings. It's Mrs Chan, ringing to give her instructions over the phone.

Read the dialogue, or listen to the recording, and then fill in the job-list by putting a tick (✔) where something needs to be done and a cross (✗) where something need not be done.

MRS CHAN: Wái, Dora àh?

DORA: Haih a.

MRS CHAN: Mgōi néih tùhng ngóh jouh géi yeuhng yéh ā. Jēung chòhng meih jāp. Mgōi néih tùhng ngóh jāp-chòhng. Dī wún meih sái. Màhfàahn néih bōng ngóh sái-jó dī wún. Dī sāam sái-jó laak, néih msái sái laak, bātgwo màhfàahn néih tùhng ngóh lohng-jó dī sāam lā. Juhng yáuh, mgōi néih tùhng ngóh maat-jó dīchēung tùhng kāp-chàhn ā.

DORA: Gám, sái-mh-sái máaih-sung a?

MRS CHAN: Msái la. Ngóh jihgéi máaih-sung dāk la.

making the bed	
washing up	
buying food for dinner	
washing the clothes	
hanging the clothes out	
vacuum-cleaning	
cleaning the windows	

Exercise 2 Mr Nice Guy

Nick is a very nice person and never says no to a favor asked. You want Nick to do three things for you: type two letters, borrow three books from the library, and buy a train ticket. Complete the conversation with polite requests for favors.

YOU:	Nick, néih dāk-mh-dākhàahn tùhng ngóh jouh géi yeuhng yéh a?
NICK:	Dāk, móuh mahntàih.
YOU:	(a) Néih hó-mh-hóyíh bōng ngóh . . .
NICK:	Hóyíh.
YOU:	(b) Gám, . . .
NICK:	(c)
YOU:	(d)
NICK:	(e)
YOU:	Mgōi saai, Nick.
NICK:	(f)

Exercise 3 The selfish family

The members of the Chow family are very selfish, and seldom offer help with housework. This is another typical evening when Mrs Chow is appealing in vain to her family for help. Everyone claims that he or she is busy doing something else. Referring to the picture, complete the conversation.

MRS CHOW:	Bīngo dākhàahn bōng ngóh sái-wún a?
JANE:	Ngóh mdākhàahn a, māmìh. Ngóh cheung-gán gō a.
MRS CHOW:	Gám, néih nē, Kelvin?

KELVIN: (a) Ngóh dōu mdākhàahn a. Ngóh . . .
MRS CHOW: Jane tùhng Kelvin dōu mdākhàahn. Gám, néih bōng
                  ngóh sái-wún dāk-mh-dāk a, bàh-bā?
MR CHOW: (b) Deui mjyuh . . .

Recognizing Chinese characters

煮飯   to cook meals

洗碗   to wash up

買餸   to buy food for meals

洗衣   to wash the clothes

晾衣	to hang the clothes
燙衣服	to iron the clothes
掃地	to sweep the floor
吸塵	to vacuum-clean
抹窗	to clean the windows

10 Hái bīndouh?

Where is it?

Vocabulary 📼

Personal belongings

Below are some things commonly found at home. They are presented with their assigned classifiers.

yāt *go* sáudói	a handbag
yāt *go* ngàhnbāau	a purse
yāt *go/fu* ngáahngéng	a pair of spectacles
yāt *deui* maht	a pair of socks
yāt *deui* sáumaht	a pair of gloves
yāt *deui* tōháai	a pair of slippers
yāt *jek* maht/sáumaht/tōháai	a sock/glove/slipper
yāt *jī* bāt	a pen
yāt *bá* jē	an umbrella
yāt *bá* sō	a comb
yāt *go* séuibūi	a glass
yāt *go* chàhbūi	a cup
yāt *go* luhkyínggēi	a video-recorder
yāt *béng* luhkyíngdáai	a video-tape

Classifiers

Apart from the most common classifier **go**, which is used for 'roundish' objects and many other less obviously roundish ones such as people (**yāt go yàhn**) and spectacles (**yāt go ngáahn-géng**), most classifiers are rationally determined. In the examples given above, **yāt deui** is literally 'a pair', while **jek** is the classifier for single pieces of footwear or gloves. **Jī** is used for long, slender objects which are cylindrical in shape, for instance, **yāt jī bāt** (a pen), while **bá** is used for long, slender objects that are not cylindrical, such as **yāt bá jē** (an umbrella) and **yāt bá sō** (a comb). **Béng**, on the other hand, is much more restricted in its use, referring only to audio or video cassette tapes.

Dialogues 🔘

Read the questions, and then read or listen to the dialogues to find the answers.

1 The Chans are an untidy family. The children, Sylvan and Sally, often leave things lying around in odd places. Their father Mr Chan is not much better. Mrs Chan is probably the only organized person in the house. At the moment Sally is about to go out, and is desperately trying to find her handbag and her gloves.

(a) Where is Sally's handbag?
(b) Where are her gloves?

SALLY: Māmìh, ngóh go sáudói mgin-jó a. Néih jī-mh-jī ngóh go sáudói hái bīndouh a?
MRS CHAN: Nē! Néih go sáudói hái sōfá seuhngmihn a.
SALLY: Haih wo. Gám, ngóh deui sáumaht nē? Ngóh wán mdóu deui sáumaht a.
MRS CHAN: Néih deui sáumaht hái ōnlohkyí seuhngmihn a. Gin-mh-gin a?
SALLY: Gin dóu la. Mgōi saai, māmìh.

2 Mr Chan is hunting around for his spectacles while his son Sylvan is frantically searching for his missing comb and socks.

(a) Where are Mr Chan's spectacles?
(b) Where is Sylvan's comb?
(c) Where are Sylvan's socks?

MR CHAN: Taai-táai a, ngóh wán mdóu ngóh go ngáahngéng a!
MRS CHAN: Nē! Néih go ngáahngéng mhaih hái chàhgēi seuhng-mihn lō! Gin-mh-gin a?
MR CHAN: Bīndouh a? . . . Gin dóu la. Hái chàhgēi seuhng-mihn ā ma.
SYLVAN: Māmìh, néih yáuh móuh gin dóu ngóh bá sō a? Ngóh bá sō mgin-jó a.
MRS CHAN: Néih bá sō àh? Nē! Néih bá sō mhaih hái dihnsi-gēi seuhngmihn lō!
SYLVAN: Haih wo. Gám, ngóh deui maht nē? Néih gin-mh-gin a?
MRS CHAN: Néih deui maht hái deihhá a. Nē, chāantói hahmihn a.
SYLVAN: Gin dóu la. Mgōi, māmìh.

Idioms and structures

The items in the list below appear in the same order as they do in the dialogue above. The *italicized* items are *new* items. In the notes, numbers in brackets refer to the expressions listed below.

1 *mgin-jó* — has gone missing
2 *Néih jī-mh-jī ngóh go sáudói hái bīndouh a?* — Do you know where my handbag is?
3 **Néih go sáudói *hái sōfá seuhngmihn* a.** — Your handbag is *on the sofa.*
4 *wán mdóu* — cannot find
5 **Gin-mh-gin a?** — Can you see it?
6 **Gin dóu la.** — I can see them now.
7 **Néih go ngáahngéng *mhaih hái chàhgēi seuhngmihn lō?*** — *Aren't those* your glasses on the coffee table?
8 **Hái chàhgēi seuhngmihn *ā ma.*** — On the coffee table, *as you said.*

9 **néih** *yáuh móuh gin dóu* *Have you seen my comb?*
  ngóh bá sō a?
10 **Néih bá sō** *àh?* *Did you say your comb?*

Mgin-jó (1)

The verb **gin** means 'to see', and the verb **mgin** (to lose) is formed from it by adding the negative prefix **m-**. **Mgin** is very often used with the aspect marker **-jó**, which indicates completion of action, to form the expression **mgin-jó**. In its stative use, describing the state of something, **mgin-jó** would translate into English as 'missing', as in **ngóh go sáudói** *mgin-jó* ('My handbag is *missing*'). In its verbal use **mgin-jó** would translate into English as 'has/have lost', as in **Ngóh** *mgin-jó* **ngóh go sáudói** ('I have *lost* my handbag').

Asking where something is (2)

To ask where something is, the question phrase **hái bīndouh** is used with the interrogative particle **a**. Note particularly the word order: the question phrase comes at the end of the sentence.

Ngóh deui tōháai *hái bīndouh* **a?**
Where are my slippers?
Néih jī-mh-jī ngóh go sáudói *hái bīndouh* **a?**
Do you know where my handbag is?

Saying where an object is (3)

To indicate location in Cantonese, the verbal form of the word **hái** is used, together with an adverb of location. However, the use is different from the use of prepositions in English. To indicate location, English employs the following pattern:

Noun A	Verb 'to be'	Preposition	Noun B
The book	is	on	the coffee table.

In Cantonese, the constituent parts come in a different order, as follows:

Noun A	*hái*	Noun B	*Adverb of location*
Bún syū	**hái**	**jēung chàhgēi**	**seuhngmihn**.
The book	is	the coffee table	on top

Note that while the definite article 'the' is used for a specified noun in English, Cantonese uses the determiner **gó** and an appropriate classifier for a specified noun, such as, **gó bún syū** (the book), **gó jēung chàhgēi** (the coffee table). However, the determiner **gó** is often omitted, hence **Bún syū hái jēung chàhgēi seuhngmihn.** Below is a list of common adverbs of location used in Cantonese. The familiar nouns **syū** (book), **chàhgēi** (coffee table), **sōfá** (sofa), **dihnsihgēi** (TV set), **syūgá** (bookshelves) and **ōnlohkyí** (easy chair) are used to form sentences to illustrate the use.

> **Bún syū *hái* jēung chàhgēi *seuhngmihn*.**
> The book *is on* the coffee table.
> **Bún syū *hái* jēung chàhgēi *hahmihn*.**
> The book *is under* the coffee table.
> **Jēung chàhgēi *hái* jēung sōfá *gaaklèih*.**
> The coffee table *is beside* the sofa.
> **Go dihnsihgēi *hái* jēung sōfá *chìhnmihn*.**
> The TV set *is in front of* the sofa.
> **Go syūgá *hái* jēung sōfá *hauhmihn*.**
> The bookshelves *are behind* the sofa.

To say Object A is between Object B and Object C, again the adverb of location comes at the end, as follows:

> **Jēung sōfá *hái* jēung chàhgēi *tùhng* jēung ōnlohkyí jūnggāan.**
> The sofa *is between* the coffee table *and* the easy chair.

To say something (say, the book) is on the floor, you can say:

> **Bún syū *hái deihhá seuhngmihn*.**

or simply:

> **Bún syū *hái deihhá*.**

The verbal particle *dóu*   *(4, 6)*

The verbal particle **dóu** is often used after a verb to indicate success in doing something. For example, the verb **wán** means 'to look for' and **wán *dóu*** means 'to be able to find'. Hence **Ngóh wán *dóu* go sáudói la** is 'I found the handbag'. The negative form of **wán *dóu*** is formed by adding the negative prefix **m-** to **dóu** and the phrase becomes **wán *mdóu***, which translates into 'to fail to find'. Thus,

Ngóh wán *mdóu* deui sáumaht is 'I cannot find the gloves'. Later in Dialogue 1, Gin *dóu* la in response to the question Gin-mh-gin a? stresses the fact that one can now see something which one failed to see a minute before.

Mhaih . . . lō! (7)

The structure mhaih . . . lō! gives positive emphasis. Although mhaih is negative by itself, the sentence-final particle lō turns the whole structure positive. This structure can be compared to the rhetorical question of 'Aren't those your glasses lying on the coffee table?' Another example can be found later in Dialogue 2: Néih bá sō *mhaih* hái dihnsihgēi seuhngmihn lō! ('Isn't that your comb on the TV set?').

The double particle ā ma (8)

Ā ma are two particles used together at the end of a statement which repeats another speaker's message to acknowledge it. In Dialogue 2, Mrs Chan tells Mr Chan his spectacles are on the coffee table (hái chàhgēi seuhngmihn), and when Mr Chan finally finds his spectacles he acknowledges receipt of the message by saying Hái chàhgēi seuhngmihn ā ma ('On the coffee table, as you said').

Yáuh móuh . . . dóu? (9)

The verb gin is very often used with the verbal particle dóu to mean 'to have seen', with emphasis on someone having seen something in the immediate past. To form a choice-type question with gin dóu, the verbs yáuh and móuh are used. Hence néih *yáuh móuh* gin *dóu* ngóh bá sō a? ('Have you seen my comb?').

Question with àh

Here the question with àh (see Lesson 5) acknowledges the first question, and buys time for a reply. In Dialogue 2, Sylvan asks the question Néih yáuh móuh gin dóu ngóh bá sō a?, and Mrs Chan responds by saying Néih bá sō àh?, to give herself time to look around for the comb. Similarly, if the question was **Néih yáuh móuh gin dóu Sylvan bún syū a?**, then the response would be **Sylvan bún syū àh?**

Vocabulary 🔘

Shops

Below is a list of different shops. Try reading out each item aloud. If you have the cassette tapes of this book, you can model your pronunciation on the recording.

màhngeuihdim 文具店	stationery shop
syūdim/syūgúk 書店 書局	bookstore
tòhnggwódim 糖果店	sweet shop
fādim 花店	flower shop
fuhkjōngdim 服裝店	dress shop _boutique_
mihnbāaupóu 麵包店	bakery
fēifaatpóu 飛髮舖	barber's shop
hàaihpóu 鞋舖	shoe shop
dihnheipóu 電器舖	electrical appliance store
yeuhkfòhng 藥房	drugstore
chīukāpsíhchèuhng 超級市場	supermarket

Shop/store

Most of the items in the list above are compound nouns ending either in **dim** or **póu**, both of which mean 'shop' or 'store'. For example, 'sweets' is **tòhnggwó**, and a 'sweet shop' is **tòhnggwódim**. Two exceptions are **yeuhkfòhng** (drugstore), in which **fòhng** (literally 'room') is used, and **chīukāpsíhchèuhng**, which is a literal translation of supermarket, with **chīukāp** meaning 'super' and **síhchèuhng** meaning 'market'. Another exception is the alternative term for 'bookstore', **syūgúk**, in which **gúk** is used to refer to a large shop. All these shops use the classifier **gāan**, hence **yāt gāan mihnbāaupóu, yāt gāan dihnheipóu**, and so on.

Dialogues 📼

Read the questions, and then read or listen to the dialogues to find
the answers. If you have the cassette tape, you may wish to
listen to the dialogues and answer the questions without reading
the texts.

3 Auntie Kate has come to visit the Chans from Canada, and is staying with them for a month. She is asking Sally where she can buy certain things.

(a) Where is the shoe shop that Sally recommends?
(b) How far away is it?
(c) Where is the dress shop that Sally recommends?

AUNTIE KATE: Sally, ngóh séung máaih deui hàaih. Néih jī-mh-jī
bīndouh yáuh hàaihpóu a?
SALLY: Ngóh jī hái deihtitjaahm deuimihn yáuh yāt gāan
hàaihpóu. Gódouh dī hàaih géi leng ga.
AUNTIE KATE: Gám, gāan hàaihpóu káhn-mh-káhn nīdouh ga?
SALLY: Hóu káhn ja. Daaihyeuk hàahng léuhng go jih
jauh dou la.
AUNTIE KATE: Gám, nīdouh fuhgahn yáuh móuh fuhkjōngdim a?
Ngóh juhng séung máaih géi gihn sāam.
SALLY: Yáuh yāt gāan, jauh hái hàaihpóu chèhdeui-
mihn.
AUNTIE KATE: Gám, ngāam saai laak.

4 Today Auntie Kate wants to see a film, and asks Sylvan about the nearest cinema.

(a) What is the name of the nearest cinema?
(b) How long does it take to walk there?
(c) How long does it take to go by taxi?

AUNTIE KATE: Sylvan, ngóh séung heui tái chēut dihnyíng.
Lèih ngūkkéi jeui káhn gāan heiyún hái bīn-
douh a?
SYLVAN: Lèih nīdouh jeui káhn gāan heiyún haih Capitol
Cinema. Bātgwo dōu géi yúhn a, yiu hàahng daaih-
yeuk ńgh go jih sīnji douh a.

AUNTIE KATE: Gám, daap dīksí yiu géinoih a?
SYLVAN: Daap dīksí jauh hóu faai, léuhng go jih jauh heui douh laak.

Idioms and structures

The items in the list below appear in the same order as they do in the dialogue above. The *italicized* items are *new* items. In the notes, numbers in brackets refer to the expressions listed below.

1 **Néih jī-mh-jī** *bīndouh* *yáuh hàaihpóu a?*
Do you know *where I can find a shoe shop?*

2 *Hái deihtitjaahm deuimihn yáuh yāt gāan hàaihpóu.*
There's a shoe shop opposite the underground station.

3 **Ngóh juhng séung máaih** *géi gihn sāam.*
I also want to buy *some clothes.*

4 **Gám,** *ngāam saai laak!*
That's great!

5 **Ngóh séung heui tái** *chēut dihnyíng.*
I want to go to see a film. (**Chēut** is the classifier for **dihnyīng.**)

6 *Lèih ngūkkéi jeui káhn gāan heiyún hái bīndouh a?*
Where is the nearest cinema from home?

7 **Bātgwo** *dōu* **géi** *yúhn* **a.**
Even so it's quite *far away.*

8 *Yiu* **hàahng daaihyeuk ńgh go jih** *sīnji* **douh a.**
It takes about 25 minutes to walk there.

Location   (1, 2)

To indicate the location of buildings, we use similar structures to those discussed earlier in this Lesson. Below are several examples using a cinema (**heiyún**) and a supermarket (**chīukāpsíhchèuhng**) as two points of orientation.

(Gāan) mihnbāaupóu hái (gāan) heiyún *gaaklèih.*
The bakery *is beside* the cinema.
(Gāan) fādim hái (gāan) heiyún *deuimihn.*
The flower shop *is opposite* the cinema.
(Gāan) syūdim hái (gāan) chīukāp síhchèuhng *chèhdeuimihn.*
The bookstore *is diagonally across from* the supermarket.
(Gāan) yeuhkfòhng hái (gāan) fādim *tùhng* **(gāan) hàaihpóu** *jūnggāan.*

The drugstore *is between* the flower shop *and* the shoe shop.
(Gāan) dihnheipóu *hái* **(gāan) heiyúhn** *fuhgahn.*
The electrical appliance shop *is near* the cinema.

To ask whether there is a certain kind of shop nearby, the existential verbs **yáuh** and **móuh** are used, as follows:

Nīdouh fuhgahn *yáuh móuh* **yeuhkfòhng a?**
Is there a drugstore nearby?

An alternative is to use the question word **bīndouh** (where):

Fuhgahn *bīndouh* **yáuh yeuhkfòhng a?**
Where can I find a drugstore around here?

To answer these questions the information about the whereabouts is usually put at the beginning of the sentence:

Hái heiyúhn deuimihn **yáuh yāt gāan yeuhkfòhng.**
There is a drugstore opposite the cinema.

Géi gihn sāam (3)

Sāam in the phrase **géi gihn sāam** refers to items of clothing, and **gihn** is the classifier for **sāam**.

Ngāam saai laak (4)

In the idiomatic expression **ngāam saai laak**, the word **ngāam** is a verb which means 'to fit' while **saai** is a particle which means 'completely', and the expression literally means 'it fits perfectly well (with my plans)'.

Serial construction (5)

As discussed in previous Lessons, in Cantonese two or more verbs can be used consecutively to express a series of actions. In this example the three verbs **séung** (to want to), **heui** (to go), and **tái** (to see) are used serially.

Distances (6)

The Cantonese words for 'near' and 'far' are **káhn** and **yúhn** respectively, but structurally they are used slightly differently. The adjective **káhn** can be used alone, as below:

> **Gāan mihnbāaupóu hóu *káhn*.**
> The bakery is very near.

It can also be used *before* a point of reference:

> **Gāan mihnbāaupóu hóu *káhn* ngūkkéi.**
> The bakery is near home.

It can also be used with the word **lèih**, which functions like the English preposition 'from', in which case **káhn** comes after the point of reference:

> **Gāan mihnbāaupóu *lèih* ngūkkéi hóu *káhn*.**
> The bakery is near home.

As for **yúhn**, it can either be used alone or with the word **lèih**, but it cannot be used before the point of reference. Below are two examples:

> **Gāan fādim hóu *yúhn*.**
> The flower shop is far away.
> **Gāan fādim *lèih* ngūkkéi hóu *yúhn*.**
> The flower shop is far from home.

To ask whether a shop is near or far away, the adjective **káhn** or **yúhn** is reduplicated in a choice-type question:

> **Gāan fēifaatpóu *káhn-mh-káhn* nīdouh a?**
> Is the barber's shop near here?
> **Gāan tòhnggwódim lèih nīdouh *yúhn-mh-yúhn* a?**
> Is the sweet shop far from here?

Dōu (7)

Here the word **dōu** is used to mark the apparent contrast between the expression **jeui káhn gāan heiyún** (the nearest cinema) and **géi yúhn** ('quite *far away*'). More explicitly, it means 'Even if I say it's the nearest cinema it is quite a long distance away'.

Subjective distances (8)

To indicate how long it takes to go, say, on foot, to a certain destination, two kinds of pattern are used, depending on whether the speaker thinks it is near or far away:

> **(Gāan) mihnbāaupóu hàahng ńgh fānjūng** *jauh* **dou** *laak*.
> It only takes five minutes to walk to the bakery.
> **(Gāan) fādim** *yiu* **hàahng bun go jūngtàuh** *sīnji* **dou**.
> It's half-an-hour's walk to go to the flower shop.

The use of the pattern **yiu . . . sīnji** to indicate the considerable effort required to get a task accomplished and the use of the pattern **jauh . . . lak** to emphasize the ease of doing something were discussed Lesson 7.

Exercises

Exercise 1 Where are the shops?

Richard has just moved into a new flat in a housing estate. Today, he wants to do some shopping, but as he is not very familiar with the nearby shops, he asks his neighbor Kathy to give him some instructions.

Read the dialogue between Richard and Kathy. Then help Richard to complete the sketch map so that he can find the shops easily.

RICHARD: Kathy, ngóh séung máaih géi bún syū. Néih jī-mh-jī fuhgahn bīndouh yáuh syūgúk a?

KATHY: Ngóh jīdou hái chīukāpsíhchèuhng gaaklèih, fādim deuimihn yáuh yāt gāan syūgúk. Gódouh géi dō syū maaih ga.

RICHARD: Gám, hái syūgúk fuhgahn yáuh móuh yeuhkfòhng a?

KATHY: Yáuh. Jauh hái syūgúk chèhdeuimihn, fādim gaaklèih jauh yáuh gāan yeuhkfòhng laak.

RICHARD: Ngóh juhng séung máaih dī dihnhei. Jeui káhn gāan dihnheipóu hái bīndouh a?

KATHY: Dihnheipóu àh? Jeui káhn gó gāan jauh haih hái heiyún chèhdeuimihn, hàaihpóu gaaklèih.

RICHARD: Gám, mihnbāaupóu nē? Bīndouh yáuh mihnbāaupóu a?

KATHY: Hái heiyún deuimihn, chīukāpsíhchèuhng gaaklèih mhaih yáuh mihnbāaupóu lō!

RICHARD: Hái chīukāpsíhchèuhng gaaklèih àh? Hóu lā. Juhng yáuh, fuhgahn yáuh móuh tòhnggwódim a? Ngóh séung máaih dī tòhnggwó.

KATHY: Yáuh. Hái heiyún tùhng fuhkjōngdim jūnggāan yáuh yāt gāan tòhnggwódim.

RICHARD: Gāan tòhnggwódim hái heiyún tùhng fuhkjōngdim jūnggāan. Hóu. Mgōi saai.

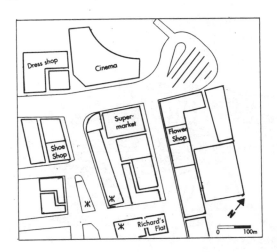

Exercise 2 Where is everything?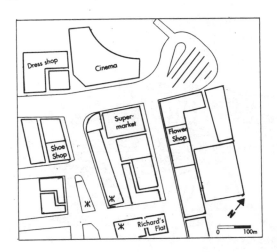

Translate into Cantonese the following statements about where things are. The first one has been done for you as an example.

(a) The book is on the easy chair.
   Bún syū hái jēung ōnlohkyí seuhngmihn.
(b) The umbrella is beside the sofa.
(c) The spectacles are on the floor.
(d) The cup is on the bookshelves.
(e) The slippers are under the coffee table.
(f) The glass is on the TV set.
(g) The pen is between the glass and the cup.

Exercise 3 The scene of the crime

The Poons came home on Saturday evening to find that their house had been burgled and the usually orderly sitting room was in a mess. They telephoned the police, and Inspector Ko and his team arrived shortly after. Inspector Ko is examining the things scattered all over the sitting room and using his recorder to make a list of where different objects are found. Referring to the picture, complete Inspector Ko's monologue.

Hái sōfá séuhngmihn yáuh yāt go sáudói, yāt jek maht . . . Hái
deihhá yáuh . . .

Exercise 4 The nearest shop

Your friend Ching Ping from Guangzhou is staying with you for a
few weeks. Before he leaves, he wants to do some shopping. He is
asking you to recommend some nearby shops where he can buy
certain things. Referring to the map, complete the dialogue.

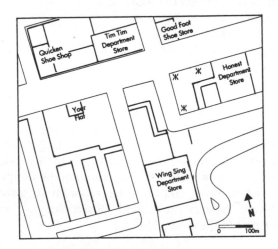

CHING PING:	Ngóh séung máaih dī sāam. Nidouh fuhgahn yáuh móuh fuhkjōngdim a?
YOU:	Yáuh. Yáuh géi gāan, Tim Tim lā, Wing Sing la, tùhng Honest.
CHING PING:	Gám, bīn gāan jeui káhn a?
YOU:	(a)
CHING PING:	Gám, nī gāan haih-mh-haih jeui daaih a?
YOU:	(b)
CHING PING:	Gám, bīn gāan jeui daaih a?
YOU:	(c)
CHING PING:	Nī gāan yúhn-mh-yúhn a?
YOU:	(d)
CHING PING:	Ngóh juhng séung máaih yāt deui hàaih. Nīdouh fuhgahn yáuh móuh hàaihpóu a?
YOU:	(e)
CHING PING:	Gám, léuhng gāan bīn gāan káhn-dī a?
YOU:	(f)

Recognizing Chinese characters

文具店	stationery shop
書店	bookstore
糖果店	sweet shop
花店	flower shop
服裝店	dress shop
藥房	drugstore
超級市場	supermarket

fuhng jáau chicken feet

11 Giu yéh sihk
Ordering food

> **In Lesson 11 you will learn about:**
>
> - ordering food and asking for the bill
> - stating preferences

Vocabulary 💿

In a noodle shop   *the bill*

The Chinese restaurants in Hong Kong mainly serve Cantonese-style food, unless otherwise specified. Also commonly found in Hong Kong are small Cantonese-style noodle shops, where noodles, rice and congee (a kind of rice porridge commonly eaten in South East Asia) are served. In a noodle shop, food is ordered by the container, such as bowls and plates. Below is a list of common dishes served in a Cantonese-style noodle shop.

yāt *wún* **wàhntānmihn**	a *bowl* of won-ton noodles
yāt *wún* **yùhdáanmihn**	a *bowl* of fish-ball noodles ✓
yāt *wún* **gahpdáijūk**	a *bowl* of congee with mixed meat
yāt *wún* **ngàuhyuhkjūk**	a *bowl* of congee with beef ✓
yāt *dihp* **yàuhchoi**	a *plate* of vegetables with oyster ✓ sauce

In a tea-house

One of the favorite pastimes of Cantonese people is to go to a tea-house in a large group for a hearty meal of **dímsām** (dumplings either steamed in bamboo baskets or fried and then served on a plate) always accompanied by a choice of Chinese teas. When Cantonese speakers say **heui yám-chàh**, which literally means 'go-drink-tea', they mean having **dímsām** in a tea-house.

When people go to a tea-house, after sitting down at a table, they first order tea, and then they order **dímsām** either from **dímsām** trolleys or by placing an order through a waiter (**fógei**). Tea is ordered by the pot (**wùh**), and **dímsām** are ordered either by the bamboo basket (**lùhng**), or by the plate (**dihp**). Below is a list of some of the most popular Chinese teas and **dímsām** offered in a tea-house.

Chinese teas:

yāt wùh *bóuléi*	a pot of *Pu-erh* (dark) tea
yāt wùh *hēungpín*	a pot of *jasmine* tea ✓
yāt wùh *lùhngjéng*	a pot of *Lung-ching* (light) tea

Dímsām:

yāt lùhng *hāgáau*	a basket of *steamed shrimp dumplings* ✓
yāt lùhng *sīumáai*	a basket of *steamed pork dumplings*
yāt lùhng *chāsīubāau*	a basket of *steamed barbecued-pork buns*
yāt lùhng *fángwó*	a basket of *steamed shrimp and bamboo-shoot dumplings*
yāt dihp *chēungyún*	a plate of *spring rolls* ✓
yāt dihp *daahntāat*	a plate of *custard tarts* ✓

Asking for the bill

After eating, you ask for the bill! There are two ways to ask for the bill in Cantonese, depending on the context. In a noodle shop, we usually say **Mgòi tái-sou!**, which literally means 'Please see amount!', i.e. 'please check the amount that I have to pay'. This is because in a small noodle shop the convention is for the waiter to call out an amount to notify the cashier what sum of money he will be receiving. The alternative expression **Mgòi màaih-dāan!** is used in a bigger eating place such as a restaurant or tea-house, where proper bills are issued by the cashier and brought to the table by the waiter – hence the word **dāan**, 'bill'. This expression literally means 'Please close (the) bill'.

Dialogues 🔘🔘

Read the questions, and then read or listen to the dialogues to find the answers.

1 John is going to his Cantonese class, which begins at 6:15 p.m. It's now 6 p.m., and he is feeling hungry, so he stops by a noodle shop to get something to eat.

(a) What does John order?

(b) What does the waiter suggest that John order?

(c) How much does John pay for his food?

WAITER: Sīnsāang, sihk dī mātyéh a?

JOHN: Mgōi néih yāt wún wàhntānmihn, tùhng yāt wún gahp-dáijūk.

WAITER: Hóuh, yāt wún wàhntānmihn, yāt wún gahpdáijūk. Yiu-mh-yiu dihp yàuhchoi tīm a? Gāmyaht dī choisām hóuh leng wo. 今日

JOHN: Hóuh lā, yiu dihp yàuhchoi tīm lā.

(Some time later.)

JOHN: Fógei, mgōi tái-sou.

WAITER: Júngguhng y'ah baat mān. Chēutmihn béi lā. —四 八

*2 It's Sunday and the Lams have gone to their favorite tea-house for a **dímsām** lunch. They are being greeted by a waiter.*

(a) What kinds of tea do the Lams order?

(b) What kinds of **dímsām** do they order?

(c) How much does the food cost?

(d) How much does Mr Lam pay?

WAITER: Sīnsāang, géidō wái a?

MR LAM: Sei wái, mgōi.

WAITER: Sei wái àh? Nīdouh lā.

MR LAM: Hóu, mgōi.

WAITER: Yám mātyéh chàh a?

MRS LAM: Mgōi yāt wùh hēungpín, yāt wùh bóuléi ā.

MRS LAM: Mgōi yāt wùh hēungpín, yāt wùh bóuléi ā.

(*After a few minutes the waiter comes back with the teas ordered.*)

WAITER: Yāt wùh hēungpín, yāt wùh bóuléi. Chíng mahn giu dī mātyéh dímsām a? 蝦餃 燒賣

MRS LAM: Mgōi léuhng lùhng hāgáau, yāt lùhng sīumáai, tùhng léuhng lùhng chāsīubāau. 叉燒飽

KENNY: Yiu dō yāt dihp daahntāat.

ANGEL: Tùhngmàaih yāt lùhng fángwó. 粉果

WAITER: Hóu, léuhng lùhng hāgáau, yāt lùhng sīumáai, yāt lùhng fángwó, léuhng lùhng chāsīubāau, tùhng yāt dihp daahntāat.

(*Some time later the Lams are ready to go.*)

MR LAM: Fógei, mgōi màaih-dāan.

WAITER: Hóu.

(*The waiter returns.*)

WAITER: Dōjeh yāt-baak gáu-sahp yih mān.

MR LAM: Nī douh yih-baak mān. Msái jáau laak.

WAITER: Dōjeh.

Idioms and structures

The items in the list below appear in the same order as they do in the dialogues above. The *italicized* items are *new* items. In the notes, numbers in brackets refer to the expressions listed below.

1 **Yiu-mh-yiu dihp yàuhchoi *tīm* a?**   Do you want a plate of vegetables *in addition*?

2 ***Chēutmihn béi* lā!**   Please *pay outside*.

3 **Yám mātyéh chàh a?**   What tea would you like to drink?

4 **Yiu *dō* yāt dihp daahntāat.**   A plate of custard tarts, *too*.

5 ***Tùhngmàaih* yāt lùhng fángwó.**   *And* a basket of fángwó.

6 ***Msái jáau* laak.**   *Keep the change.*

Suggesting something additional   (1)

The word **tīm** means 'in addition' and is used for suggesting an additional item. It is always put *at the end of a proposition*, hence **Yiu-mh-yiu dihp yàuhchoi *tīm* a?** and **yiu dihp yàuhchoi *tīm* lā**, but never *ngóh tīm yiu yāt dihp yàuhchoi.

Chēutmihn 出面 *(2)*

Chēutmihn is another adverb of location: it means 'outside', while the word for 'inside' is **léuihmihn**. Here, in the context of the noodle-shop, the waiter is asking the customer to 'pay outside' because conventionally he does not bring the customer the bill. The customer has to go to the cashier who usually sits at the entrance to the shop.

Asking for something additional (4)

The word **dō** is used with a verb to suggest either an addition or an extension to the action concerned. For example, **Yiu *dō* yāt dihp daahntāat** means '(I) *also* want a plate of custard tarts', while **Ngóh séung dá *dō* bun go jūngtàuh móhngkàuh** means 'I want to play tennis for half an hour *more*'. Notice that **dō** is always positioned immediately after the verb.

To summarize, there are three ways to ask for an additional item, say, a plate of custard tarts:

> **Ngóh séung yiu *dō* yāt dihp daahntāat.**
> **Ngóh séung yiu (yāt) dihp daahntāat *tīm*.**
> **Ngóh *juhng* séung yiu (yāt) dihp daahntāat.**

See Lesson 9 for **juhng** as 'also'.

唔使找 嘞

Msái jáau laak (6)

The idiom **Msái jáau laak** has exactly the same function as 'Keep the change' in English, though they have different literal meanings. The verb **jáau** means 'to give money back as change', and so **Msái jáau laak** more explicitly means 'There is no need for you to give me the change'.

Vocabulary 🔲

At a fast-food shop

Below is some of the food one might eat at a fast-food shop. Note the classifier used for each item.

Snacks

yāt go *honbóubāau*	a *hamburger*
yāt go *jīsí honbóubāau*	a *cheeseburger*
yāt go *yùhláuhbāau*	a *fishburger*
yāt jek *yihtgáu*	a *hot-dog*
yāt bāau *syùhtíu*	a packet of *chips/French fries*

Drinks

yāt būi *chàh*	a cup of *tea*
yāt būi *gafē*	a cup of *coffee*
yāt būi *hólohk*	a cup of *cola*
yāt būi *cháangjāp*	a cup of *orange juice*

As most fast-food shops are self-service, there is not much negotiation between the customer and the salesperson. One question, though, that the salesperson often asks the customer is: **Hái (nī) douh sihk dihng līk jáu a?**, which means 'Eat-in or take-away?'

Dialogues 🔲

Read the questions, and then read or listen to the dialogues to find the answers.

3 Carmen is on her way to her Cantonese lesson. She is hungry and stops by a fast-food shop.

(a) What does Carmen buy?
(b) Is she eating in or taking the food away?
(c) How much does the food cost?

SALESPERSON: Fūnyìhng gwònglàhm.
CARMEN: Mgòi béi yāt go jīsí honbóubāau, yāt bāau daaih syùhtíu, tùhng yāt būi sai hólohk.
SALESPERSON: Hái douh sihk dihng līk jáu a?
CARMEN: Līk jáu ga.
SALESPERSON: Dòjeh sahp-chāt go bun.
CARMEN: Nīdouh yih-sahp mān.
SALESPERSON: Dòjeh. Jáau fāan léuhng go bun.
CARMEN: Mgòi.

4 Carmen is discussing with Richard the kinds of food they like.

(a) Which does Carmen prefer, Japanese food or Chinese food?
(b) Which does Richard prefer, Chinese food or French food?
(c) What is John's favorite food?

RICHARD: Carmen, néih jūng-mh-jūngyi sihk Yahtbún choi a?

CARMEN: Jūngyi a. Ngóh hóu jūngyi sihk Yahtbún choi ga.

RICHARD: Gám, néih haih-mh-haih jeui jūngyi sihk Yahtbún choi a?

CARMEN: Mhaih wo. Ngóh dōu hóu jūngyi sihk Jūnggwok choi wo.

RICHARD: Gám, néih jūngyi bīn yeuhng dō-dī a?

CARMEN: Yahtbún choi tùhng Jūnggwok choi, ngóh dōu haih jūngyi Jūnggwok choi dō-dī. Néih nē, Richard?

RICHARD: Ngóh mjūngyi sihk Yahtbún choi. Ngóh jūngyi Faatgwok choi tùhng Jūnggwok choi. Bātgwo ngóh dōu haih jūngyi Faatgwok choi dō-gwo Jūnggwok choi.

CARMEN: Gám néih tùhng John yāt yeuhng laak. John dōu haih jeui jūngyi sihk Faatgwok choi.

Idioms and structures

The items in the list below appear in the same order as they do in the dialogues above. The *italicized* items are *new* items. In the notes, numbers in brackets refer to the expressions listed below.

1 *Fūnyìhng gwōnglàhm*   A formal and respectful way of saying '*Welcome*'.

2 **yāt bāau daaih syùhtíu**   one large French fries

3 **yāt būi sai hólohk**   one small Coke

4 *Jáau fāan léuhng go bun.*   Here's $2.50 change.

5 *Yahtbún choi tùhng Jūng-gwok choi, ngóh dōu haih jūngyi Jūnggwok choi dō-dī.*   *I think I like Chinese food better than Japanese food.*

Adjectives of size (2)

Daaih is 'large' in Cantonese while **sai** is 'small'. Notice here that **daaih** and **sai** are put immediately before **syùhtíu** and **hólohk** and not the containers **bāau** and **būi**.

The verbal particle *fāan* (4)

我 迎

The verbal particle **fāan** in **jáau** *fāan* **léuhng go bun** indicates that the action is 'in response' to a previous action. Hence the expression more explicitly means 'I am giving you $2.50 as change in response to your payment'. Similarly, when returning a borrowed object to the owner, you say **Béi** *fāan* **néih** to indicate that it is a return action.

Stating preferences (5)

In Cantonese, there is no exact equivalent to the expression 'I prefer A to B'. Below are sentences showing how preferences are expressed in Cantonese, using Chinese food (**Jūnggwok choi**) and Japanese food (**Yahtbún choi**) as examples. 比 較

> **Jūnggwok choi tùhng Yahtbún choi, ngóh** *béigaau jūngyi* **Jūnggwok choi.**
> (lit.) Chinese food and Japanese food, I comparatively like Chinese food.
> **Jūnggwok choi tùhng Yahtbún choi, ngóh** *jūngyi* **jūnggwok choi** *dō-dī*. 多 啲
> (lit.) Chinese food and Japanese food, I like Chinese food more.
> **Ngóh** *jūngyi* **Jūnggwok choi** *dō-gwo* **Yahtbún choi.**
> (lit.) I like Chinese food more than Japanese food.

Béigaau functions like the English word 'comparatively' and is put immediately before a verb or an adjective. For example, **Jūk tùhng mihn, ngóh béigaau héifūn sihk jūk** means 'I prefer eating congee to eating noodles'; while **Nī deui hàaih béigaau pèhng** is 'This pair of shoes is comparatively cheap'.

The distinction between the usage of **dō-dī** and **dō-gwo** is very similar to that described in the discussion about comparison of prices. (See Lesson 6.) When only the preferred item is mentioned in the clause of comparison, **dō-dī** is used, but when both compared items are mentioned, then **dō-gwo** is used, and is positioned *after* the preferred item and *before* the less preferred one. In other words, **dō-dī** always comes in a sentence-final position while **dō-gwo** never does. Below are examples:

> **Tái jùkkàuh tùhng tái páaumáh, ngóh jūngyi tái jùkkàuh *dō-dī*.**
> **Ngóh jūngyi tái jùkkàuh *dō-gwo* tái páaumáh.**
> I prefer watching soccer to watching horse-racing.

Exercises

Exercise 1 Taking food orders

Imagine you work for a fast-food shop. Read or listen to the dialogue. Then note down the food items ordered.

CUSTOMER: Mgōi néih, ngóh séung yiu léuhng go honbóubāau, sāam go yihtgáu, tùhng léuhng bāau syùhtíu.

YOU: Hóu. Léuhng go honbóubāau, sāam go yihtgáu, tùhng léuhng bāau syùhtíu. Syùhtíu yiu daaih dihng sai a?

CUSTOMER: Yiu daaih ge.

YOU: Gám, yiu-mh-yiu dī yéh yám tīm a?

CUSTOMER: Yiu a. Yiu léuhng būi chàh, léuhng būi gafē, tùhng yāt būi cháangjāp.

YOU: Dāk. Léuhng būi chàh, léuhng būi gafē, tùhng yāt būi cháangjāp.

CUSTOMER: Haih laak. Mgōi.

Exercise 2 Dream holidays

John, Carmen and Richard are discussing their favorite places for a holiday. Read or listen to the dialogue. Then note down each speaker's favorite or preferred places for a holiday.

JOHN: Richard, néih jeui jūngyi heui bīndouh léuihhàhng a?

RICHARD: Ngóh heui-gwo hóu dō gwokgā. Ngóh jeui jūngyi Fēileuihtbān tùhng Yandouh.

CARMEN: Gám, Fēileuihtbān tùhng Yandouh néih jūngyi bīndouh dō-dī a?

RICHARD: Ngóh béigaau jūngyi Yandouh. Néihdeih nē? Néihdeih jeui jūngyi heui bīndouh a?

CARMEN: Ngóh jeui jūngyi heui Jūnggwok. Yahtbún ngóh dō

jūngyi. Bātgwo dōu haih jūngyi Jūnggwok dō-dī. Néih
nē, John? 私

JOHN:　　Ngóh jauh jūngyi Yahtbún dō-gwo Jūnggwok laak.
　　　　Ngóh gokdāk Yahtbún béigaau hóuwáan. 好玩

Exercise 3 The noodle shop waiter

Ah Wing works as a waiter in a noodle shop. When a customer
leaves, it is customary for him to work out the total immediately so
that the customer knows how much to pay. Complete the following
conversations according to the price-list. The first conversation has
been completed for you as an example.

a) stēam wún, yahn dēen mihn y'eh sei mēn, leuhng dihp yeuh choi

Price-list: *sahp yih mēn yāt wún gaht dēi juk sahp yāt man*
jūng guhng sei sahp sēi ah chēt mēn

won-ton noodles	$9.00 a bowl
fish-ball noodles	$8.00 a bowl
congee with mixed meat	$11.00 a bowl
congee with beef	$10.00 a bowl
vegetables with oyster sauce	$6.00 a plate

1 Two customers have just had two bowls of won-ton noodles and
one bowl of congee with beef.

CUSTOMER:　Mgōi tái-sou. 唔該 算

AH WING:　　Hóu. Léuhng wún wàhntān mihn, sahp-baat mān.
　　　　　　Yāt wún ngàuhyuhkjūk, sahp mān. Júngguhng y'ah-
　　　　　　baat mān lā. 牛肉粥 十

CUSTOMER:　Nīdouh sā'ah mān. 三吖

AH WING:　　Jáau fāan léuhng mān.

CUSTOMER:　Mgōi.

AH WING:　　Dōjeh. Mgōi

2 Three customers have just finished three bowls of fish-ball noodles, two plates of vegetables, and one bowl of congee with mixed
meat.

CUSTOMER:　Mgōi tái-sou.

AH WING:　　(a)

CUSTOMER:　Nīdouh yāt-baak mān. ngh ch

AH WING:　　(b) Jáau fāan ngh sahp sāam mān

CUSTOMER:　Mgōi saai.

AH WING:　　(c)

158

3 Four customers have just eaten four bowls of won-ton noodles, two bowls of fish-ball noodles, three bowls of congee with beef, and two plates of vegetables.

CUSTOMER:	Mgōi tái-sou.
AH WING:	(d)
CUSTOMER:	Nīdouh ńgh-baak mān.
AH WING:	(e) *Jáan tāen sei baak hhng luhk men*
CUSTOMER:	Mgōi.
AH WING:	(f)

Exercise 4 Ordering dímsām

You enjoy having **dímsām** in a tea-house. Today you are taking some foreign friends to a tea-house. As you are the only one who speaks Cantonese, you have to order the tea and **dímsām**. Complete the conversation.

WAITER:	Géidō wái a?
YOU:	(a)
WAITER:	Nīdouh lā.
YOU:	(b) *Mh gōi*
WAITER:	Yám mātyéh chàh a?
YOU:	(c)
WAITER:	Sihk dī mātyéh dímsām a?
YOU:	(d)

Exercise 5 Preferences

Translate each sentence from English into Cantonese by using any of the three structures discussed. The first one has been done for you as an example.

(a) I prefer touring Korea to touring the Philippines.
   Ngóh jūngyi heui Hòhngwok léuihhàhng dō-gwo heui Fēileuhtbān léuihhàhng.
 or **Hòhngwok tùhng Fēileuhtbān, ngóh jūngyi heui Hòhngwok léuihhàhng dō-dī.**
 or **Hòhngwok tùhng Fēileuhtbān, ngóh béigaau jūngyi heui Hòhngwok léuihhàhng.**
(b) My father likes going to the tea-house more than going to the cinema.
(c) My elder brother prefers playing basketball to playing tennis.
(d) His mother likes listening to the radio more than watching television.

(e) My younger sister prefers learning French to learning German.

Recognizing Chinese characters

普洱	Pu-erh tea
香片	jasmine tea
龍井	Lung-ching tea
點心	**dímsām**
蝦餃	steamed shrimp dumplings
燒賣	steamed pork dumplings
义燒包	steamed barbecued-pork buns
粉果	steamed shrimp and bamboo-shoot dumplings
春卷	spring rolls
蛋撻	custard tarts

ngoh bch bā

12 Tīnhei

The weather

In Lesson 12 you will learn about:

- understanding broadcast weather reports
- talking about the weather
- making predictions
- giving advice
- dates
- festive greetings

Vocabulary 🔲

Describing the weather

The list below gives the most common words used in Cantonese for describing the weather. Try reading them aloud. If you have the cassette tapes of this book with you, you can model your pronunciation on the tape recording.

tīnhei	the weather
yiht	hot
dung	cold
nyúhn	warm
lèuhng	cool
sāp	humid
gōn	dry
hóutīn	fine/sunny
yāmtīn	overcast
mahtwàhn	cloudy
daaihfūng	windy
tòihfūng	typhoon

The weather forecast

The broadcast weather forecast is usually written in fairly formal Chinese and then read aloud. As a result, some rather bookish expressions are used. These expressions are usually two-syllable versions of their more colloquial counterparts. For example, **yiht** (hot) becomes **yìhmyiht** and **nyúhn** (warm) becomes **wānnyúhn**. The formal version of **dung** is **hòhnláahng**. Below is a list of expressions which are likely to come up in weather forecasts.

yìhmyiht	hot
hòhnláahng	cold
wānnyúhn	warm
chīnglèuhng	cool
chìuhsāp	humid
gōnchou	dry
tīnchìhng	fine
tīnyām	overcast
mahtwàhn	cloudy
fūngsai kèuhnggihng	windy

When rain, fog, snow or thunderstorms are predicted, the 'existential' **yáuh** is used. For example:

yáuh yúh	(there will be) rain
yáuh mèihyúh	light rain
yáuh jaauhyúh	showers
yáuh lèuihbouh	thunderstorms
yáuh mouh	fog
yáuh syut	snow

For forecasting rain or snow, we use verb-object constructions with the verb **lohk**, which means 'to come down' but, unlike the English, takes an object:

lohk-yúh	to rain
lohk-syut	to snow

When *change* in weather is predicted, the verb **jyún**, which means 'to change', is used:

jyún yiht	to turn hot
jyún lèuhng	to turn cool
jyún láahng	to turn cold
jyún chìhng	to turn fine

Weather forecasts often predict wind directions. In Cantonese, the verb **chēui** is used before the word for the direction and the word for 'wind', **fūng**. For example, **chēui dūng fūng** predicts 'easterly winds'.

chēui dūng fūng	easterly winds
chēui nàahm fūng	southerly winds
chēui sāi fūng	westerly winds
chēui bāk fūng	northerly winds

Weather forecasts also predict highest temperatures, lowest temperatures, and relative humidities. Below are the related vocabulary items:

heiwān	air temperature
jeui gōu heiwān	highest temperature
jeui dāi heiwān	lowest temperature
sēungdeui sāpdouh	relative humidity

Temperature and humidity

Normally, the Celsius scale (centigrade) is used, and since this is taken for granted, only the word for 'degree', namely, **douh**, is used when referring to temperatures. Hence, 10 °C is **sahp douh**, while 20 °C is **yih-sahp douh**. Relative humidities, on the other hand, are expressed in percentages. Note the Cantonese structure. For example, 50% is **baak fahn jī *ńgh-sahp***. Here, the figure 50 (**ńgh-sahp**) comes *after* the expression for %: **baak fahn jī**; **baak** means 'one hundred', and **fahn** means 'parts', and the whole expression **baak fahn jī ńgh-sahp** translates literally into 'one hundred parts fifty'. Hence, 60% is **baak fahn jī luhk-sahp** and 65% is **baak fahn jī luhk-sahp ńgh**, etc.

Dialogues 🔘

Read the questions, and then read or listen to the dialogues to find the answers.

1 Paul is telephoning his brother Peter long distance from Hong Kong. Peter studies in New Zealand and they are talking about the weather in Hong Kong and in New Zealand. It is mid-June.

(a) What is the weather like in New Zealand?
(b) What about Hong Kong?

PAUL: Peter, Náusāilàahn yìhgā dī tīnhei dímyéung a?
PETER: Náusāilàahn yìhgā dōu géi dung a, heiwān daaihyeuk sahp douh, bātgwo hóu hóutīn. Gám, Hēunggóng nē?
PAUL: Hēunggóng yìhgā hóu yiht la, daaihyeuk sāam-sahp douh. Tīnhei hóu chìuhsāp, mhaih géi syūfuhk.

2 Here is a radio weather forecast for Hong Kong. It is winter.

(a) What will the weather be like tomorrow?
(b) Will it rain tomorrow?
(c) What are the predicted highest and lowest temperatures?

FORECASTER: Yuhchāak tīngyaht wúih chēui bāk fūng, tīnhei hòhnláahng, yáuh mèihyúh. Jeui gōu heiwān daaihyeuk sahp-ńgh douh, jeui dāi heiwān daaih-yeuk sahp-yāt douh.

Idioms and structures

The items in the list below appear in the same order as they do in the dialogues above. The *italicized* items are *new* items. In the notes, numbers in brackets refer to the expressions listed below.

1 **Náusāilàahn yìhgā dī tīnhei dímyéung a?** How is the weather in New Zealand at present?
2 **mhaih géi *syūfuhk*** it doesn't feel very *comfortable*

3 *Yuhchāak* tīngyaht *wúih*   *It is predicted* that winds will be
   chēui bāk fūng   northerly tomorrow.

The possessive *dī*   *(1)*

The **dī** in this context is used to indicate possession, specifying that
the weather being discussed is that of the present moment in New
Zealand. Notice that the 'possessor' of the weather is **yìhgā** rather
than **Náusāilàahn**; thus the expression is very similar in structure to
'the present moment's weather in New Zealand' in English. A
similar expression is **Hèunggóng gāmyaht** *dī* **tīnhei**, which means
'today's weather in Hong Kong'.

Asking about the weather   *(1)*

To ask a general question about the weather, you can use the
question word **dímyéung**:

   Tīngyaht dī tīnhei *dím-*   What will the weather be like
   yéung **a?**   tomorrow?

or you can ask a choice-type question:

   Tīngyaht dī tīnhei *hóu-mh-*   Will the weather be good
   hóu **a?**   tomorrow?

You can also ask about certain characteristics of the weather with a
choice-type question:

   Tīngyaht *yiht-mh-yiht* **a?**   Will it be cold tomorrow?
   Tīngyaht *hóu-mh-hóutīn* **a?**   Will it be fine tomorrow?
   Tīngyaht *yáuh móuh yúh*   Will there be rain tomorrow?
   lohk **a?**

Predicting the future   *(3)*

When predicting things that are likely to happen in the future, we
use the modal **wúih**. **Wúih** can be used before an adjective, as in:

   Tīngyaht *wúih* **hóutīn.**   It will be fine tomorrow.

It can be used before the 'existential' verb **yáuh**, as in:

Tīngyaht *wúih* yáuh mouh.	It will be foggy tomorrow.

It can also be used before other verbs, as in:

Hauhyaht *wúih* lohk-yúh.	It will rain the day after tomorrow.
Jāumuht *wúih* jyún lèuhng.	It will turn cool during the weekend.

Vocabulary 🔘

Wishing well

Below are a number of idiomatic expressions used in wishing others well during festive seasons or on special occasions:

Singdaan faailohk!	Merry Christmas!
Sānnìhn faailohk!	Happy New Year!
Sāangyaht faailohk!	Happy birthday!
Yātlouh seuhnfūng!	Have a good flight!
Gūnghéi faatchòih!	greeting said at Chinese New Year

The months of the year

In Cantonese, the months do not have special names, but are simply called 'the first month' (**yāt-yuht**), 'the second month' (**yih-yuht**) and so on. Here is a list of the twelve months in Cantonese:

yāt-yuht	January
yih-yuht	February
sāam-yuht	March
sei-yuht	April
ńgh-yuht	May
luhk-yuht	June
chāt-yuht	July
baat-yuht	August
gáu-yuht	September
sahp-yuht	October
sahp-yāt-yuht	November
sahp-yih-yuht	December

Days of the month

To refer to a particular day of the month, the word **houh** (lit. number) is used. The 'first' is **yāt-houh**, the 'second' is **yih-houh**, the 'third' is **sāam-houh**, etc. If the month is also given in a date, then the month comes *before* the day. Below are a few examples:

yāt-yuht yāt-houh	first of January
chāt-yuht gáu-houh	ninth of July
sahp-yih-yuht yih-sahp-	twenty-fifth of December
ńgh-houh	

Dialogues 📼

Read the questions, and then read or listen to the dialogues to find the answers.

3 It is Christmas Day and Jimmy is flying out to New York to visit his brother Oscar this evening. He is telephoning Oscar from Hong Kong, asking him about the weather in New York.

(a) What is the weather in New York like now?
(b) What is the average temperature?
(c) What is the outlook for next week?
(d) What advice does Oscar give to Jimmy about the clothes to bring to New York?

JIMMY: Singdaan faailohk!
OSCAR: Singdaan faailohk!
JIMMY: Oscar, Náuyeuk yìhgā dī tīnhei dímyéung a?
OSCAR: Náuyeuk yìhgā hóu dūng a, lohk-gán syut a, heiwān daaih-yeuk lìhng hah yih-sahp douh.
JIMMY: Gám, sái-mh-sái daaih dō-dī sāam lèih Náuyeuk a?
OSCAR: Jeui hóu daaih dō-dī sāam lèih lā.
JIMMY: Hóu lā.
OSCAR: Bātgwo mhóu daaih taai dō sāam wo, yānwaih hah go láih baai tīnhei wúih nyúhn fāan dī.
JIMMY: Hóu lā. Gám, tīngyaht gin lā.
OSCAR: Hóu lā. Yātlouh seuhnfūng.

4 It's a December day in Hong Kong. On the radio the weatherman is giving some weather information as well as advice for drivers.

(a) What will the weather be like today?
(b) What advice is given to people who are leaving home?
(c) What advice is given to drivers?

WEATHERMAN: Yuhchāak gāmyaht tīnhei wúih hòhnláahng tùhng yáuh yúh. Daaihgā chēut-gāai geidāk jeuk dō gihn sāam, tùhngmàaih daai fāan bá jē la. Juhng yáuh, yìhgā lohk-gán yúh. Daaihgā yiu síusām jā-chē a.

Idioms and structures

The items in the list below appear in the same order as they do in the dialogues above. The *italicized* items are *new* items. In the notes, numbers in brackets refer to the expressions listed below.

1	*lìhng hah* yih-sahp douh	20° *below zero*
2	*Jeui hóu* daaih dō dī sāam lèih lā.	*It might be better* to bring more clothes.
3	Bātgwo *mhóu* daaih taai dō sāam wo	But *don't* bring too many clothes
4	nyúhn fāan dī	it will become warm again
5	*tīngyaht gin lā*	*see you tomorrow*
6	*Daaihgā* chēut gāai *geidāk* jeuk dō gihn sāam	Everyone must *remember* to put on more clothes when we go out
7	Daaihgā yiu *síusām* jā-chē a.	Everyone has to drive *carefully*.

Sub-zero temperatures   (1)

Lìhng means 'zero' and **hah** means 'below' or 'under'; thus **lìhng hah yih-sahp douh** is 'twenty degrees below zero'. Similarly, **lìhng hah sahp douh** is 'minus ten degrees'.

Giving advice (2, 3)

When giving advice in Cantonese, the two modals **jeui hóu** (similar in meaning to 'had better') and **yiu** (similar in meaning to 'should') can be used before the verb. To advise somebody *not* to do something, **mhóu** ('don't') is used before the verb. To say that it is not necessary to do something, **msái** is used. Below are some examples:

> **Gāmyaht wúih yáuh jaauyúh. Néih chēut gāai** *jeui hóu* **daai bá jē.**
> There will be showers today. You'd better take your umbrella when you go out.
> **Gāmmáahn wúih hóu dung. Néih** *yiu* **jeuk dō gihn sāam a.**
> It will be cold tonight. You have to put on more clothes.
> **Gāmyaht tīnhei hóu dūng.** *Mhóu* **heui yàuhséui la.**
> It's very cold today. Don't go swimming.
> **Tīnhei wúih jyún yiht.** *Msái* **jeuk taai dō sāam la.**
> The weather is getting hotter. There's no need to wear too many clothes.

Fāan *to indicate change back to normal* (4)

The word **fāan** here has the meaning of 'back to normal'. Thus the expression **nyúhn fāan dī** has the connotation of 'going back to the warm weather which we had before'.

'See you' (5)

The verb **gin** means 'to see'. **Tīngyaht** *gin* **lā** is equivalent to 'See you tomorrow' in English and is often used to close a conversation.

Everyone (6)

Daaihgā is a pronoun which means 'everyone', and is very often used in broadcast messages to appeal to the general public. For example, *Daaihgā* **yiu síusām jā-chē a** is an appeal to the listeners to drive carefully.

Adverbs of manner (7)

Adverbs of manner, like most other adverbs, are put *before* the verbs they modify. For example:

Daaihgā yiu *síusām* jā-chē a. We must drive *carefully*.
Daaihgā *maahn-máan* hàahng a. Please walk slowly.

Exercises

Exercise 1 Weather forecast ⚟

Here is a forecast of tomorrow's weather in Guangzhou. Read the forecast or listen to the tape recording. Then complete the table.

Tīngyaht tīnhei yìhmyiht tùhng chìuhsāp. Jeui gōu heiwān daaih-yeuk sāam-sahp yih douh. Jeui dāi heiwān yih-sahp-baat douh. Sēungdeui sāpdouh baak fahn jī chāt-sahp baat ji baak fahn jī baat-sahp gáu.

General description:	
Highest temperature:	
Lowest temperature:	
Relative humidity:	% – %

Exercise 2 The weather in China

The two newspaper cuttings provide information about two major cities in China, namely, Shanghai (**Seuhnghói**) and Guangzhou (**Gwóngjāu**). You have friends who plan to go to these cities at different times of the year, and they have come to consult you for the appropriate weather information. Complete the following conversation by using the information provided on page 170.

Shanghai Temperature Range and Average Rainfall

	Temperature high (°C)	Temperature low (°C)	Number of days with rainfall	Monthly rainfall (in centimetres)
January	8	0	10	4.8
April	19	9	13	9.1
July	33	24	11	14.7
October	24	13	9	7.4

WHEN TO GO. Although Shanghai's climate is subtropical, it does have a distinct change of seasons. Spring weather is usually warm but unsettled. Summer is hot and humid, with the highest incidence of rainy days of all the seasons. Autumn is the best season for visiting: warm and relatively dry. Winter, the longest season, is cold, but although the temperatures often go below freezing, snow is unusual.

Guangzhou Temperature Range and Average Rainfall

	Temperature high (°C)	Temperature low (°C)	Number of days with rainfall	Monthly rainfall (in centimetres)
January	18	9	7	2.2
April	25	18	15	17.3
July	33	25	16	20.5
October	29	19	6	8.6

WHEN TO GO. Guangzhou is in a subtropical weather belt. In summer it is hot and humid, the rainfall heavy, with numerous thunderstorms. No pronounced winter season exists; although occasional days can be very cold, generally winter is mild and pleasant. In spring the weather starts to get warmer and the humidity higher; the rainy season begins in April and continues through September, about 80 percent of the yearly average of 64 inches falling in these six months. Autumn is a delightful season with warm days, low humidity, and infrequent rainfall.

The province is frequently affected by typhoons in August and September. Northerly breezes prevail October through February; southerly winds are more evident in the other months.

The most pleasant time to visit Guangzhou is October through March.

Conversation 1:

JOHN: Ngóh yāt-yuht yiu heui Seuhnghói. Seuhnghói yāt-yuht dung-mh-dung a?

YOU: (a) Seuhnghói yāt-yuht dōu géi dung a. Heiwān daaihyeuk . . .

JOHN: Gám, sái-mh-sái daaih hóu dō sāam a?

YOU: (b)

JOHN: Seuhnghói yāt-yuht yáuh móuh yúh lohk a? Sái-mh-sái daai bá jē a?

YOU: (c)

Conversation 2:

CARMEN: Ngóh sei-yuht wúih heui Gwóngjāu. Gwóngjāu sei-yuht dī tīnhei dím a?

YOU: (d) Gwóngjāu sei-yuht . . .

CARMEN: Gám, heiwān daaihyeuk géidō douh a?

YOU: (e)

CARMEN: Gám, chìuh-mh-chìuhsāp a?

YOU: (f)

Conversation 3:

RICHARD: Ngóh sahp-yuht heui Gwóngjāu. Néih jī-mh-jī Gwóngjāu sahp-yuht dī tīnhei wúih dím ga?

YOU: (g)

RICHARD: Wúih-mh-wúih lohk-yúh a?

YOU: (h)

RICHARD: Gám, sái-mh-sái daai bá jē heui a?

YOU: (i)

Exercise 3 Predicting the future ▦

Translate the following sentences into Cantonese, using **wúih** for predictions. The first one has been done for you as an example.

(a) It will rain tomorrow.
   Tīngyaht wúih lohk-yúh.
(b) The weather will become cooler the day after tomorrow.
(c) The weather will become hot next week.
(d) It will be very windy on Saturday.
(e) There will be thunderstorms on Sunday.
(f) It will be humid tomorrow.

Exercise 4 When will they come home?

Mr and Mrs Chan's children all live abroad, but they are all coming home this year to celebrate their parents' fortieth wedding anniversary. Mr and Mrs Chan are looking at their calendar to remind themselves when each of their children will come home to Hong Kong. Using the information provided below, complete the conversation between Mr Chan and Mrs Chan.

MR CHAN: Simon géisìh fāan Hēunggóng a?
MRS CHAN: Simon baat-houh sīngkèih-yih jauh fāan Hēunggóng la.
MR CHAN: Gám, Samuel nē?
MRS CHAN: Samuel àh? (a) Samuel ...
MR CHAN: Gám, Keith nē?
MRS CHAN: (b)
MR CHAN: Teresa yauh géisìh fāan lèih a?
MRS CHAN: (c)

March

M	T	W	T	F	S	S
Simon back in HK	1	2	3 *Samuel back from UK*	4	5	6
7	(8)	9	(10)	11	12	13
(14)	15	16	17	(18)	19	20
Teresa back 21	22	23	24	25	26	27
28	29	30	31	*Keith back from Australia*		

Recognizing Chinese characters

炎熱 hot   晴朗 fine

寒冷 cold   陰暗 overcast

溫暖 warm   密雲 cloudy

清涼 cool   有雨 rainy

13 Yīfuhk

The clothes we wear

hō hāaih wuhn dúhng hàaih trainers .

In Lesson 13 you will learn about:

- describing what people are wearing
- colors

Vocabulary 🔲

Clothing

Below is a list of clothing. Notice the different classifiers that are used. Try reading out each item aloud. If you have the cassette tapes of this book, you can model your pronunciation on the tape recording.

chēun hah chāu dūng jūng

jeui sān

Men's wear

yāt gihn sēutsāam	a shirt
yāt tou sāijōng	a suit
yāt tìuh (sāijōng) fu	a pair of trousers/slacks
yāt tìuh tāai	a tie
yāt gihn ngoihtou	a jacket
yāt deui (pèih)hàaih	a pair of (leather) shoes
yāt deui maht	a pair of socks
yāt déng móu	a hat/a cap

半截裙

Ladies' wear

yāt gihn sēutsāam	a blouse
yāt tìuh kwàhn	a dress, a skirt
yāt tìuh bunjihtkwàhn	a skirt
yāt tìuh (sāijōng) fu	a pair of slacks

yāt tou toujōng	a suit
yāt gihn ngoihtou	a jacket
yāt deui sīmaht	a pair of pantyhose
yāt deui (pèih)hàaih	a pair of (leather) shoes
yāt deui gōujāanghàaih	a pair of high-heeled shoes

Casual wear

yāt gihn tīsēut	a T-shirt
yāt tìuh ngàuhjáifu	a pair of jeans
yāt tìuh dyúnfu	a pair of shorts
yāt deui bōhàaih	a pair of sports shoes
yāt deui lèuhnghàaih	a pair of sandals

Warm clothes

yāt gihn lāangsāam	a woollen sweater/jumper
yāt gihn (daaih)lāu	a(n) (over)coat
yāt tìuh génggān	a scarf
yāt deui sáumaht *sòutou*	a pair of gloves

Classifiers for items of clothing

Gihn is the classifier used for tops such as **sēutsāam** (shirt) and **ngoihtou** (jacket), **tìuh** is the classifier used for **fu** (slacks) and **kwàhn** (dress and skirt), while **deui** is the classifier for all things that come in pairs, such as kinds of **hàaih**, **maht** and **sáumaht** (shoes, socks and gloves).

Dialogues

Read the questions, and then read or listen to the dialogues to find the answers.

1 Carmen and Emily have been shopping together. They have met John in a cafe, and they are showing him what they bought.

(a) What did Emily buy?
(b) What did Carmen buy?
(c) What did Carmen buy for John?

JOHN: Wā! Néihdeih máaih-jó gam dō yéh àh?
CARMEN: Haih a. Dī yéh hóu pèhng a.
EMILY: Haih a. Néih tái. Ngóh máaih-jó léuhng gihn sēutsāam, léuhng tìuh bunjihtkwàhn, tùhng yāt deui hàaih a.
JOHN: Gám néih nē, Carmen? Néih máaih-jó dī mātyéh a?
CARMEN: Ngóh máaih jó yāt tou toujōng, yāt gihn ngoihtou, tùhng léuhng gihn sēutsāam. Néih tái leng-mh-leng?
JOHN: Haih géi leng wo.
CARMEN: Juhng yáuh. Ngóh máaih-jó yāt yeuhng yéh béi néih.
JOHN: Mātyéh lèih ga?
CARMEN: Ngóh máaih-jó nī tìuh tāai béi néih. Néih jūng-mh-jūngyi a?
JOHN: Jūngyi. Dōjeh.

2 John and Carmen are looking at a photograph of John's colleagues, which was taken on a trip to Beijing. John is telling Carmen who's who in his office.

(a) Who is the man wearing a coat and a cap?
(b) Who is the man wearing a scarf?
(c) Who is the woman wearing a skirt and high-heeled shoes?

CARMEN: Yí, nī go jeuk daaihláu, daai móu ge haih bīngo a?
JOHN: Nī go daai-jó móu ge haih Ben, ngóhdeih go lóuhbáan.
CARMEN: Kéuih jauh haih Ben àh? Gám, nī go laahm-jó géng gān ge, fèih-féi-déi ge yauh haih bīngo a?
JOHN: Laahm-jó génggān nī go haih Teddy. Teddy gaaklèih, jeuk kwàhn tùhng gōujāanghàaih gó go haih kéuih taai-táai.
CARMEN: Nī go jauh haih Teddy go taai-táai àh?
JOHN: Haih a, jeuk kwàhn tùhng gōujāanghàaih, chèuhng tàuhfaat nī go jauh haih Teddy go taai-táai laak.

Idioms and structures

The items in the list below appear in the same order as they do in the dialogue above. The *italicized* items are *new* items. In the notes, numbers in brackets refer to the expressions listed below.

1 *Wā*	an exclamation showing surprise
2 **Néihdeih máaih-jó gam dō yéh àh?**	You bought so many things?
3 **Néih tái.**	Look.
4 **Néih tái leng-mh-leng?**	Do you think they are pretty?
5 *Haih* **géi leng** *wo.*	They *are* quite pretty.
6 **Ngóh máaih-jó yāt yeuhng yéh** *béi néih.*	I've bought something *for you.*
7 **Mātyéh lèih ga?**	What is it? (showing curiosity)
8 **Nī go** *jeuk daaihláu, daai móu* **ge haih bīngo a?**	Who is this one *wearing a coat and a hat?*
9 *lóuhbáan*	*boss*

Question to indicate recognition and slight surprise (2)

Here **Néihdeih máaih-jó gam dō yéh àh?** is another question which shows recognition and slight surprise. The word **gam** helps indicate the recognition. A genuine question (for instance, if John is asking Carmen on the phone) would be **Néihdeih máaih-jó hóu dō yéh àh?** To both questions a positive response is **Haih a** while a negative one would be **Mhaih aak** (No, not really).

Haih . . . wo (5)

To comment on something being quite pretty, you can say **Géi leng wo.** However, when you are *asked* to judge whether something is pretty and a positive answer is expected, you can make the emphatic statement *Haih* **géi leng** *wo.* The **haih** used before the adjective **leng** coupled with the particle **wo** (see Lesson 5) help convey the message 'They *are* quite pretty'.

The verbs for 'putting on' (8)

Jeuk is the Cantonese verb which means 'to wear' or 'to put on'. However, there are a few other verbs which are used specifically for certain kinds of clothes. For example, for **tāai** (tie), the verb **dá** is used, while **daai** is used for **móu** (hat/cap). For **génggān** (scarf), the verb **laahm,** which literally means 'to wrap around the body', is used.

To say what clothes somebody has put on, the aspect marker **-jó** is often used, as follows:

Mary *jeuk-jó* **tou toujōng tùhng gōujāanghàaih.**
Mary is wearing a suit and high-heeled shoes.
Tīnhei hóu dung. Jimmy *laahm-jó* **tìuh génggān.**
The weather is cold. Jimmy has put on a scarf.

When information about clothes is used to describe people for identification purposes, the aspect marker **-jó** is not used, and the classifiers are omitted. For example:

/*Jeuk sāijōng* **gó go haih ngóh bàh-bā.**
The one wearing a suit is my father.
/*Daai móu* **gó go haih Peter.**
The one wearing a cap is Peter.
/*Jeuk tīsēut, ngàuhjáifu* **gó go néuihjái hóu leng.**
The girl wearing a T-shirt and jeans is very pretty.

Vocabulary ▨

Colors

hùhngsīk	red
wòhngsīk	yellow
làahmsīk	blue
luhksīk	green
baahksīk	white
hàaksīk	black
jísīk	violet, purple
fēsīk	brown
cháangsīk	orange
fūisīk	gray

Sīk by itself means 'color'. Thus **hùhngsīk,** for example, literally means 'red color'.

Dialogue 🔳

Read the questions and then read or listen to the dialogues to find
the answers.

3 Sam and Elza are discussing the clothes they wear to work. Sam teaches at a university while Elza works in a bank.

(a) What does Sam wear to work?
(b) Does he usually wear a tie?
(c) What does Elza wear to work?
(d) What does Elza wear when she does not have to go to work?

ELZA: Sam, néih pìhngsìh jeuk mātyéh sāam fāan-gūng ga?

SAM: Ngóh hái daaihhohk gaau-syū, sóyíh msái jeuk dāk taai
sīmàhn. Ngóh dōsou dōu haih jeuk sēutsāam tùhng sāi
fu.

ELZA: Sái-mh-sái dá tāai a?

SAM: Msái yātdihng dá tāai. Bātgwo ngóh dūngtīn tīnhei dung
jauh dōsou dá tāai, hahtīn tīnhei yiht jauh hóu síu dá laak.
Néih nē, Elza? Néih fāan-gūng sái-mh-sái jeuk dāk hóu
sīmàhn a?

ELZA: Yiu a. Ngóh fāan ngàhnhòhng, yātdihng yiu jeuk kwàhn
tùhng jeuk gōujāanghàaih. Dūngtīn jauh dōsou jeuk toujōng. Bātgwo ngóh fongga msái fāan-gūng jauh jeuk fāan
tīsēut, ngàuhjáifu tùhng bōhàaih, gámyéung syūfuhk dī.

Idioms and structures

The items in the list below appear in the same order as they do in
the dialogue above. The *italicized* items are *new* items. In the notes,
numbers in brackets refer to the expressions listed below.

1 **Ngóh hái** *daaihhohk gaau-syū*	I *teach* at a *university*
2 **msái jeuk dāk taai** *sīmàhn*	(I) do not have to be very smartly dressed
3 *Msái yātdihng* **dá tāai**	I *don't necessarily* have to wear a tie

4 ngóh *dūngtīn* tīnhei dung
   jauh dōsou dá tāai
5 *hahtīn*
6 Ngóh fāan *ngàhnhòhng*
7 ngóh ... jauh jeuk *fāan*
   tīsēut ...

In winter when the weather is cold I usually put on a tie
(in) summer
I work for a *bank*
I will go *back to* wearing T-shirts ...

'University' (1)

Daaihhohk is 'university', and it literally means 'big school'. **Síuhohk** (literally 'little school'), on the other hand, is 'primary school', and **jūnghohk** (literally 'middle school') is 'secondary school'.

Gaau-syū (1)

The verb-object construction **gaau-syū** means 'teach', literally 'teach books' (**syū** = book).

Dress code (2)

To comment on *how* somebody is dressed, the resultative particle **dāk** is used after the verb **jeuk**, which is then followed by an adjective. Below are some examples:

> **Kéuih** *jeuk dāk* **hóu sīmàhn.** He is very smartly dressed.
> **Kéuih** *jeuk dāk* **hóu** She is very casually dressed.
> **chèuihbín.** 便
> **Dī hohksāang** *jeuk dāk* **hóu** The students are very neatly
> **jíngchàih.** dressed.

To say whether one needs to dress up for an occasion, the modals **yiu** (have to), **msái** (don't have to) and **hóyíh** (can) are used. For example:

> **Chàhn sīnsāang fāan-gūng** *yiu* **jeuk dāk hóu sīmàhn.**
> Mr Chan has to dress up smartly when he goes to work.
> **Richard fāan-gūng** *msái* **jeuk dāk taai sīmàhn.**
> Richard does not have to dress up too smartly when he goes to work.

Ngóh sīngkèih-luhk fāan-gūng *hóyíh* jeuk ngàuhjáifu tùhng bōhàaih.
On Saturdays I can go to work in jeans and sports shoes.

The idiomatic use of the verb **fāan** to mean 'to work in' (6)

The expression **Ngóh fāan ngàhnhòhng** is another way of saying **Ngóh hái ngàhnhòhng fāan-gūng** (I work in a bank); **fāan** is the verb taken from **fāan-gūng**.

The particle **fāan** to mean 'back to' (7)

Fāan in the expression **ngóh jauh jeuk *fāan* tīsēut** . . . has the meaning of 'going back to', and conveys the idea that it is T-shirts and other casual wear that Elza usually wears.

Exercises

Exercise 1 The spending spree 🆗
The Chans are going to Canada. Mrs Chan has just gone shopping for warm clothes, and Mr Chan is finding out what she has bought for the family.

Read or listen to the conversation between Mr and Mrs Chan. Then note down what Mrs Chan has bought.

MRS CHAN: Néih tái. Ngóh máaih-jó géi dō sāam.
MR CHAN: Haih wo. Néih máaih-jó dī mātyéh a?
MRS CHAN: Néih tái. Ngóh máaih-jó sāam gihn daaihlāu, sei gihn lāangsāam. Juhng yáuh sāam tìuh génggān.
MR CHAN: Haih wo. Dī génggān hóu leng wo.
MRS CHAN: Haih a. Dī génggān hóu leng ga. Bātgwo dōu msyun hóu gwai.
MR CHAN: Gám, nī bāau haih mātyéh lèih ga?
MRS CHAN: Nī bāau haih sáumaht. Ngóh júngguhng máaih-jó nǵh deui sáumaht.
MR CHAN: Wā! Gam dō àh?

Exercise 2 Grace's friends

Grace is showing a photograph of her friends in Japan to John and Carmen. Read the conversation or listen to the recording. Then label the picture with the information.

GRACE:	Nī géi go dōu haih ngóh hái Yahtbún dī hóu pàhng-yáuh.
JOHN:	Nī go jeuk dāk hóu sīmàhn ge haih bīngo a?
GRACE:	Kéuih haih Saito. Kéuih haih ngóh tùhnghohk.
CARMEN:	Nī go nē? Nī go jeuk hùhngsīk kwàhn ge néuihjái nē?
GRACE:	Nī go néuihjái haih Saito go mùih-múi. Kéuih giujouh Mariko.
JOHN:	Gám, nī léuhng go nē? Nī léuhng go jeuk dāk hóu chèuih-bín ge nàahmjái nē?
GRACE:	Kéuihdeih haih Hama tùhng Hideki. Nī go jeuk hāaksīk tīsēut tùhng ngàuhjáifu ge haih Hama. Kéuih haih Hideki go gòh-gō. Jeuk hāaksīk tīsēut tùhng dyúnfu ge haih Hideki. Kéuih haih dàih-dái.

Exercise 3 Old friends

Your friends have come to your home for dinner. After dinner you show them your photos. You are looking at a photo taken ten years ago, on the snowy mountains, of your college friends. You are telling your dinner guests the names of each of them by describing their appearance and the clothes they were wearing. Complete the monologue by referring to the picture.

YOU: Jóbīn nī go jeuk fu, laahm-jó génggān, daai-jó sáumaht ge néuihjái . . .

Exercise 4 What you wear to work

You are talking with a friend about the clothes that you have to wear to work and the clothes that you like wearing when going out in the evening and at weekends. Complete the conversation below with true information about yourself.

YOUR FRIEND: Ngóh múih yaht fāan-gūng yiu jeuk sāijōng dá tāai. Néih nē? Néih sái-mh-sái a?

YOU: Ngóh . . .

YOUR FRIEND: Bātgwo ngóh yehmáahn tùhng sīngkèih-luhk sīngkèih yaht heui gāai jauh mjūngyi jeuk sāijōng dá tāai laak. Ngóh jūngyi jeuk dāk chèuihbín dī. Ngóh jūngyi jeuk ngàuhjáifu tùhng tīsēut dō-dī. Gám, néih nē?

YOU: Ngóh . . .

Recognizing Chinese characters

紅色	red
黃色	yellow
藍色	blue
綠色	green
白色	white
黑色	black
橙	orange chéng
啡	brown gafē

14 Léuihhàhng gīngyihm

Traveling experiences

156-157
87

In Lesson 14 you will learn about:

- discussing past experiences
- asking 'how often', 'how long' and 'when'
- describing countries and cities

Vocabulary 📼

Below are some commonly used expressions about past time. Try reading out each item aloud. If you have the cassette tapes of this book, you can model your pronunciation on the tape recording.

gāmnín	this year
gauhnín	last year
chìhnnín	the year before last
nī go yuht	this month
seuhng go yuht	last month
chìhn go yuht	the month before last
nī go láihbaai	this week
seuhng go láihbaai	last week
chìhn go láihbaai	the week before last
sāam nìhn chìhn	three years ago
sāam go yuht chìhn	three months ago
sāam go láihbaai chìhn	three weeks ago

Note that in the last three expressions, *chìhn* means 'ago'. However, both **yuht** and **láihbaai** take the classifier **go**, while **nìhn** does not. **Nìhn** is the same word as **nín** in **gāmnín**, **gauhnín** and **chìhnnín**, but the pronunciation has undergone a tone change.

Dialogues 🔲

Read the questions, and then read or listen to the dialogues to find the answers.

1 Richard and John are discussing their traveling experiences.

(a) How many times has John been to China?
(b) When did he go to China?
(c) Has Richard been to China?
(d) When did Richard go to Taiwan?

RICHARD: John, néih yáuh móuh heui-gwo Jūnggwok a?
JOHN: Yáuh a, ngóh heui-gwo Jūnggwok la.
RICHARD: Gám, néih heui-gwo géidō chi Jūnggwok a?
JOHN: Ngóh heui-gwo léuhng chi.
RICHARD: Néih géisìh heui ga?
JOHN: Ngóh chìhnnín heui-gwo yāt chi, gauhnín heui-gwo yāt chi. Néih nē? Néih heui-gwo Jūnggwok meih a?
RICHARD: Ngóh meih heui-gwo Jūnggwok, bātgwo ngóh heui-gwo Tòihwāan.
JOHN: Néih géisìh heui Tòihwāan ga?
RICHARD: Ngóh seuhng go yuht heui Tòihwāan ge.

2 Emily and Carmen are talking about the sports they have played lately.

(a) Has Carmen played any tennis this year?
(b) Why hasn't Carmen done any swimming this year?
(c) Why hasn't Emily played any sports this year?

EMILY: Carmen, néih gāmnín yáuh móuh yàuh-gwo séui a?
CARMEN: Móuh a, ngóh gāmnín móuh yàuh-gwo séui a. Gāmnín tīnhei taai dung la. Bātgwo ngóh dá-gwo géi chi móhngkàuh. Néih nē, Emily? Néih gāmnín yáuh móuh jouh-gwo wahnduhng a?
EMILY: Móuh a. Ngóh gāmnín hóu mòhng, móuh sìhgaan jouh wahnduhng, sóyíh móuh yàuh-gwo séui, yauh móuh dá-gwo móhngkàuh.

Idioms and structures

The items in the list below appear in the same order as they do in the dialogue above. The *italicized* items are *new* items. In the notes, numbers in brackets refer to the expressions listed below.

1 *néih yáuh móuh heui-gwo*   Have you ever been to China?
   Jūnggwok a?
2 *néih heui-gwo géidō chi*   How many times have you been
   Jūnggwok a?   to China?
3 *Néih géisìh heui ga?*   When did you go?
4 **Néih gāmnín yáuh móuh**   Have you *done any sports* this
   jouh-gwo *wahnduhng* a?   year?
5 **Ngóh gāmnín** *hóu mòhng*   I have been *very busy* this year.
6 **móuh** *sìhgaan* **jouh-**   (I have) no *time* to do sports
   wahnduhng

Asking about and describing experiences   *(1)*

To ask whether somebody has had the experience of doing something, you can form a choice-type question with the two existential verbs **yáuh** and **móuh**, and use the aspect marker **-gwo** after the main verb:

Néih *yáuh móuh* **heui**-*gwo*   Have you been to Australia?
Oujāu a?
Néih *yáuh móuh* **gin**-*gwo*   Have you seen kangaroos
doihsyú a?   before?

A positive answer to the first question would then be:

Yáuh **a, ngóh heui**-*gwo*   Yes, I have been to Australia.
Oujāu.

And a negative answer would be:

Móuh **a, ngóh** *móuh* **heui-**   No, I have not been to
gwo **Oujāu.**   Australia.

A second way to ask the same first question is to offer the two choices of **heui-gwo** and **meih heui-gwo**, **meih** being the adverb for incomplete action. However, in such an interrogative pattern the verb **heui** and the aspect marker **-gwo** are not repeated in the negative option, resulting in the following question:

Néih heui-gwo Oujāu _meih_ a? Have you been to Australia?

And to ask the second question in the same way, you say:

Néih gin-gwo doihsyú _meih_ a? Have you seen kangaroos
before?

Positive answers to the questions above can be either long or short,
as follows:

Ngóh heui-gwo Oujāu. / Heui-gwo.
Ngóh gin-gwo doihsyú. / Gin-gwo.

Negative answers can also be long or short:

Ngóh meih heui-gwo Oujāu. / Meih heui-gwo.
Ngóh meih gin-gwo doihsyú. / Meih gin-gwo.

Asking about frequency (2)

A possible follow-up question to whether somebody has experi-
enced something is to ask how many times. The Cantonese expression for asking this is **géidō chi**. Read the following exchange:

A: **Néih yáuh móuh heui-gwo Oujāu a?**
    Have you been to Australia?
B: **Yáuh a, ngóh heui-gwo Oujāu.**
    Yes, I have been to Australia.
A: **Néih heui-gwo _géidō chi_ Oujāu a?**
    How many times have you been to Australia?
B: **Ngóh heui-gwo _léuhng chi_ Oujāu.**
    I've been to Australia twice.

The point to bear in mind about the pattern is the word order.
The expression of frequency comes between the verb-and-aspect
marker **heui-gwo** and its object **Oujāu**, so that the literal translation
of the Cantonese **Ngóh heui-gwo léuhng chi Oujāu** is 'I have been
two times (to) Australia.' Here is a further exchange to illustrate
the structure:

A: **Néih gāmnín yàuh-gwo séui meih a?**
    Have you done any swimming this year?
B: **Yàuh-gwo.**
    Yes, I have.
A: **Néih gāmnín yàuh-gwo _géidō chi_ séui a?**

How many times have you been swimming this year?

B: **Ngóh gāmnín yàuh-gwo *sāam chi* séui.**
I've been swimming three times this year.

Asking when ⟨géisìh⟩ (3)

When discussing experiences, another possible follow-up question is 'When . . .?' The Cantonese word for 'when' is **géisìh**. Read the following exchanges:

A: **Néih yáuh móuh heui-gwo Oujāu a?**
Have you been to Australia?
B: **Yáuh a, ngóh heui-gwo Oujāu.**
Yes, I have been to Australia.
A: **Néih *géisìh* heui ga?**
So, when did you go?
B: **Ngóh *gauhnín* heui ge.**
I went last year.

C: **Néih yáuh móuh gin-gwo sāyùh a?**
Have you ever seen sharks before?
D: **Yáuh a, ngóh gin-gwo sāyùh la.**
Yes, I have seen sharks before.
C: **Néih *géisìh* gin ga?**
When did you see them?
D: **Ngóh *sāam nìhn chìhn* hái Oujāu gin ge.**
I saw them in Australia three years ago.

Notice that in the follow-up question to 'When . . .?' the destination or the object can be omitted, and so can the aspect marker **-gwo**. **Ga** is often used instead of **a** as the interrogative (question) particle in such a follow-up question. In answer to a follow-up question, **ge** is often used as a sentence-final particle.

In Cantonese, time expressions always come *before* the verb, hence **Ngóh *gauhnín* heui ge.**

Vocabulary 🔛

Major cities of the world

Here is a list of some of the world's major cities. Read each item aloud, or if you have the cassette tapes of this book, you can model your pronunciation on the tape recording.

Lèuhndēun	London
Lohkchaamgēi	Los Angeles
Máhnèihlāai	Manila
Náuyeuk	New York
Bālàih	Paris
Sāamfàahnsíh	San Francisco
Dūnggīng	Tokyo
Dōlèuhndō	Toronto
Wāngōwàh	Vancouver

Describing countries

You may want to say what you like about a particular country. Below are some of the probable reasons for liking a country.

Fūnggíng hóu leng. 乾淨	The scenery is good.
Wàahngíng hóu gōnjehng.	The environment is clean.
Gāautūng hóu fōngbihn.	The transportation is convenient.
Dī yàhn hóu hóu.	The people are nice.
Máaih-yéh hóu pèhng.	Things are very cheap.
Dī yéh hóu hóusihk.	The food is delicious.

Dialogues 🔛

Read the questions first, and then read or listen to the dialogues to find the answers.

3 Peter is asking John about his recent trip to the United States.

(a) When did John go to the United States?
(b) Which cities did he visit?
(c) How long did he stay in each?

PETER: John, néih seuhng go yuht haih-mh-haih heui-gwo
Méihgwok a?
JOHN: Haih a. Ngóh ngāam-ngāam hái Méihgwok fāan lèih.
PETER: Néih heui-jó Méihgwok bīndouh a?
JOHN: Ngóh heui-jó Sāamfàahnsíh tùhng Lohkchaamgēi. Ngóh
heui taam-pàhngyáuh.
PETER: Néih heui-jó Sāamfàhnsíh géinoih a?
JOHN: Ngóh heui-jó Sāamfàahnsíh ńgh yaht.
PETER: Gám, Lohkchaamgēi nē? Néih hái Lohkchaamgēi làuh-
jó géidō yaht a?
JOHN: Ngóh hái Lohkchaamgēi jauh làuh-jó luhk yaht.

4 Jimmy is asking William about his impressions of Japan, which he visited once.

(a) How does William find Japan?
(b) What are the things he likes about Japan?
(c) What are the things he doesn't like about Japan?

JIMMY: William, néih gak, heui-gwo Yahtbún haih-mh-haih a?
WILLIAM: Haih a.
JIMMY: Néih géisìh heui ga?
WILLIAM: Ngóh chìhnnín heui ge.
JIMMY: Gám, néih jūng-mh-jūngyi Yahtbún a?
WILLIAM: Ngóh hóu jūngyi Yahtbún a. Yahtbún dī fūnggíng hóu
leng, jāuwàih dōu hóu gōnjehng, dī yàhn hóu hóu,
hóu yáuh láihmaauh, bātgwo máaih-yéh hóu gwai.
JIMMY: Dī yéh hóu-mh-hóusihk ga?
WILLIAM: Màh-má-déi lā, tùhngmàaih sihk-yéh dōu hóu gwai.

Idioms and structures

The items in the list below appear in the same order as they do in
the dialogue above. The *italicized* items are *new* items. In the notes,

numbers in brackets refer to the expressions listed below.

1 **néih seuhng go yuht haih-mh-haih heui gwo Méihgwok a?**	You went to the United States last month, didn't you?
2 **Ngóh** *ngāam-ngāam* **hái Méihgwok fāan lèih.**	I have *just* come back from the United States.
3 **Ngóh heui** *taam-pàhngyáuh*	I went to *visit friends*
4 *Néih heui-jó Sāamfàhnsíh* **géinoih a?**	*How long did you stay in San Francisco?*
5 **Néih hái Lohkchaamgēi** *làuh-jó* **géidō yaht a?**	How many days did you *stay* in Los Angeles?
6 *jāuwàih* **dōu hóu gōnjehng**	It's very clean *everywhere.*
7 **hóu** *yáuh láihmaauh*	very *polite*

Asking for confirmation hcih m hcih   (1)

The question asks for confirmation of some information, hence **haih-mh-haih heui-gwo Méihgwok a?** rather than **yáuh móuh heui-gwo Méihgwok a?** or **heui-gwo Méihgwok meih a?** The most appropriate translation into English is the tag question: 'You went to the United States last month, didn't you?'

Taam 探   (3)

The verb **taam** can only take human objects and means 'to pay somebody a visit'. Thus, **heui Méihgwok** *taam*-**pàhngyáuh** is correct but **taam* **Méihgwok** is wrong.

Asking about the length of an activity   (4)

Apart from asking when somebody has visited a country, one might also enquire how long he or she stayed there. For this the question word **géinoih** ('how long') is used. Read the exchange below:

A: **Néih yáuh móuh heui-gwo Yahtbún a?**
       Have you been to Japan before?
B: **Yáuh a. Heui-gwo yāt chi. Gauhnín heui ge.**
       Yes, I have, once. I went last year.
A: **Gám, néih heui-jó** *géinoih* **a?**

How long did you stay there?

B: **Ngóh heui-jó sahp yaht.**

I was there for ten days.

Notice that two different aspect markers, namely **-gwo** and **-jó**, are used with the verb **heui** in this dialogue. **-gwo** is used to refer to experience, as evident in the question **Néih yáuh móuh *heui-gwo* Yahtbún a?** (*Have* you *ever been* to Japan?) and the statement *Heui-gwo* **yāt chi** (I *have been* once). **-jó**, on the other hand, focuses on new information about a completed action which is already known about. In the dialogue above, after A has confirmed that B has been to Japan once, A then asks **néih *heui-jó* géinoih a?** (How long *were* you *there*?), and B answers **Ngóh *heui-jó* sahp yaht** (I *was there* for ten days), both of which show recognition of the fact, now known, that B has been to Japan.

Another point worth noting is the word order. Whereas time expressions in Cantonese usually precede the verb, phrases of duration usually *follow* the verb, hence **Ngóh heui-jó sahp yaht.**

Jāuwàih 周圍   *(6)*

The Cantonese word **jāuwàih** is a noun which means 'the surroundings', and so the sentence *jāuwàih* **dōu hóu gōnjehng** is literally 'The surroundings are all very clean.'

Yáuh láihmaauh   *(7)*

In the expression **yáuh láihmaauh**, **yáuh** is a verb which means 'to have' while **láihmaauh** is a noun which means 'good manners', hence 'polite'. The expression for 'impolite' is **móuh láihmaauh**.

Exercises

Exercise 1 Globe-trotters

Winnie, Kitty and Sally are bragging about their wide traveling experiences. Read the conversation. Then make a record of the girls' traveling experiences and decide which of the three has traveled the most.

WINNIE: Ngóh jeui jūngyi heui-léuihhàhng ga laak. Ngóh heui-gwo sāam chi Āujāu, léuhng chi Méihgwok, yāt chi Yahtbún, tùhng yāt chi Oujāu.

KITTY: Gám, néih yáuh móuh heui-gwo Jūnggwok tùhng Tòihwāan a?

WINNIE: Móuh wo.

KITTY: Ngóh heui-gwo ńgh chi Jūnggwok, sei chi Tòihwāan, léuhng chi Yahtbún. Ngóh dōu yáuh heui-gwo Āujāu, Méihgwok, tùhng Oujāu, múih douh heui-gwo léuhng chi.

SALLY: Gám ngóh heui dāk jeui dō léuihhàhng la. Ngóh heui-gwo yāt chi Yandouh, sāam chi Fēileuihtbān, léuhng chi Yahtbún, sei chi Jūnggwok, tùhng ńgh chi Tòihwāan. Āujāu ngóh heui-gwo yāt chi, Méihgwok sei chi, Gānàhdaaih sāam chi. Juhng yáuh, ngóh heui-gwo sāam chi Oujāu, tùhng léuhng chi Náusāilàahn.

Exercise 2 *Where have they been?* 🔲

Translate the following sentences into Cantonese using -**gwo** to refer to experiences. The first one has been done for you as an example.

(a) I went to England last year.
   Ngóh gauhnín heui-gwo Yīnggwok.
(b) I went to Japan the month before last.
(c) He went to France last week.
(d) She went to China two months ago.
(e) We went to Taiwan five years ago.
(f) They went to Canada four weeks ago.

Exercise 3 *Expressing frequency* 🔲

To familiarize yourself with the structures for expressing frequency of past experiences, answer the following questions with the number given. The first one has been done for you.

(a) **Néih heui-gwo géidō chi Yahtbún a?**   (3)
   Ngóh heui-gwo sāam chi Yahtbún.
(b) **Néih heui-gwo géidō chi Dākgwok a?**   (5)
(c) **Néih nī go yuht tái-gwo géidō chi hei a?**   (2)
(d) **Néih nī go láihbaai dá-gwo géidō chi móhngkàuh a?**   (2)
(e) **Néih gāmnín heui-gwo géidō chi léuihhàhng a?**   (4)

Exercise 4 Where have the Chans been?

Mr and Mrs Chan love traveling. They have done quite a bit this year, and their neighbours Mr and Mrs Wong are asking them about their travels. Complete the conversation with the information given on the calendar.

fēi leuht bān   tòih wāan
yàn douh

April

M	T	W	T	F	S	S
	Philippines			1	2	3
4	5	6	7	8	9	10
11	12	13	14	15 *India*	16	17
18	19	20	21	22	23	24
25	26 *India*	27	28	29	30	

May

M	T	W	T	F	S	S
						1
2	3	4	5	6	7	8
9	10	11	12 *Taiwan*	13	14	15
16	17	18	19	20	21	22
23	24	25	26	27	28	29
30	31					

MR WONG: Chàhn sīnsāang, Chàhn táai, néihdeih gāmnín yáuh móuh heui-gwo léuihhàhng a?

MR CHAN: Yáuh a. Ngóhdeih gāmnín heui-gwo sāam go gwokgā la.

MR WONG: Bīn sāam go gwokgā a?

MRS CHAN: (a) Ngóhdeih heui-jó . . .

MRS WONG: Néihdeih géisìh heui . . . ga?

MR CHAN: (b) Ngóhdeih . . .

MR WONG: Néihdeih heui-jó géinoih a?

MRS CHAN: (c)

MRS WONG: Gám, juhng yáuh nē?

MRS CHAN: (d)

MRS WONG: Gám, juhng yáuh yāt go gwokgā nē?

MRS CHAN: (e)

Exercise 5 Where have you been?

Modeling on Exercise 1 above, write out your traveling experiences in Cantonese below.

YOU: Ngóh heui-gwo . . .

Execise 6 Your favorite place

Of all the places you have visited, which is your favorite country or city? Modeling on Dialogue 4, explain why you like this place best.

YOU: Ngóh jeui jūngyi . . . yānwaih . . .

Recognizing Chinese characters

倫敦	London
馬尼拉	Manila
紐約	New York
巴黎	Paris
三藩市	San Francisco
東京	Tokyo
多倫多	Toronto
温哥華	Vancouver

15 Dá-dihnwá

On the telephone

In Lesson 15 you will learn about:

- telephone conversations
- how to invite somebody out
- how to arrange to meet somebody

Vocabulary 📼

Cantonese speakers have certain conventions in talking on the telephone. Below is a list of the common expressions used. Try reading out each item aloud. If you have the cassette tapes of this book, you can model your pronunciation on the tape recording.

dá-dihnwá	to make a phone call
tēng-dihnwá	to answer the phone
dáng (yāt) dáng/ dáng (yāt) jahn	to wait a minute
mhái douh	not here
hàahnghōi-jó *chēut jó heui*	has/have gone out
làuh (yāt go) háuseun	leave a message
dá gwo (dihnwá) lèih	to call again
dá fāan (dihnwá) béi néih	to call you back
daap cho sin	wrong number
góng-gán	line engaged
noihsin	extension

Dialogues 📼

Read the questions, and then read or listen to the dialogues to find the answers.

1 John is out of the office for a while and his colleague Jimmy is answering the phone for him.

(a) Who is calling?
(b) What message does he leave?
(c) What is his phone number?

MR WONG:	Wái, mgōi néih giu John tēng-dihnwá.
JIMMY:	Deui mjyuh, John hàahnghōi-jó. Chíng mahn bīnwái wán kéuih a?
MR WONG:	Ngóh haih Wòhng sīnsāang a. Néih haih bīnwái a?
JIMMY:	Ngóh haih John go tùhngsih Jimmy. Wòhng sīnsāang, sái-mh-sái làuh go háuseun a?
MR WONG:	Hóu ā. Mgōi néih giu kéuih dá fāan dihnwá béi ngóh ā. Ngóh go dihnwá haih sāam-luhk-lìhng-sāam-luhk-chāt-baat.
JIMMY:	Sāam-luhk-lìhng-sāam-luhk-chāt-baat. Hóu, ngóh giu John dá fāan dihnwá béi néih lā.
MR WONG:	Hóu. Mgōi saai, Jimmy.
JIMMY:	Bāai-baai.
MR WONG:	Bāai-baai.

2 John is alone at home. The telephone rings and John picks it up.

(a) Where is Carmen?
(b) What message does she leave?
(c) Does she want Carmen to call her back?

JOHN:	Wái.
SUSAN:	Wái, chíng mahn Carmen hái-mh-hái douh a?
JOHN:	Deui mjyuh, Carmen chēut-jó gāai wo. Néih bīnwái wán kéuih a?
SUSAN:	Ngóh haih Susan a. Néih haih-mh-haih John a?
JOHN:	Haih a.
SUSAN:	John, néih hó-mh-hóyíh tùhng ngóh làuh go háuseun béi Carmen a?
JOHN:	Hóyíh. Néih góng lā.
SUSAN:	Mgòi néih wah béi Carmen tēng, tīngyaht lohk-yúh jauh mheui dá-móhngkàuh laak.
JOHN:	Hóu lā. Ngóh wah béi kéuih tēng lā. Gám, sái-mh-sái giu Carmen dá-fāan béi néih a?

SUSAN:	Msái la.
JOHN:	Hóu lā. Bāai-baai.
SUSAN:	Bāai-baai.

Idioms and structures

The items in the list below appear in the same order as they do in the dialogue above. The *italicized* items are *new* items. In the notes, numbers in brackets refer to the expressions listed below.

1 *Wái, mgōi néih giu John*   Hello, can I speak to John, please?
   tēng-dihnwá.

2 *Deui mjyuh, John*   I'm afraid John is not in at the
   hàahnghōi-jó.   moment.

3 Ngóh haih John go *tùhngsih.*   I am John's *colleague.*

4 *Mgōi néih giu kéuih*   Please tell him to return my call.
   dá fāan dihnwá béi ngóh ā.

5 *Bāai-baai.*   Bye-bye.

Greeting on the phone (1)

To open a telephone conversation, Cantonese-speakers say **wái**, whether calling or answering.

Asking for somebody on the phone (1)

To ask for somebody on the phone, you can go straight into it by saying:

Wái, mgōi néih giu ...   Hello, can I speak to ... ,
   tēng-dihnwá.   please?

Or you can first ask whether somebody is there:

Wái, chíng mahn ...   Hello, is ... there, please?
   hái-mh-hái douh a?

Answering the phone (2)

When a caller asks to speak to somebody else, you might answer:

Hóu, mgōi dáng yāt jahn.   Please wait a minute.

When a caller asks whether somebody else is in, you might say:

Hái douh. Mgōi dáng yāt jahn.   Yes, he's here. Just a minute.

If someone asks to speak to you, you say:

Ngóh haih.   Speaking.

If somebody asked for is not in, you might say:

Deui mjyuh, kéuih mhái   I'm sorry, he's not in.
douh wo.

or

Deui mjyuh, kéuih   I'm sorry, he's gone out.
hàahnghōi-jó wo.

You may wish to ask who is calling, by saying:

Chíng mahn bīnwái wán   Can I know who's calling,
kéuih a?   please?

You may also want to ask whether the caller needs to leave a message:

Néih sái-mh-sái làuh go   Would you like to leave a
háuseun a?   message?

Colleagues and classmates   *(3)*

The noun **tùhngsih** ('colleague') is made up of **tùhng**, which means 'together with', and **sih**, which means 'to work'. Thus **tùhngsih** is 'someone you work with', while **tùhnghohk** ('classmate') is 'someone you learn with', **hohk** meaning 'to learn'.

Leaving a message   *(4)*

To ask to leave a message, you can say:

Mgōi néih tùhng ngóh làuh go háuseun ā.
Could you leave a message for me, please?

In leaving a message, you can say who you are, and then say you'll call back another time:

Mgōi néih wah béi kéuih tēng Chàhn sīnsāang wán-gwo kéuih. Ngóh wúih sei dím jūng dá gwo làih.
Please tell him/her that Mr Chan called, and I'll call again at 4 o'clock.

(Notice the use of the construction **wah béi** + someone + **tēng** to mean 'to tell someone'; e.g. 'I'll tell John' in Cantonese is **ugóh wah béi John tēng**.) You can also ask to have the person return your call:

Ngóh haih Chàhn sīnsāang. Mgōi néih giu kéuih dá fāan dihn-wá béi ngóh ā.
This is Mr Chan. Please tell him/her to call me back.

You may also leave your own telephone number for someone to call back. 'Telephone number' is **dihnwá houhmáh** in Cantonese (though many people just say **dihnwá** in colloquial speech), and the actual number is cited digit by digit:

Ngóh go dihnwá (houhmáh) haih ńgh-chāt-lìhng-gáu-baat-lìhng-sei.
My phone number is 5709804.

Saying goodbye (5)

The conventional way of saying goodbye at a meeting or on the telephone is **joi gin**, which literally means 'see you again'. However, in Hong Kong, because of the Western influence, people tend to say **bāai-baai** instead. **Bāai-baai** is borrowed from the colloquial English 'bye-bye', but when we say it in Cantonese we have to abide by the rules of Cantonese, and get the tones right!

Vocabulary

Leisure activities

Below is a list of popular activities that you might invite somebody out for. Try reading out each item aloud. If you have the cassette tapes of this book, you can model your pronunciation on the tape recording.

heui tái-hei	to go to the cinema
sihk máahnfaahn	to have dinner

heui yám-yéh	to have a drink
heui yám-jáu	to go for a drink
heui yám-gafē	to go for a coffee
heui tiu-móuh	to go to a dance
heui yàuh-séui	to go swimming
heui dá-bō	to play a ballgame
heui tēng-yāmngohk	to go to a concert

Specifying the day

When arranging to meet somebody, we need to make it clear which day we are talking about. Read the examples below:

(nī go) sīngkèih-yaht	this/coming Sunday
(nī go) sīngkèih-yāt	this/coming Monday
(nī go) sīngkèih-yih	this/coming Tuesday
hah (go) sīngkèih-yaht	Sunday week
hah (go) sīngkèih-yāt	Monday week
hah (go) sīngkèih-yih	Tuesday week

Dialogue 🔘

Read the questions, and then read or listen to the dialogue to find the answers.

3 John and Carmen are at home. The telephone rings, and John answers.

(a) What activity is Richard suggesting?
(b) Who's going?
(c) When and where will they meet?

JOHN:	Wái.
RICHARD:	Wái, haih-mh-haih John a? Ngóh haih Richard a.
JOHN:	Haih a, Richard, ngóh haih John a.
RICHARD:	John, néih tùhng Carmen tīngmáahn dāk-mh-dākhàahn a? Yáuh móuh hingcheui heui tēng-yāmngohk a?
JOHN:	Tīngmáahn yīnggōi dākhàahn.
RICHARD:	Carmen nē?

JOHN:	Dáng ngóh mahn-háh kéuih sīn. (*Off the phone.*) Carmen, néih tīngmáahn dāk-mh-dākhàahn a? Séung-mh-séung heui tēng-yāmngohk a?
CARMEN:	Ngóh tīngmáahn mdākhàahn a. Néih jihgéi heui lā.
JOHN:	Wái, Richard. Carmen tīngmáahn mdākhàahn. Ngóhdeih léuhng go heui lā. Géi dímjūng hái bīndouh dáng a?
RICHARD:	Gám, ngóh máaih-fēi lā. Chāt dím bun hái Màhnfa Jūngsām mùhnháu dáng, hóu-mh-hóu?
JOHN:	Hóu lā. Dou sìh gin lā. Bāai-baai.
RICHARD:	Bāai-baai.

Idioms and structures

The items in the list below appear in the same order as they do in the dialogue above. The *italicized* items are *new* items. In the notes, numbers in brackets refer to the expressions listed below.

1 *Néih tùhng Carmen tīng-máahn dāk-mh-dākhàahn a?*

Are you and Carmen free tomorrow evening?

2 Néih *yáuh móuh hingcheui* tùhng ngóh heui tēng-yāmngohk a?

Are you interested in going to a concert with me?

3 Tīngmáahn *yīnggōi* dākhàahn.

(I) *should* be free tomorrow evening.

4 *Dáng ngóh* mahn-háh kéuih sīn.

Let *me* just ask her first.

5 Néih *jihgéi* heui lā.

You can go *by yourself.*

6 *Chāt dím bun hái Màhnfa Jūngsām mùhnháu dáng, hóu-mh-hóu?*

Shall we meet at the entrance to the Cultural Center at 7:30?

Inviting someone out (1, 2)

To invite someone out, it is common to begin by asking if he or she is free on a certain day:

Néih sīngkèih yaht yehmáahn *dāk-mh-dākhàahn* a?
Are you free on Sunday evening?

Dākhàahn is the adjective for 'free', and in the example above it is used to form a choice-type question. If the answer is positive, another question can be asked, this time to find out if the person is interested in a certain type of activity:

> **Néih** *yáuh* *móuh* *hingcheui* **tùhng ngóh heui tēng-yāmngohk a?**
> *Are you interested in* going to a concert with me?

The choice-type question above is formed with the existential verbs **yáuh** and **móuh**, followed by the noun for 'interest', **hingcheui**. Here the activity suggested is **tēng-yāmngohk**, which literally means 'listen to music', but it should be obvious from the context whether it means 'listening to records at home' or 'going to a concert'. An unambiguous, though less commonly used, way of saying 'to go to a concert' is **heui yāmngohkwúi**, with **yāmngohkwúi** meaning 'a musical concert'. The phrase **tùhng ngóh** means 'with me' in this context, though it means 'for me' when asking for a favor, as in **Mgōi tùhng ngóh làuh go háuseun ā** (Please, can you take a message for me?)

Another way of suggesting an activity is to use the expression **bātyùh** with the sentence-final particle **ā**:

> **Tīnhei gam yiht,** *bātyùh* **heui yàuh-séui** *ā*.
> The weather is so hot. *Why don't we* go swimming?
> **Daaihgā dōu dākhàahn.** *Bātyùh* **heui tái-hei** *ā*.
> We're all free. *Why don't we* go to see a film?

Or you can come straight to the point in inviting somebody out:

> **Ngóh séung chéng néih heui yāmngohkwúi. Mjī néih dāk-mh-dākhàahn nē?**
> I'd like to invite you to a concert. I was wondering whether you were free?

The pattern **Mjī . . . nē** is a way of asking a question, and functions exactly like the English pattern 'I was wondering whether . . . '.

The modal **yīnggōi** to indicate anticipation (2)

Yīnggōi in this context can be translated into 'should', but it denotes anticipation rather than obligation. Another example of the use of **yīnggōi** with this meaning can be found in the following sentence:

Ngóh *yīnggōi* ńgh dím jūng làih douh néih gūngsī ga laak.
I *should* be at your office by five o'clock.

The aspect marker *-háh* (3)

-háh is an aspect marker used after a verb to indicate that an action is to be taken for a short while. For example, for John to ask Carmen whether she will be free should take just a couple of seconds, and so should the looking at the clock indicated in **Dáng ngóh tái-*háh* yìhgā géi dím jūng** ('Let me see what time it is').

The reflexive pronoun *jihgéi* (4)

Jihgéi is a reflexive pronoun in Cantonese, but unlike the reflexive pronouns in English, it only has one form. Thus, 'You can go by yourself' is **Néih *jihgéi* heui lā**; 'He wants to do it himself' is **Kéuih séung *jihgéi* jouh**; while 'They want to see it for themselves' is **Kéuihdeih séung *jihgéi* tái**.

Specifying a place to meet (5)

To specify a place to meet, use the word **hái** before the place word, *before* the verb, which can be either **dáng** (literally 'wait' but 'meet' in this context) or **gin** (literally 'see'). To specify the time of the meeting, again the word **hái** is used before the time word, though it is often omitted. The word order is time expression *before* place expression *before* verb. Below are three examples:

Ngóhdeih chāt dím jūng hái heiyún mùhnháu dáng ā.
We'll meet outside the cinema at seven o'clock.
Ngóhdeih sāam dím jūng hái néih ngūkkéi gin ā.
We'll see each other at three o'clock at your home.
Ngóhdeih baat dím jūng hái Daaihwuihtòhng Yāmngohktēng chēutmihn dáng ā.
We'll meet at eight outside the City Hall Concert Hall.

The word **mùhnháu** means 'entrance'. **Daaihwuihtòhng** is the City Hall, which is one of the several venues where cultural activities are held in Hong Kong. Two others are:

Màhnfa Jūngsām	Cultural Center
Yínngaih Hohkyún	Academy for Performing Arts

Exercises

Exercise 1 Housewarming 🔳

Amy has moved into a new flat and wants to invite Kitty to her new home for dinner. She phones Kitty to discuss a date. Read the conversation, listen to the recording. Then answer the following questions:

(a) Why can't Kitty make it on Tuesday evening?
(b) Why can't she make it on Wednesday evening?
(c) What day do Amy and Kitty eventually agree on?
(d) What time does Amy expect Kitty?

AMY: Wái, haih-mh-haih Kitty a?
KITTY: Haih a. Néih haih Amy àh?
AMY: Kitty, ngóh séung chéng néih làih ngóh ngūkkéi sihk máahn-faahn a. Néih hah sīngkèih-yih dāk-mh-dākhàahn a?
KITTY: Hah sīngkèih-yih mdāk a. Ngóh yiu tùhng Peter heui tēng-yāmngohk a.
AMY: Gám, láihbaai-sāam máahn nē?
KITTY: Láihbaai-sāam máahn dōu mdāk a. Ngóh yiu fāan-hohk a. Bātyùh láihbaai-ńgh máahn ā, hóu-mh-hóu? Láihbaai-ńgh máahn ngóh béigaau dākhàahn.
AMY: Hóu lā. Gám jauh láihbaai-ńgh máahn lā. Néih yehmáahn chāt dím bun lèih douh ngóh ngūkkéi, dāk-mh-dāk?
KITTY: Dāk, móuh mahntàih.

Exercise 2 Taking messages 🔳

Your colleague, Pam, has gone out for a while and says she's coming back at about four o'clock. You have promised to take messages for her. Complete the following conversation between you and a caller.

CALLER: Wái, mgōi néih giu Pam tēng-dihnwá.
YOU: (a) Deui mjyuh, Pam . . .
CALLER: Chíng mahn kéuih géi dím jūng fāan lèih a?

YOU:	(b) Pam wah kéuih . . .
CALLER:	Mgōi hó-mh-hóyíh tùhng ngóh làuh go háuseun a?
YOU:	(c)
CALLER:	Mgōi néih giu kéuih hái ńgh dím jūng chìhn dá fāan dihnwá béi ngóh ā.
YOU:	(d) Hóu, ngóh giu kéuih . . .
CALLER:	Hóu laak. Mgōi saai. Bāai-baai.
YOU:	(e) Msái mgōi . . .

Exercise 3 When are you free?

Your friend Stephen is leaving Hong Kong at the end of the week, and has phoned to suggest having a drink together after work some time this week. You have a very busy week, and you are trying desperately to fit in a time for Stephen. Complete the conversation with reference to the diary:

STEPHEN:	Wái, ngóh haih Stephen a. Ngóh sīngkèih-luhk jauh fāan Méihgwok la. Néih nī go láihbaai géisìh dākhàahn tùhng ngóh yám-yéh a?
YOU:	Ngóh nī go láihbaai hóu mòhng a.
STEPHEN:	Sīngkèih-sāam máahn dāk-mh-dāk?
YOU:	(a) Mdāk a. Ngóh yiu . . .
STEPHEN:	Gám sīngkèih-sei nē?
YOU:	(b) Sīngkèih-sei . . .
STEPHEN:	Sīngkèih-yih nē?

YOU: (c) . . . Bātyùh . . .
STEPHEN: Hóu lā. Dou sìh gin lā.

Recognizing Chinese characters

大會堂　　City Hall

文化中心　Cultural Center

藝術中心　Arts Center

演藝學院　Academy for Performing Arts

Key to exercises

Lesson 1

Dialogues: 1 (a) Mangoes. (b) 4. (c) $20. **2** (a) Oranges. (b) 6. (c) $15. **3** (a) Grapes. (b) One pound. (c) $12.

Exercise 1: (a) (i). (b) (iii). (c) (i). (d) (ii).

Exercise 2: (a) Dī léi . . . yāt go. (b) Dī sāigwā . . . yāt bohng. (c) Dī muhkgwā . . . yāt bohng. (d) Dī bōlòh . . . yāt go. (e) Dī laihjī . . . yāt bohng.

Exercise 3: (a) Sei mān yāt bohng. (b) Ńgh mān yāt go. (c) Luhk mān yāt bohng. (d) Sahp mān sei go. (e) Gáu mān yāt go.

Exercise 4: (a)(i) Sahp mān sāam go. (ii) Hóu, yāt dā pìhnggwó. (iii) Dōjeh sei-sahp mān lā. (iv) Dōjeh. (b)(i) Baat mān yāt bohng. (ii) Hóu, sāam bohng laihjī. (iii) Dōjeh yih-sahp sei mān lā. (iv) Jáau fāan luhk mān. (v) Dōjeh.

Exercise 5: (a) Hawker A. (b) $86.

Exercise 6: Grapes – $15 a pound; kiwifruit – $3 each; apples – $3 each; papayas – $8 a pound; water-melons – $2 a pound; oranges – $10 for 4; pears – $10 for 4.

Lesson 2

Dialogues: 1 (a) New Zealand. (b) The USA. **2** (a) Australia. (b) English and German. (c) Canada. (d) English and French. **3** (a) Japan. (b) Japanese, English and Putonghua/(Mandarin).

Exercise 1: (a) (i). (b) (i). (c) (ii). (d) (ii).

Exercise 3: (b) Kéuih giujouh Pierre Gagnon. Kéuih haih Faatgwok yàhn. Kéuih sīk góng Faatmán tùhng Sāibāanngàhmán. (c) Kéuih giujouh Paola Giannini. Kéuih haih Yidaaihleih yàhn. Kéuih sīk góng Yidaaihleihmán, Faatmán tùhng Yīngmán.

(d) Kéuih giujouh Kim Yoo Sung. Kéuih haih Hòhngwok yàhn. Kéuih sīk góng Hòhnmán, Yahtmán tùhng Yīngmán.

Exercise 4: Raul: Filipino; speaks English, Spanish and Tagalog. Jane: Australian; speaks English, French and Italian. Bruce: American; speaks English, German, French and Spanish. Antonia: Canadian; speaks English, French and Italian. (a) 4. (b) 6. (c) Bruce. (d) English. (e) Spanish and Italian. (f) Tagalog (Filipino) and German.

Exercise 5: (b) Ngóh yiu yih-sahp go Méihgwok cháang. (c) Ngóh yiu léuhng bohng Méihgwok tàihjí. (d) Ngóh yiu sāam go Fēileuhtbān bōlòh. (e) Ngóh yiu baat go Fēileuhtbān mōnggwó. (f) Ngóh yiu yāt dā (*or* sahp-yih go) Oujāu léi.

Lesson 3

Dialogues: 1 (a) Swimming, playing tennis and listening to music. (b) Listening to music, reading and watching television. **2** (a) Window-shopping and going to the cinema. (b) He likes going to the cinema, traveling and taking pictures, but he doesn't like window-shopping. **3** (a) Once a week. (b) Saturday. **4** (a) About twice a week. (b) About twice a year.

Exercise 1: (a) (iii). (b) (iii). (c) (ii).

Exercise 2: (b) Kéuih mjūngyi yàuh-séui. (c) Kéuih géi jūngyi tái-syū. (d) Ngóhdeih mhaih géi jūngyi tái-dihnsih. (e) Kéuihdeih mjūngyi cheung-gō.

Exercise 3: (b) Ngóh yāt go láihbaai hàahng léuhng chi gāai. (c) Ngóh yāt go yuht tái léuhng chi hei/dihnyíng. (d) Ngóh yāt go láihbaai yàuh sāam chi séui. (e) Ngóh yāt nìhn heui sei chi léuih-hàhng.

Exercise 5: Possible answers: Emily tùhng John dōu jūngyi tái-dihnyíng. Carmen tùhng Emily dōu jūngyi cheung-gō. Richard tùhng John dōu mjūngyi cheung-gō.

Exercise 6: Kéuih yauh jūngyi tek-jūkkàuh. Kéuih fùhng sīngkèih-yaht tek-jūkkàuh. Kéuih yauh jūngyi páau-bouh. Kéuih fùhng

sīngkèih-sāam tùhng sīngkèih-ńgh páau-bouh. Kéuih yauh jūngyi
dá-làahmkàuh. Kéuih fùhng sīngkèih-yih tùhng sīngkèih-sei dá-
làahmkàuh. Kéuih yauh jūngyi cháai-dāanchē. Kéuih fùhng
sīngkèih-luhk cháai-dāanchē.

Lesson 4

Quick Practice 1: (a) seuhngjau gáu dīm sahp. (b) seuhngjau sahpyāt dím chāt. (c) seuhngjau sahp dím sei. (d) hahjau ńgh dím
sahpyāt. (e) hahjau luhk dím ńgh. (f) hahjau sāam dím baat.
(g) seuhngjau chāt dím bun.

Quick Practice 2: (b) sei dím yāt go jih. (c) sahp dím léuhng go jih.
(d) gáu dím sahp go jih. (e) sāam dím gáu go jih.

Dialogues: 1 (a) 4:30. (b) 5:30. **2** (a) 7 p.m. (b) 4:30 p.m. (c) 9:45 a.m.
3 (a) 7:15 a.m. (b) 11:30 p.m. (c) John gets up at 8 a.m. and goes to
bed at about 12 midnight. **4** (a) 9:30 p.m. (b) 7 p.m. and 11:30 p.m.
(c) 7:30 p.m. **5** (a) At 6 this evening. (b) At 8:30 this evening.
(c) Horse-racing is shown at 9:35 tomorrow evening.

Exercise 1: (a) (i). (b) (ii). (c) (iv). (d) (ii).

Exercise 2: (b) Yìhgā (haih) sāam dím chāt. / Yìhgā (haih) sāam
dím sāam-sahp ńgh fān. (c) Yìhgā (haih) gáu dím sahp-baat fān.
(d) Yìhgā (haih) sahp-yāt dím ńgh-sahp yih fān. (e) Yìhgā (haih)
ńgh dím sāam. / Yìhgā (haih) ńgh dím sahp-ńgh fān. /Yìhgā (haih)
ńgh dím yāt go gwāt.

Exercise 3: (a) . . . Kéuih yehmáahn baat dímjūng sihk-máahnfaahn, yìhnhauh sahp-yih dím fan-gaau. (b) Carmen seungjau chāt
dím bun héi-sān, gáu dímjūng fāan-gūng. Kéuih hahjau sahp-yih
dím bun sihk-ngaan, yìhnhauh ńgh dím sāam fong-gūng. Kéuih
yehmáahn baat dímjūng sihk-máahnfaahn, yìhnhauh yāt dímjūng
fan-gaau. (c) Richard seungjau chāt dím sāam héi-sān, gáu dímjūng
fāan-gūng. Kéuih hahjau yāt dímjūng sihk-ngaan, yìhnhauh ńgh
dím bun fong-gūng. Kéuih yehmáahn chāt dímjūng sihk-máahnfaahn, yìhnhauh sahp-yāt dím bun fan-gaau.

Exercise 4: (a) Gāmmáahn chāt dím yāt tùhng sahp-yāt dím gáu
yáuh sānmán tái. (b) Gāmmáahn chāt dím ńgh tùhng sahp-yih dím

yih yáuh tīnhéi tái. (c) Yáuh. Gāmmáahn baat dím bun yáuh géiluhkpín tái. (d) Gāmmáahn gáu dím bun yáuh dihnyíng tái. (e) Gāmmáahn móuh móhngkàuh tái.

Lesson 5

Dialogues: 1 (a) John is tall, not too fat and not too thin, and wears glasses. (b) Susan is a little thin, not too tall, has short hair, and does not wear glasses. **2** (a) He is very tall and thin, wears glasses, has short hair, and is quite good-looking. (b) She is rather short, has long hair, does not wear glasses, is quite pretty and looks very young. **3** (a) Both are 49. (b) 12. (c) 11.

Exercise 1: From left to right: Li Ming (Chinese), Michael (American), Christine (French) and Judy (British).

Exercise 2: (b) 52. (c) 38. (d) 71. (e) 96. (f) 49.

Exercise 3: (b) Martin gāmnín ńgh-sahp yih seui. Kéuih fèih-féidéi, mhaih géi gōu, daai ngáahngéng, dyún tàuhfaat. (c) Pam gāmnín sei-sahp gáu seui. Kéuih mhaih géi fèih, mhaih géi sau, daai ngáahngéng. (d) Clara gāmnín sahp-chāt seui. Kéuih géi gōu, géi sau, chèuhng tàuhfaat, móuh daai ngáahngéng. Kéuih géi leng ga. (e) Jimmy gāmnín sahp-sāam seui. Kéuih géi ngái, géi sau, daai ngáahngéng, dyún tàuhfaat.

Lesson 6

Quick Practice 1: (b) yih-baak ńgh-sahp luhk māan. (c) yāt-chīn chāt-baak baat-sahp gáu māan. (d) ńgh-chīn luhk-baak yih-sahp māan. (e) yāt-maahn ńgh-chīn māan. (f) sāam-maahn chāt-chīn ńgh-baak māan. (g) gáu-sahp sāam maahn chāt-chīn māan. (h) ńgh-sahp-luhk maahn yih-chīn yāt-baak māan. (i) yāt-baak ńgh-sahp yih maahn māan. (j) sei-baak luhk-sahp baat maahn gáu-chīn māan.

Quick Practice 2: (b) yāt-chīn lìhng sāam-sahp māan. (c) yih-maahn chāt-chīn lìhng ńgh māan. (d) ńgh-sahp maahn lìhng sei-baak māan. (e) yāt-baak gáu-sahp maahn lìhng baat-baak māan.

Quick Practice 3: (b) ńgh-baak géi māan. (c) sei-chīn yih-baak géi

mān. (d) sāam-maahn luhk-chīn géi mān. (e) sahp-géi maahn mān.
(f) gáu-sahp yih maahn géi mān. (g) yāt-baak yih-sahp-géi maahn
mān. (h) sei-baak-géi maahn mān.

Dialogues: 1 (a) $12,500. (b) $7,000; $800 each. (c) $4,600.
2 (a) About $1,000. (b) About $500. (c) About $8,000.

Quick Practice 4: (b) gáu go yāt. (c) nǵh go bun. (d) baat go yih.
(e) go sei. (f) luhk hòuhjí.

Dialogue: 3 (a) $0.80. (b) $2.30. (c) $1.80. (d) $1.70.

Exercise 1: Japan – $12,000; Hawaii – $12,000; Korea – $8,500; the
Philippines – $4,000.

Exercise 2: 5 oranges – $12.50; 4 apples – $6.80; 1 water-melon
– $14; total – $33.30.

Exercise 3: (b) Nī jēung chāantói maaih baat-chīn yih-baak nǵh-
sahp mān. (c) Dī chāanyih gáu-baak yāt-sahp mān yāt jēung.
(d) Jēung sōfá chāt-chīn baat-baak mān. (e) Nī jēung ōnlohkyí yāt-
chīn lìhng nǵh-sahp mān.

Exercise 4: (b) Chris jeui ngái. (c) Diana jeui sau. (d) Chris jeui
fèih. (e) Sally fèih-dī. (f) Raul sau-dī. (g) Elsie yáuh daai ngáahngéng. (h) Terry yáuh wùsōu.

Exercise 5: (b) Méihgwok pìhnggwó sāam mān yāt go. (c) Jūnggwok pìhnggwó léuhng mān yāt go. (d) Yahtbún pìhnggwó y'ah-nǵh
mān yāt go. (e) Jūnggwok pìhnggwó jeui pèhng. (f) Yahtbún pìhnggwó jeui gwai. (g) Méihgwok pìhnggwó pèhng-dī.

Exercise 6: (a) John gōu-gwo Carmen. (b) Carmen sau-gwo Emily.
(c) Nī jēung chàhgēi dái-gwo go jēung. (d) Go jēung chāanyí leng-
dī. (e) Ngóh go móhngkàuhpáak gwai-dī. (f) Nī jēung sōfá jeui
pèhng. (g) Carmen ga dāanchē jeui dái.

Lesson 7

Dialogues: 1 (a) The underground; 45 minutes. (b) He drives; 25
minutes. (c) On foot; 30 minutes. **2** (a) By ferry; 1 hour 10 minutes.

(b) By taxi; 10 minutes. **3** (a) 2. (b) 10 minutes. (c) 30 minutes. (d) 20 minutes. (e) 1 hour. **4** (a) 1 hour. (b) 5 minutes. (c) 25 minutes. d) 20 minutes. (e) 10 minutes.

Exercise 1: Jim: Home → walk (15 minutes) → ferry (50 minutes) → walk (10 minutes) → office.
Bill: Home → walk (5 minutes) → bus (15 minutes) → MTR (30 minutes) → office.

Exercise 2: (b) ńgh go jūngtàuh ńgh-sahp ńgh fānjūng. (c) luhk yaht. (d) yāt go sīngkèih/láihbaai lìhng sei yaht. (e) sāam go yuht. (f) léuhng nìhn lìhng sahp-yāt go yuht.

Exercise 3: (b) léuhng go bun jūngtàuh. (c) sei go bun jūngtàuh. (d) ńgh yaht bun. (e) gáu go bun sīngkèih/láihbaai. (f) chāt go bun yuht. (g) ńgh nìhn lìhng luhk go yuht.

Exercise 4: (b) sāam-sahp luhk fānjūng. (c) sei-sahp ńgh fānjūng *or* gáu go jih. (d) ńgh-sahp ńgh fānjūng *or* sahp-yāt go jih. (e) yāt go jūngtàuh ńgh-sahp fānjūng *or* yāt go jūngtàuh sahp go jih. (f) léuhng go jūngtàuh chāt fānjūng.

Exercise 6: (b) Sue: Ngóh daap bun go jūngtàuh bāsí jauh fāan dou gūngsī laak. Rob: Ngóh yiu daap bun go jūngtàuh bāsí sīnji fāan dou gūngsī a. (c) Ben: Ngóh hàahng sei go ji louh jauh fāan dou gūngsī laak. Pam: Ngóh yiu hàahng sei go ji louh sīnji fāan dou gūngsī a. (d) Dan: Ngóh daap ńgh-sahp fānjūng fóchē tùhng hàahng sāam go ji louh jauh fāan dou gūngsī laak. Ray: Ngóh yiu daap ńgh-sahp fānjūng fóchē tùhng hàahng sāam go ji louh sīnji fāan dou gūngsī a.

Exercise 7: **1** (i) Daap-féigéi yiu sei-baak yāt-sahp mān. (ii) Yiu daap sāam-sahp fānjūng. (iii) Daap-syùhn yiu yih-baak yih-sahp sāam mān. (iv) Daap-syùhn yiu baat go jūngtàuh. **2** (i) Daap-bāsí pèhng-dī. Daap-fóchē yiu yāt-baak baat-sahp sāam mān, daap-bāsí yiu yāt-baak sei-sahp ńgh mān jēk. (ii) Daap-fóchē yiu léuhng go jūngtàuh gáu go jih, daap-bāsí jauh yiu luhk go jūngtàuh laak. (iii) Daap-syùhn yiu yih-baak yih-sahp sāam mān, yiu daap baat go jūngtàuh.

Lesson 8

Dialogues: 1 (a) 6. 1 sitting-room, 1 dining-room, 3 bedrooms and 1 study. (b) 6. Mrs Lam and her husband, her parents, her son Kenny and her daughter Angel. (c) Kenny is eight and Angel is seven. **2** (a) Mr Lam is still in the office. (b) He is in his room. (c) She is in the kitchen. (d) Kenny has gone to the swimming pool. (e) Angel has gone to her school.

Exercise 1: (a) He is having a meeting. (b) He is watching television. (c) She is cooking. (d) He is swimming. (e) She is singing.

Exercise 2: (b) Mary jyú-gán faahn. (c) Kéuih cheung-gán gō. (d) Kéuih dá-gán làahmkàuh. (e) Kéuih tái-gán dihnsih.

Exercise 3: (c) Kéuih jūngyi tái-dihnyíng. (d) Ngóh múihfùhng láihbaai-yih dá-móhngkàuh. (e) Ngóh màh-mā fan-gán gaau. (f) Ngóh bàh-bā jūngyi tēng-yāmngohk. (g) Ngóh taai-táai jūngyi jyúh-yéhsihk. (h) Ngóh jèh-jē wáan-gán yàuhheigēi.

Exercise 4: (a) Ngóhdeih gāan ngūk yáuh yāt go haaktēng, yāt go faahntēng, léuhng gāan seuihfóng, yāt go chyùhfóng tùhng yūt go chisó. (b) Ngóhdeih gāan ngūk yáuh yāt go haaktēng, yāt go faahntēng, sāam gāan seuihfóng, sāam gāan chūnglèuhngfóng, yāt go chyùhfóng tùhng yāt gāan gūngyàhnfóng.

Exercise 5: (a) Chàhn sīnsāang hái faahntēng yám-gán bējáu. (b) Kéuih hái haaktēng tái-gán dihnsih. (c) Kéuih hái haaktēng tái-gán syū.

Exercise 6: (a) Kéuih heui-jó hàahng-gāai. (b) Kéuih heui-jó tái-jūkkàuh. (c) Kenny heui-jó dá-móhngkàuh. (d) Angel heui-jó tēng-yāmngohk.

Lesson 9

Dialogues: 1 (a) Washing clothes. (b) Kenny. **2** (a) Kenny. (b) Angel. (c) Mr Lam. **3** (a) Vicky. (b) Mary. **4** (a) Angel. (b) Mr Lam. (c) Kenny.

Exercise 1:   making the bed   ✓
washing up   ✓
buying food for dinner   ✗
washing the clothes   ✗
hanging the clothes out   ✓
vacuum-cleaning   ✓
cleaning the windows   ✓

Exercise 2: (a) Néih hó-mh-hóyíh bōng ngóh dá léuhng fūng seun a? (b) Gám, hó-mh-hóyíh bōng ngóh je sāam bún syū a? (c) Dāk, móuh mahntàih. (d) Gám, tùhng ngóh máaih jēung fóchēfēi, dāk-mh-dāk? (e) Hóu aak. (f) Msái mgōi.

Exercise 3: (a) Ngóh dōu mdākhàahn a. Ngóh wáan-gán yàuh-heigēi a. (b)Deui mjyuh. Ngóh dōu mdāk a. Ngóh tái-gán boují a.

Lesson 10

Dialogues: 1 (a) On the sofa. (b) On the easy chair. **2** (a) On the coffee table. (b) On the television set. (c) On the floor under the dining table. **3** (a) Opposite the underground station. (b) About 10 minutes' walk away. (c) Diagonally across from the shoe shop. **4** (a) Capitol Cinema. (b) About 25 minutes. (c) 10 minutes.

Exercise 1: (a) bookstore – next to supermarket, opposite flower shop; drugstore – diagonally across from bookstore, next to flower shop; electrical appliance store – diagonally across from cinema, next to shoe shop; bakery – opposite cinema, next to supermarket; sweet shop – between cinema and dress shop.

Exercise 2: (b) Bá jē hái sōfá gaaklèih. (c) Go ngáahngéng hái dei-hhá seuhngmihn. (d) Go chàhbūi hái syūgá seuhngmihn. (e) Deui tōháai hái chàhgēi hahmihn. (f) Go séuibūi hái dihnsih gei seuhng-mihn. (g) Jī bāt hái séuibūi tùhng chàhbūi jūnggāan.

Exercise 3: Hái sōfá seuhngmihn yáuh yāt go sáudói, yāt jek maht, yāt jek sáumaht, tùhng yāt bá jē. Hái sōfá gaaklèih ge deihhá yáuh yāt go ngàhnbāau, yāt bá sō, yāt jek tōháai. Hái dihnsihgēi seuhng-mihn yáuh yāt go séuibūi. Hái dihnsihgēi gaaklèih ge deihhá yáuh yāt jek chàhbūi, léuhng jī bāt, tùhng sāam béng luhkyíngdáai. Dihnsihgēi hahmihn go luhkyínggēi mgin-jó.

Exercise 4: (a)Tim Tim jeui káhn. (b) Mhaih. (c) Wing Sing jeui daaih. (d) Dōu msyun hóu yúhn, daaihyeuk yiu hàahng sāam go jih. (e) Yáuh léuhng gāan, Quicken tùhng Good Foot. (f) Quicken káhn-dī. (g) Hàahng léuhng go jih jauh dou laak.

Lesson 11

Dialogues: 1 (a) A bowl of won-ton noodles and a bowl of congee with mixed meat. (b) A plate of vegetables with oyster sauce. (c) $28. **2** (a) A pot of jasmine tea and a pot of Pu-erh tea. (b) 2 baskets of shrimp dumplings, 1 basket of pork dumplings, 2 baskets of barbecued-pork buns, 1 basket of shrimp and bamboo shoot dumplings, and a plate of custard tarts. (c) $192. (d) $200. **3**(a) 1 cheeseburger, 1 large French fries, and 1 small Coke. (b) Taking away. (c) $17.50. **4**(a) Chinese food. (b) French food. (c) French food.

Exercise 1: Food: 2 hamburgers, 3 hot-dogs, 2 large French fries. Drinks: 2 cups of tea, 2 cups of coffee, and 1 orange juice.

Exercise 2: Richard's favorite place: India. Carmen's: China. John's: Japan.

Exercise 3: (a) Sāam wún yùhdáanmihn y'ah sei mān, léuhng dihp yàuhchoi sahp-yih mān, yāt wún gahpdáijūk jauh sahp-yāt mān. Júngguhng sei'ah chāt mān lā. (b) Jáau fāan ńgh'ah sāam mān. (c) Dōjeh. (d) Sei wún wàhntānmihn, sā'ah luhk mān, léuhng wún yùhdáanmihn, sahp-luhk mān, sāam wún ngàuhyuhkjūk, sā'ah mān, léuhng dihp yàuhchoi, sahp-yih mān. Júngguhng gáu'ah sei mān lā. (e) Jáau fāan sei-baak lìhng luhk mān. (f) Dōjeh.

Exercise 5: (b) Ngóh bàh-bā jūngyi heui yám-chàh dō-gwo heui tái-hei. *or* Heui yám-chàh tùhng heui tái-hei, ngóh bàh-bā jūngyi heui yám-chàh dō-dī, *or* Heui yám-chàh tùhng heui tái-hei, ngóh bàh-bā béigaau jūngyi heui yám-chàh. (c) Ngóh gòh-gō jūngyi dá-làahmkàuh dō-gwo dá-móhngkàuh, *or* Dá-làahmkàuh tùhng dá-móhngkàuh, ngóh gòh-gō jūngyi dá-làahmkàuh dō-dī, *or* Dá-làahmkàuh tùhng dá-móhngkàuh, ngóh gòh-go béigaau jūngyi dá-làahmkàuh. (d) Kéuih màhmā jūngyi tēng-sāuyāmgēi dō-gwo tái-dihnsih, *or* Tēng-sāuyāmgēi tùhng tái-dihnsih, kéuih màh-mā jūngyi tēng-sāuyāmgēi dō-dī, *or* Tēng-sāuyāmgēi tùhng tái-dihnsih, kéuih màh-mā béigaau jūngyi tēng-sāuyāmgēi. (e) Ngóh mùih-múi jūngyi hohk-Faatmán dō-gwo hohk-Dākmán, *or* Hohk Faatmán tùhng hohk-Dākmán, ngóh mùih-múi jūngyi hohk-Faatmán dō-dī, *or* Hohk-Faatmán tùhng hohk-Dākmán, ngóh mùih-múi béigaau jūngyi hohk-Faatmán.

Lesson 12

Dialogues: 1 (a) Quite cold, with temperatures around 10 °C, but fine. (b) Very hot, around 30 °C, very humid. **2** (a) Cold, with northerly winds and light rain. (b) Yes. (c) 15 °C; 11 °C. **3** (a) Very cold, with snow. (b) Around –20 °C. (c) Warmer. (d) To bring more clothes but not too many. **4** (a) Cold and rainy. (b) To wear more clothes. (c) To drive carefully.

Exercise 1: Hot and humid; 32 °C; 28 °C; 78%–89%.

Exercise 2: (a) Seuhnghói yāt-yuht dōu géi dung a. Heiwān lìhng douh ji baat dou. (b) Yiu a. (c) Seuhnghói yāt-yuht mhaih géi dō yúh lohk, hóyíh mdaai jē. (d) Gwóngjāu sei-yuht béigaau nyúhn, tùhngmàaih wúih lohk-yúh. (e) Heiwān daaihyeuk sahp-baat douh ji yih-sahp ńgh douh. (f) Hóu chìusāp. (g) Gwóngjāu sahp-yuht wānnyúhn tùhng gōnchou, béigaau syūfuhk. (h) Mhaih géi dō yúh lohk. (i) Msái la.

Exercise 3: (b) Hauhyaht wúih jyún lèuhng. (c) Hah go láihbaai tīnhei wúih jyún yiht. (d) Sīngkèih-luhk wúih hóu daaihfūng. (e) Sīngkèih-yaht wúih yáuh lèuihbouh. (f) Tīngyaht wúih chìuhsāp.

Exercise 4: (a) Samuel sahp-houh sīngkèih-sei hái Yīnggwok fāan lèih. (b) Keith jauh sahp-baat-houh sīngkèih-ńgh hái Oujāu fāan lèih. (c) Teresa jauh sahp-sei-houh sīngkèih-yāt fāan Hēunggóng.

Lesson 13

Dialogues: 1 (a) 2 blouses, 2 skirts, and 1 pair of shoes. (b) 1 suit, 1 jacket, and 2 blouses. (c) A tie. **2** (a) Ben. (b) Teddy. (c) Teddy's wife. **3** (a) A shirt and slacks. (b) Not always. He usually wears one in winter, but not in summer. (c) A skirt and high-heeled shoes, and usually a suit in winter. (d) A T-shirt, jeans and sports shoes.

Exercise 1: 3 coats, 4 woollen jumpers, 3 scarfs, and 5 pairs of gloves.

Exercise 2: From left to right: Hideki, Hama, Mariko and Saito.

Exercise 3: Jóbín nī go jeuk fu, laahm-jó génggān, daai-jó sáumaht ge néuihjái haih Sandy. Gaaklèih nī go daai-jó móu, jeuk daaihlāu, daai ngáahngéng ge nàahmjái haih Andy. Nī go dá tāai, laahm-jó génggān ge haih Timmy. Kéuih gaaklèih nī go daai-jó móu tùhng sáumaht ge néuihjái haih Beverly.

Lesson 14

Dialogues: 1 (a) Twice. (b) Last year and the year before last. (c) No. (d) Last month. **2** (a) Yes. (b) It was too cold. (c) None. **3** (a) Last month. (b) San Francisco and Los Angeles. (c) 5 days in San Francisco and 6 in Los Angeles. **4** (a) He likes it very much. (b) The beautiful scenery, the clean surroundings, and the nice, polite people. (c) Shopping and food are very expensive.

Exercise 1: Winnie: 3 times to Europe, twice to the USA, once to Japan, and once to Australia. Kitty: 5 times to China, 4 times to Taiwan, twice to Japan, twice to Europe, the USA and Australia. Sally: once to India, 3 times to the Philippines, twice to Japan, 4 times to China, 5 times to Taiwan, once to Europe, 4 times to the USA, 3 times to Canada, 3 times to Australia, and twice to New Zealand. Sally is the most-traveled girl.

Exercise 2: (b) Ngóh chìhn go yuht heui-gwo Yahtbún. (c) Kéuih seuhng go yuht heui-gwo Faatgwok. (d) Kéuih léuhng go yuht chìhn heui-gwo Jūnggwok. (e) Ngóhdeih ngh nìhn chìhn heui-gwo Tòiwāan. (f) Kéuihdeih sei go láihbaai chìhn heui-gwo Gānàhdaai.

Exercise 3: (b) Ngóh heui-gwo ngh chi Dākgwok. (c) Ngóh nī go yuht tái-gwo léuhng chi hei. (d) Ngóh nī go láihbaai dá-gwo léuhng chi móhngkàuh. (e) Ngóh gāmnín heui-gwo sei chi léuihhàhng.

Exercise 4: Ngóhdeih heui-jó Fēileuhtbān, Yandouh, tùhng Tòih-wāan . . . Ngóhdeih sei-yuht heui Fēileuhtbān ge . . . Ngóhdeih ˋheui-jó luhk yaht . . . Ngóhdeih juhng yáuh heui Yandouh. Dōu haih sei-yuht heui. Heui-jó baat yaht . . . Juhng yáuh, ngóhdeih ngh-yuht heui-jó luhk yaht Tòihwāan.

Lesson 15

Dialogues: 1 (a) Mr Wong. (b) He wants John to ring him back.
(c) 3603678. **2** (a) She has gone out. (b) That they will not be playing tennis if it rains tomorrow. (c) No. **3** (a) Going to a concert. (b)
John and Richard. (c) 7:30 at the entrance to the Cultural Center.

Exercise 1: (a) She has to go to a concert with Peter. (b) She has a
class on Wednesday evening. (c) Friday. (d) 7:30 p.m.

Exercise 2: (a) Deui mìjyuh, Pam mhái douh wo, *or* Deui mìjyuh,
Pam hàahnghō-jó wo. (b) Pam wah kéuih daaihyeuk sei dím jūng
fāan lèih. (c) Dāk, móuh mahntaih. (d) Hóu, ngóh giu kéuih hái
ngh dím jūng chìhn dá fāan dihnwá béi néih. (e) Msái mgōi. Bāai-
baai.

Exercise 3: (a) Mdāk a. Ngóh yiu dá-móhngkàuh a. (b) Sīngkèih-
sei máahn ngóh yiu hōi-wúi a. (c) Sīngkèih-yih máahn dōu mdāk
wo. Ngóh yiu heui tái-hei. Bātyùh sīngkèih-ngh ā . . .

Cantonese–English glossary

Abbreviations for grammatical
terms

adv	adverb
adj	adjective
asp	aspect marker
conj	conjunction
cl	classifier
dem	demonstrative
i	interjection
ie	idiomatic expression
m	measure
mv	modal verb
n	noun
num	numeral
prep	preposition
prt	particle
prn	pronoun
pw	place word
qw	question word
tw	time word
v	verb
v-o	verb-object construction
v-prt	verbal particle

ā (*prt*)
a (*prt*)
àh (*prt*)
ak (*prt*)
ā ma (*prt*)

Aujāu (*pw*)	Europe
bá (*cl*)	*classifier* for long slender objects such as combs and umbrellas
baahksīk (*adj*)	white
bāai-baai (*ie*)	bye-bye!
baak (*num*)	hundred
baakmaahn (*num*)	million
baat (*num*)	eight
baat'ah (*num*)	eighty (elided form)
baat-yuht (*tw*)	August
bāau (*m*)	packet
Bāgēisītáan (*pw*)	Pakistan
Bāgēisītáanwá (*n*)	any of the languages of Pakistan
bàh-bā (*n*)	father
bāk (*adj*)	north
Bākgīng (*pw*)	Beijing/Peking
Bālàih (*pw*)	Paris
bāsí (*n*)	bus
bāsíjaahm (*n*)	bus stop
bāt (*n*)	pen
bātgwo (*conj*)	but
bātyùh (*ie*)	why don't . . .?
béi (*v*)	to give
béi-chín (*v-o*)	to pay

béigaau (*adv*) comparatively
bējáu (*n*) beer
béng (*cl*) *classifier* for audio- and video-tapes
bīn(+ *cl*/*dem*) (*qw*) which?
bīndouh (*qw*) where?
bīngo (*qw*) who?
bīnwái (*qw*) who?
bōhàaih (*n*) sports shoe
bohng (*m*) pound (in weight)
bōlòh (*n*) pineapple
bōng(sáu) (*v*) to help
bougou (*n*) report
boulām (*n*) plum
bóuléi (*n*) Pu-erh (dark) tea
būi (*n/m*) cup
bún (*cl*) *classifier* for books
bun (*n*) half
búngóng (*adj*) local (in Hong Kong)
bunjihtkwàhn (*n*) skirt
bunyeh (*tw*) after midnight
cháai-dāanchē (*v-o*) to ride a bicycle
chāandang (*n*) dining chair
cháang (*n*) orange
cháangjāp (*n*) orange juice
cháangsīk (*adj*) orange (color)
chāantói (*n*) dining table
chāanyí (*n*) dining chair
chàh (*n*) tea
chàhbūi (*n*) cup
chàhgēi (*n*) coffee table
chàhmmáahn (*tw*) yesterday evening, last night
chàhmyaht (*tw*) yesterday
chāsīubāau (*n*) steamed barbecued-pork bun

chāt (*num*) seven
chāt'ah (*num*) seventy (elided form)
chāt-yuht (*tw*) July
chē (*n*) car
chēfòhng (*n*) garage
chèhdeuimihn (*adv*) diagonally across the road
chéng (*v*) to invite
chèuhng (*adj*) long
chēui (*v*) to blow
chèuihbín (*adj*) casual (in dress)
chēung (*n*) window
cheung-gō (*v-o*) to sing
chēungyún (*n*) spring roll
chēut (*cl*) *classifier* for films and documentaries
chēut-gāai (*v-o*) to go out
chēutmihn (*adv*) outside
chēut-mùhnháu (*v-o*) to leave home
chi (*n*) a time
chìhn (*adv*) ago, the one (week, month, year, etc.) before last
chìhng (*adj*) fine (weather)
chìhnmihn (*adv*) in front (of)
chìhnnín (*tw*) the year before last
chín (*n*) money
chīn (*num*) thousand
chīnglèuhng (*adj*) cool
chíng mahn (*ie*) may I ask
chisó (*n*) toilet
Chìuhjāuwá (*n*) Chiu Chow dialect
chìuhsāp (*adj*) humid
chīukāp-síhchèuhng (*n*) supermarket
chòhng (*n*) bed

choi (*n*) food, cuisine

choimáh (*n*) horse-racing

choisām (*n*) a Chinese green vegetable, choisum

chūng-lèuhng (*v-o*) to take a bath/shower

chūnglèuhng-fóng (*n*) bathroom

chyùhfóng (*n*) kitchen

dá (*v*) to hit, to type

dā (*num*) a dozen

daahntāat (*n*) custard tart

daai (*v*) to put on (spectacles, a cap, a hat, etc.); to take, to bring

daaih (*adj*) large

daaihfūng (*adj*) windy

daaihgā (*prn*) everyone

daaihhohk (*n*) university

daaihlāu (*n*) overcoat

daaihlóu (*n*) elder brother

Daaihwuih-tòhng-Yāmngohk-tēng (*pw*) City Hall Concert Hall

daaihyeuk (*adv*) roughly, approximately

dāan (*n*) bill

dāanchē (*n*) bicycle

daap (*v*) to take (a means of transport)

daap cho sin (*ie*) wrong number (on the phone)

dá-bō (*v-o*) to play a ballgame

dá-dihnwá (*v-o*) to make a phone call

dái (*adj*) good value

dāi (*adj*) low

dàih-dái (*n*) younger brother

dá-jih (*v-o*) to type

dāk (*v-prt*)

dāk (*adj*) OK, all right

Dākgwok (*pw*) Germany

dākhàahn (*adj*) free, not busy

Dākmán (*n*) German (language)

dāk-mh-dāk (*ie*) is it all right?

dá-làahmkàuh (*v-o*) to play basketball

dá-móhngkàuh (*v-o*) to play tennis

dáng (*v*) to wait

dang (*n*) chair

dáng ngóh lèih gaaisiuh ... (*ie*) let me introduce ...

dáng yāt jahn/ dáng (*ie*) wait a minute

dá-tāai (*v-o*) to put on a tie

deihhá (*n*) floor

deihtit (*n*) underground railway (in Hong Kong, MTR or Mass Transit Railway)

deihtitjaahm (*n*) underground, subway (MTR) station

déng (*cl*) *classifier* for headgear

deui (*m*) pair

deuimihn (*adv*) opposite, across the road

deui mjyuh (*ie*) Sorry!

dī (*prn*) some

-dī (*prt*)

dihnchē (*n*) tram

dihnchējaahm (*n*) tram stop

dihng (*conj*) or (in questions with two alternatives)

dihnheipóu (*n*) electrical appliance store
dihnsih (*n*) television
dihnsihgēi (*n*) television set
dihnsihkehk (*n*) television drama
dihnwá (*n*) telephone
dihnyíng (*n*) film
dihp (*m*) plate
dīksí (*n*) taxi
dīksíjaahm (*n*) taxi rank
dím (*qw*) how?
dim (*n*) shop, store
dím(jūng) (*tw*) o'clock
dím maaih a? what is the price?
(*ie*)
dímsām (*n*) snacks, generally
steamed, served
in a tea-house
dímyéung (*qw*) what does he/she
look like?; how?,
what?
díp (*n*) plate
dō (*adj*) many, much
doihsyú (*n*) kangaroo
dōjeh (*ie*) thank you (for a
gift)
dōjeh saai (*ie*) thank you very
much
Dōlèuhndō (*pw*) Toronto
dōsou (*adv*) mostly
dóu (*v-prt*)
dōu (*adv*) also, still
dou (*prt*)
douh (*adv*) there
dóu-laahpsaap to empty the
(*v-o*) rubbish bin
duhk-syū (*v-o*) to study
dūng (*adj*) east
dung (*adj*) cold
Dūnggīng (*pw*) Tokyo
dūngtīn (*tw*) winter
dyún (*adj*) short

dyúnfu (*n*) shorts
faahntēng (*n*) dining room
faai (*adj*) quick; in a short
time
fāan (*v-prt*)
fāan (*v*) to return
fāan . . . (*ie*) to work at/in . . .
fāan-gūng (*v-o*) to go to work
fāan-hohk (*v-o*) to go to school
Faatgwok (*pw*) France
Faatmán (*n*) French (language)
fādim (*n*) flower shop
fan-gaau (*v-o*) to sleep
fān(jūng) (*n*) minute
fángwó (*n*) steamed shrimp
and bamboo-
shoot dumpling
fāyún (*n*) garden
fēi (*n*) ticket
fēifaatpóu (*n*) barber's shop
fēigēi (*n*) aeroplane
fēigēichèuhng airport
(*n*)
fèih (*adj*) fat
Fēileuhtbān the Philippines
(*pw*)
Fēileuhtbānwá any of the
(*n*) languages of the
Philippines
fēsīk (*adj*) brown
fóchē (*n*) train
fóchējaahm (*n*) railway station
fógei (*n*) waiter
fóng (*n*) room
fōngbihn (*adj*) convenient
fong-gūng (*v-o*) to leave work
fu (*cl*) *classifier* for
spectacles
fu (*n*) trousers/slacks
fuhgahn (*adv*) nearby
fuhkjōngdim (*n*) dress shop
fùhng (*adv*) whenever

fūisīk (*adj*)	gray		**gáu** (*num*)	nine
fūng (*cl*)	*classifier* for a letter		**gáu'ah** (*num*)	ninety (elided form)
fūng (*n*)	wind		**gauhnín** (*tw*)	last year
fūnggíng (*n*)	scenery		**gáu-yuht** (*tw*)	September
fūngsai kèuhng-	windy		**ge** (*prt*)	
gihng (*adj*)			**géi** (*adv*)	quite
fūnyìhng gwōng-	Welcome!		**géi** (*num*)	several
làhm (*ie*)			**gei** (*v*)	to send something
ga (*cl*)	*classifier* for			by post
	vehicles		**gēichèuhng** (*n*)	airport
ga (*prt*)			**geidāk** (*v*)	to remember
gāai (*n*)	street, road		**géidímjūng** (*qw*)	what time?
gāaisíh (*n*)	market		**géidō** (*qw*)	how much, how
gaaklèih (*adv*)	beside			many?
gāan (*cl*)	*classifier* for		**géidō seui** (*ie*)	how old?
	houses, rooms		**géiluhkpín** (*n*)	documentary
	and shops		**géinoih** (*qw*)	how long (a
gaau-syū (*v-o*)	to teach (in school			period of time)?
	or university)		**gei-seun** (*v-o*)	to send something
gāautūng (*n*)	transportation			by post
gafē (*n*)	coffee		**géisìh** (*qw*)	when?
gahpdáijūk (*n*)	congee with mixed		**génggān** (*n*)	scarf
	meat		**gihn** (*cl*)	*classifier* for items
gājē (*n*)	elder sister			of clothing
gakèih (*n*)	holiday		**gin** (*v*)	to see
ga la (*prt*)			**giujouh** (*v*)	to be called,
ga laak (*prt*)				named
gám . . . (*ie*)	so . . ., then . . .		**gó** (*dem*)	that
gam (*adv*)	so, such		**go** (*cl*)	*classifier* for
gāmmáahn (*tw*)	this evening,			people, roundish
	tonight			objects such as
gāmnín (*tw*)	this year			apples and
gam noih (*ie*)	such a long time			custard tarts,
gāmyaht (*tw*)	today			containers such
gámyéung (*adv*)	in this way, like			as bowls and
	this			cups, physical
-gán (*asp*)	*progressive aspect*			spaces such as
	marker			rooms and
Gānàhdaaih	Canada			airports, and
(pw)				many abstract
gānjyuh (*adv*)	and then			concepts such as
gāsī (*n*)	furniture			measures of time

go (*num*) — unit
góbīn (*adv*) — over there
gòh-gō (*n*) — elder brother
gokdāk (*v*) — to feel
gōn(chou) (*adj*) — dry
góng (*v*) — to speak
góng-gán (*ie*) — line engaged (on the phone)
gōnjehng (*adj*) — clean
gōu (*adj*) — tall, high
gōudaaih (*adj*) — big (in body build)
gōu-gōu-sau-sau (*ie*) — tall and thin
gōujāanghàaih (*n*) — high-heeled shoe
Gūnghéi faat-chòih (*ie*) — greeting at Chinese New Year
gūngsī (*n*) — office
gūngyàhnfóng (*n*) — servant's room
gwai (*adj*) — expensive
gwai (*adv*) — honorably
gwāt (*n*) — a fifteen-minute unit of time
-gwo (*prt*)
-gwo (*asp*) — *experiential aspect marker*
gwokgā (*n*) — country
Gwóngjāu (*pw*) — Guangzhou/Canton
Gwóngjāuwá/ Gwóngdūngwá (*n*) — Cantonese (language)
hàahng (*v*) — to walk
hàahng-gāai (*v-o*) — to go window-shopping
hàahnghōi-jó (*ie*) — not in, gone out
hàahng-louh (*v-o*) — to walk
hàaih (*n*) — shoe

hàaihpóu (*n*) — shoe shop
haakfóng (*n*) — guest room
hāaksīk (*adj*) — black
haaktēng (*n*) — sitting room
hāgáau (*n*) — steamed shrimp dumpling
háh (*asp*) — *delimitative aspect marker*
hah (*adj*) — next (week, month or year)
hah (*prep*) — below, under
hahjau (*tw*) — afternoon
hahmihn (*adv*) — under, beneath
hahtīn (*tw*) — summer
Hahwāiyìh (*pw*) — Hawaii
hái (*v*) — to be in/at
hái (*prep*) — in/at a place, at a time
hái douh sihk (*ie*) — eat-in
haih (*v*) — to be
haih nē (*ie*) — by the way
hauhmihn (*adv*) — behind
hauhsāang (*adj*) — young
háuseun (*n*) — message
héifūn (*v*) — to like
héi-sān (*v-o*) — to get up
heiwān (*n*) — temperature
heiyún (*n*) — cinema, movies
heui (*v*) — to go
heui-gāai (*v-o*) — to go out
heui-léuihhàhng (*v-o*) — to go traveling
Hēunggóng (*pw*) — Hong Kong
hēungjīu (*n*) — banana
hēungpín (*n*) — jasmine tea
hingcheui (*n*) — interest
hohkhaauh (*n*) — school
hohksāang (*n*) — student
Hòhngwok (*pw*) — Korea

hòhnláahng (*adj*)	cold	**jek** (*cl*)	*classifier* for single pieces of footwear, gloves, windows, animals, boats, dumplings, bananas and hot-dogs
Hòhnmán (*n*)	Korean (language)		
hóitāan (*n*)	beach		
hōi-wúi (*v-o*)	to be at/have a meeting		
hólohk (*n*)	cola		
honbóubāau (*n*)	hamburger		
hóu (*adj*)	good, decent		
hóu (*adv*)	very, quite	**jeui** (*adv*)	most
hòuhjí (*n*)	a ten-cent unit of money	**jeui hauh** (*adv*)	finally
		jeui hóu ... (*ie*)	it might be better to ...
houh(máh) (*n*)	number	**jeuk** (*v*)	to wear
hóusihk (*adj*)	delicious	**jēung** (*cl*)	*classifier* for pieces of furniture with flat surfaces and for other flat objects
hóutái (*adj*)	good to see (of a film or television program)		
hóutīn (*adj*)	fine, sunny (weather)	**jī** (*cl*)	*classifier* for long, slender objects such as pens
hóuwáan (*adj*)	fun to do, fun to visit, etc.		
hóyíh (*mv*)	can, could	**jī(dou)** (*v*)	to know
hùhngsīk (*adj*)	red	**jih** (*n*)	a five-minute unit of time
hūngyàuh (*n*)	air-mail		
ja (*prt*)		**jihgéi** (*prn*)	self
jáau (*v*)	to give as change	**jíngchàih** (*adj*)	neat (in dress)
jaauhyúh (*n*)	shower (of rain)	**jīsí honbóubāau** (*n*)	cheeseburger
jā-chē (*v-o*)	to drive a car		
jái (*n*)	son	**jísīk** (*adj*)	purple, violet
jān haih (*ie*)	really	**jīujóu** (*tw*)	early morning
jāp (*v*)	to tidy up	**-jó** (*asp*)	*perfective aspect marker*
jāp-chòhng (*v-o*)	to make the bed		
		jóbīn (*adv*)	on the left
jāp-tói (*v-o*)	to clear the table	**joi** (*adv*)	and, again
jáu (*v*)	to leave	**jóuchāan** (*n*)	breakfast
jāu (*n*)	continent	**jouh** (*v*)	to do; is shown (of a film or television program)
jauh (*conj*)	(if ...) then		
jāuwàih (*n*)	surroundings		
jē (*n*)	umbrella		
je (*v*)	to borrow	**jouh-wahnduhng** (*v-o*)	to play sports
jèih-jē (*n*)	elder sister		
jēk (*prt*)		**juhng** (*adv*)	still; in addition

jūnggāan (*adv*) in the middle, between
júngguhng (*adv*) in total, altogether
Jūnggwok (*pw*) China
jūnghohk (*n*) secondary school
júngjaahm (*n*) terminal, terminus
Jūngmán (*n*) Chinese (language)
jūngtàuh (*n*) hour
jūngyi (*v*) to like
jyú (*v*) to cook
jyú-faahn (*v-o*) to cook a meal
jyuh (*v*) to live
jyún (*v*) to become, to turn; to change
jyun (*v*) to change (transport)
jyú-yéhsihk (*v-o*) to cook (food)
kàhmmáahn (*tw*) yesterday evening, last night
kàhmyaht (*tw*) yesterday
káhn (*adj*) near
kāp-chàhn (*v-o*) to vacuum-clean
kèihsaht (*adv*) actually
kèihyihgwó (*n*) kiwifruit
kèuhnggihng (*adj*) strong
kéuih (*prn*) he, him, she, her, it
kéuihdeih (*prn*) they, them
kwàhn (*n*) dress, skirt
lā (*prt*)
la (*prt*)
laahm (*v*) to put on (a scarf)
làahmsīk (*adj*) blue
láahng (*adj*) cold
laahpsaap (*n*) rubbish
laak (*prt*)
lāangsāam (*n*) woollen sweater/jumper
làh (*prt*)
láihbaai (*n*) week

láihbaai-luhk (*tw*) Saturday
láihbaai-ńgh (*tw*) Friday
láihbaai-sāam (*tw*) Wednesday
láihbaai-sei (*tw*) Thursday
láihbaai-yaht (*tw*) Sunday
láihbaai-yāt (*tw*) Monday
láihbaai-yih (*tw*) Tuesday
laihjī (*n*) lychee
láihmaauh (*n*) good manners
lāu (*n*) coat
làuh (*v*) to stay, to leave something behind (e.g. a message)
léi (*n*) pear
lèih (*prep*) from
lèihdóu (*n*) outlying island
leng (*adj*) pretty; fresh (of fruit)
lengjái (*adj*) handsome
Lèuhndēun (*pw*) London
léuhng (*num*) two
lèuhng (*adj*) cool
lèuhnghàaih (*n*) sandals
leuhtsī (*n*) lawyer
lèuihbouh (*n*) thunderstorm
léuihmihn (*adv*) inside
lìhng (*num*) zero
lìhng hah (*ie*) below zero (of temperatures)
lihngngoih (*adv*) besides
līk jáu (*ie*) take-away
lō (*prt*)
lohk (*v*) to fall (rain, snow)
Lohkchaamgēi (*pw*) Los Angeles
lohk-syut (*v-o*) to snow
lohk-yúh (*v-o*) to rain

lohng-sāam (v-o)	to hang clothes out to dry	**māmìh** (n)	mum
lóuh (adj)	old	**mān** (m)	dollar
lóuhbáan (n)	boss	**mātyéh** (qw)	what?
lóuhsī (n)	teacher	**mdāk a** (ie)	not OK
luhk (num)	six	**meih** (adv)	not yet
luhk'ah (num)	sixty (elided form)	**Méihgwok** (pw)	the USA
luhksīk (adj)	green	**mèihyúh** (n)	light rain, drizzle
luhkyíngdáai (n)	video-tape	**méng** (n)	name
luhkyínggēi (n)	video-recorder	**mgin-jó** (ie)	(gone) missing
luhk-yuht (tw)	June	**mgōi** (ie)	thank you (for a favour); please
lùhng (n/m)	bamboo basket for steaming dimsum	**mgōi màaih-dāan** (ie)	The bill, please!
lùhngjéng (n)	Lung-ching (light) tea	**mgōi saai** (ie)	Thanks a lot!
		mgōi tái-sou (ie)	The bill, please!
m- (adv)	negative marker	**mhái douh** (ie)	not here
máahn (tw)	evening	**mhaih géi** (adv)	not that much
maahn (num)	ten thousand	**mihnbāaupóu** (n)	bakery
máahnfaahn (n)	dinner		
maahn-máan (adv)	slowly	**mìhngseunpín** (n)	postcard
máaih (v)	to buy	**mjī** (v)	to wonder
maaih (v)	to sell	**mòhng** (adj)	busy
máaih-fēi (v-o)	to buy tickets	**móhngkàuh-páak** (n)	tennis racket
máaih-sung (v-o)	to buy food (for meals)	**mōnggwó** (n)	mango
máaih-yéh (v-o)	to go shopping	**móu** (n)	hat, cap
maat-chēung (v-o)	to clean the windows	**móuh** (v)	negative of **yáuh**
		mouh (n)	fog
màhfàahn (adj)	problematic, troublesome	**móuh mahntàih** (ie)	No problem!
màh-mā (n)	mother	**msái** (mv)	need not
màh-má-déi (ie)	not that much	**msái jáau laak** (ie)	Keep the change!
Máhnèihlāai (pw)	Manila	**msái mgōi** (ie)	Not at all! (polite response to **mgōi**)
Màhnfa-Jūngsām (pw)	Cultural Centre		
màhngeuihdim (n)	stationery shop	**muhkgwā** (n)	papaya
		mùhnháu (n)	entrance
maht (n)	sock	**(mùih-)múi** (n)	younger sister
máhtàuh (n)	ferry pier	**nàahm** (adj)	south
mahtwàhn (adj)	cloudy	**nàahmjái** (n)	boy, young man

nàahmyán (*n*)   man
Náusāilàahn (*pw*)   New Zealand
Náuyeuk (*pw*)   New York
nē (*prt*)
nē (*i*)
néih (*prn*)   you (singular)
néihdeih (*prn*)   you (plural)
néih hóu (*ie*)   How are you?
néui (*n*)   daughter
néuihjái (*n*)   girl, young woman
néuihyán (*n*)   woman
ngáahngéng (*n*)   spectacles
ngāam-ngāam (*adv*)   just, a short while ago
ngāam saai laak (*ie*)   That's great!
ngàhnbāau (*n*)   purse
ngàhnhòhng (*n*)   bank
ngái(sai) (*adj*)   short (in body build)
ngàuhjáifu (*n*)   jeans
ngàuhyuhkjūk (*n*)   congee with beef
nǵh (*num*)   five
nǵh'ah (*num*)   fifty (elided form)
nǵh-yuht (*tw*)   May
ngóh (*prn*)   I, me
ngóhdeih (*prn*)   we, us
ngoihtou (*n*)   jacket
ngūk (*n*)   house, flat
ngūkkéi (*n*)   home
ngūkkéiyàhn (*n*)   family member
nī (*dem*)   this
nībīn (*adv*)   over here
nīdouh (*adv*)   here
nìhn (*n/m*)   year
noih (*adj*)   long (time)
noihsin (*n*)   telephone extension
nyúhn (*adj*)   warm
ōnlohkyí (*n*)   easy chair

Oujāu (*pw*)   Australia
páau-bouh (*v-o*)   to run (for exercise)
páaubouhhàaih (*n*)   running shoe
pàhngyáuh (*n*)   friend
pèhng (*adj*)   cheap
pèihhàaih (*n*)   leather shoe
pìhnggwó (*n*)   apple
pìhngsìh (*adv*)   usually, generally
pìhngyàuh (*n*)   surface mail
-póu (*n*)   shop, store
Póutūngwá (*n*)   Putonghua/ Mandarin (language)
sā'ah (*num*)   thirty (elided form)
saai (*v-prt*)
sāam (*n*)   clothes
sāam (*num*)   three
Sāamfàahnsíh (*pw*)   San Francisco
sāam-yuht (*tw*)   March
sāanggwó (*n*)   fruit
sāanggwódong (*n*)   fruit-stall
sāangyaht faailohk (*ie*)   Happy birthday!
sahp (*num*)   ten
sahp-maahn (*num*)   hundred thousand
sahp-yāt-yuht (*tw*)   November
sahp-yih-yuht (*tw*)   December
sahp-yuht (*tw*)   October
sái (*v*)   to wash
sāi (*adj*)   west
sai (*adj*)   small
Sāibāanngàh (*pw*)   Spain
Sāibāanngàh-mán (*n*)   Spanish (language)

sái-díp (v-o)	to wash the plates	sihk (v)	to eat
sāigwā (n)	water-melon	sihk-jóuchāan (v-o)	to have breakfast
sāijōng (n)	men's suit		
sāijōngfu (n)	trousers, slacks	sihk-máahn-faahn (v-o)	to have dinner
sailóu (n)	younger brother		
sái-sāam (v-o)	to wash clothes	sihk-ngaan (v-o)	to have lunch
sái-wún (v-o)	to wash up, to wash the bowls	sihk-yéh (v-o)	to eat
		sihou (n)	hobby
sānmán (n)	news	sīk (mv)	can, to know how to
sānnìhn faailohk (ie)	Happy New Year!		
		sīk (n)	color
sāp (adj)	humid	Sīknèih (pw)	Sydney
sau (adj)	thin	sīmàhn (adj)	smart (in dress)
sáudói (n)	handbag	sīmaht (n)	pantyhose
sáumaht (n)	glove	sīn (adv)	first, firstly
sáusīn (adv)	first of all	sing (v)	to be surnamed
sāyùh (n)	shark	singdaan faailohk (ie)	Merry Christmas!
sèhng (adj/adv)	whole; fully, completely		
		sīngkèih (n)	week
sei (num)	four	sīngkèih-luhk (tw)	Saturday
sei'ah (num)	forty (elided form)		
sei-yuht (tw)	April	sīngkèih-ńgh (tw)	Friday
seuhng (adj)	previous (week, month or year)		
		sīngkèih-sāam (tw)	Wednesday
seuhng (adv)	on, above, over		
Seuhnghói (pw)	Shanghai	sīngkèih-sei (tw)	Thursday
Seuhnghóiwá (n)	Shanghainese (language)	sīngkèih-yaht (tw)	Sunday
seuhngjau (tw)	in the morning	sīngkèih-yāt (tw)	Monday
seuhngmihn (adv)	on, above	sīngkèih-yih (tw)	Tuesday
		sīnji (adv)	only then
séui (n)	water	sīnsāang (n)	Mr, teacher, husband
seui (n)	years of age		
séuibūi (n)	(drinking) glass	síubā (n)	minibus
seuihfóng (n)	bedroom	síuhohk (n)	primary school
seun (n)	letter	síujé (n)	Miss, young lady
séung (mv)	to want to, to wish to	síumáai (n)	steamed pork dumpling
séungdeui-sāpdouh (n)	relative humidity		
		síusām (adj/adv)	careful(ly)
		síusíu (adj/adv)	a little, some
sēutsāam (n)	shirt, blouse	sō (n)	comb
sìhgaan (n)	time	sōfá (n)	sofa

sou-deih (v-o) to sweep the floor
sóyíh (conj) so, as
sung (n) food for cooking a meal
syū (n) book
syūdim (n) bookstore
syūfóng (n) study
syūfuhk (adj) comfortable
syūgá (n) bookcase, bookshelves
syūgúk (n) bookstore
syùhn (n) boat, ferry
syùhtíu (n) chips, French fries
syun (v) can be regarded as . . .
syut (n) snow
-táai (n) Mrs
tāai (n) (neck-)tie
taai-táai (n) Mrs, wife
taam-pàhngyáuh to visit friends (v-o)
tái (v) to see, to watch, to look at, to read
tái-boují (v-o) to read the newspaper
tái-dihnsih (v-o) to watch television
tái-dihnyíng (v-o) to watch a film
tái-hei (v-o) to watch a film
tàihjí (n) grape
tái-jūkkàuh (v-o) to watch football, soccer
tái-syū (v-o) to read (books)
táiyuhk (n) sports
tàuhfaat (n) hair
tek-jūkkàuh (v-o) to play football, soccer
tēng (v) to listen (to)
tēng (n) sitting room, dining room
tēng-dihnwá (v-o) to answer the phone

tēng-sāuyāmgēi (v-o) to listen to the radio
tēng-yāmngohk (v-o) to listen to music
tìm (adv) in addition
tìnchìhng (adj) fine (weather)
tìngmáahn (tw) tomorrow evening/night
tìngyaht (tw) tomorrow
tìngyaht gin lā (ie) See you tomorrow!
tìnhei (n) weather
tìnyām (adj) overcast
tìsēut (n) T-shirt
tìuh (cl) classifier for long slender objects such as trousers, streets and sharks
tiu-móuh (v-o) to dance
tōháai (n) slipper
tòhnggwó (n) sweets
tòhnggwódim (n) sweet shop
tòihfūng (n) typhoon
Tòihwāan (pw) Taiwan
tong-sāam (v-o) to iron clothes
tou (cl) classifier for a matching suit of clothes
tòuhsyūgún (n) library
toujōng (n) ladies' suit
tùhng (prep) for, with
tùhng(màaih) (conj) and
tùhnghohk (n) classmate, schoolmate
tùhngsih (n) colleague
tūngsèuhng (adv) usually
wā (i) interjection showing surprise
wá language

wàahngíng (n)	the environment
wáan-yàuhheigēi (v-o)	to play electronic games
wah ... tēng (v)	to tell
wahnduhng (n)	sports
wàhntānmihn (n)	won-ton noodles
wái (cl)	classifier for people
wái (ie)	Hello! (greeting on the phone)
wán (v)	to look for
Wāngōwàh (pw)	Vancouver
wānnyúhn (adj)	warm
wihngchìh (n)	swimming pool
wo (prt)	
wòhngsīk (adj)	yellow
wùh (m)	pot
wùhsōu (n)	moustache, beard
wúih (mv)	shall, will
wūjōu (adj)	dirty
wún (n/m)	bowl
y'ah (num)	twenty (elided form)
yàhn (n)	person, people
yaht (n)	day
Yahtbún (pw)	Japan
Yahtmán (n)	Japanese (language)
yám (v)	to drink
yám-bējáu (v-o)	to go for a beer
yám-chàh (v-o)	to have dimsum in a tea-house
yám-gafē (v-o)	to have coffee
yám-jáu (v-o)	to go for a drink
yāmngohk (n)	music
yāmngohkwúi (n)	concert
yāmtīn (adj)	overcast
yám-yéh (v-o)	to go for a drink
Yandouh (pw)	India

Yandouhwá (n)	any of the languages of India
yānwaih (conj)	because
yāt (num)	one
yātdihng (adv)	sure, surely
yātlouh seuhnfūng (ie)	Have a good flight!
yāt yeuhng (adj)	the same
yāt-yuht (tw)	January
yáuh (v)	to have
yáuh (v)	there is/are
yàuh (prep)	from
yauh (adv)	also
yauhbīn (adv)	on the right
yàuhchoi (n)	vegetables with oyster sauce
yàuhgáan (n)	aerogram
yáuh géi daaih (ie)	how old?
yáuh móuh (v)	is/are there?
yàuh-séui (v-o)	to swim
yéh (n)	thing
yehmáahn (tw)	evening, night
yeuhkfòhng (n)	drugstore
yeuhng (cl)	classifier for events, things in general
yeuhng (n)	kind, sort
yéung (n)	appearance
yí (i)	interjection showing mild surprise
yí (n)	chair
Yidaaihleih (pw)	Italy
Yidaaihleihmán (n)	Italian (language)
yih (num)	two
yìhgā (adv)	now
(yìhm)yiht (adj)	hot
yìhnhauh (adv)	and then, later on

yihtgáu (*n*)	hot-dog
yih-yuht (*tw*)	February
yīnggōi (*mv*)	should
Yīnggwok (*pw*)	England, the UK
Yīngmán (*n*)	English (language)
yíng-séung (*v-o*)	to take pictures
yíngyan (*v*)	to make photo-copies
Yínngaih-Hohkyún (*pw*)	Academy for Performing Arts
yīsāng (*n*)	doctor

yiu (*v*)	to need, to want, to take (time), to cost
yiu (*mv*)	must, to have to
yúh (*n*)	rain
yuhchāak (*v*)	to predict
yùhdáanmihn (*n*)	fish-ball noodles
yùhláuhbāau (*n*)	fishburger
yúhn (*adj*)	far
yùhn (*v-prt*)	
yuht (*n*)	month

English–Cantonese glossary

The respective classifiers are given in square brackets where appropriate.

above	seuhng(mihn)	back (to go/to give)	fāan
Academy for Performing Arts	Yínngaih-Hohkyún	bakery	mihnbāaupóu [gāan]
actually	kèihsaht	banana	hēungjīu [jek]
addition, in	juhng, tīm	bank	ngàhnhòhng [gāan]
aerogram	yàuhgáan [go]		
aeroplane	fēigēi [ga]	barbecued-pork bun	chāsīubāau [go]
afternoon	hahjau		
again	joi	barber's shop	fēifaatpóu [gāan]
ago	chìhn	basketball	làahmkàuh
air-mail	hūngyàuh	bath, to have/take a	chūng-lèuhng
airport	(fēi)gēichèuhng [go]		
		bathroom	chūnglèuhngfóng [gāan]
all right	dāk		
also	yauh, dōu, tīm	be, to	haih
altogether, in total	júngguhng	beach	hóitāan [go]
		beard	wùhsōu [jāp]
and	tùhng(màaih)	be at/in (place), to	hái
and then	gānjyuh, yìhnhauh		
		because	yānwaih
answer the phone, to	tēng-dihnwá	become, to	jyún
		bed	chòhng [jēung]
appearance	yéung	bed, to make the	jāp-chòhng
apple	pìhnggwó [go]		
approximately	daaihyeuk	bedroom	seuihfóng [gāan]
April	sei-yuht	behind	hauhmihn
at (a place) (to be)	hái	Beijing	Bākgīng
		below zero	lìhng hah
August	baat-yuht	beneath	hah(mihn)
Australia	Oujāu	beside	gaaklèih

besides	lihngngoih	bye-bye	bāai-baai
better, it might be . . . to	jeui hóu	called, to be	giujouh
		can (to be able to)	sīk
between	jūnggāan		
bicycle	dāanchē [ga]	can (may)	hóyíh
big (in body build)	gōudaaih	Canada	Gānàhdaaih
		Canton	Gwóngjāu
bill	dāan [jēung]	Cantonese (language)	Gwóngjāuwá/ Gwóngdūngwá
(the) bill, please!	mgōi màaih-dāan/ mgōi tái-sou	cap	móu [déng]
black	hāaksīk	car	chē [ga]
blouse	sēutsāam [gihn]	careful(ly)	síusām
blow, to	chēui	casual (in dress)	chèuihbín
blue	làahmsīk	chair	dang, yí [jēung]
boat	syùhn [jek]	chair, dining	chāandang, chāanyí [jēung]
book	syū [bún]		
bookcase/ bookshelves	syūgá [go]	chair, easy	ōnlohkyí [jēung]
		change (transport), to	jyun
bookstore	syūdim, syūgúk [gāan]	change (money), to give	jáau
borrow, to	je		
boss	lóuhbáan [go]	cheap	pèhng
bowl	wún [go]	cheeseburger	jīsí honbóubāau [go]
boy	nàahmjái [go]		
breakfast	jóuchāan [go]	China	Jūnggwok
breakfast, to have	sihk-jóuchāan	Chinese (language)	Jūngmán
bring, to	daai	chips/French fries	syùhtíu
brother, elder	daaihlóu, gòh-gō [go]	Chiu Chow dialect	Chìuhjāuwá
brother, younger	dàih-dái, sailóu [go]	cinema	heiyún [gāan]
brown	fēsīk	City Hall Concert Hall	Daaihwuihtòhng- Yāmngohktēng
bus	bāsí [ga]	classmate	tùhnghohk [go]
bus stop	bāsíjaahm [go]	clean	gōnjehng
busy	mòhng	clean the windows, to	maat-chēung
but	bātgwo		
buy, to	máaih	clear the table, to	jāp-tói
buy food (for meals), to	máaih-sung		
buy tickets, to	máaih-fēi	clothes	sāam [gihn]
by the way	haih nē	cloudy	mahtwàhn

coat	**lāu [gihn]**
coffee	**gafē**
coffee table	**chàhgēi [jēung]**
cola	**hólohk**
cold	**dung, (hòhng)láang**
colleague	**tùhngsih [go]**
color	**sīk**
comb	**sō [bá]**
come, to	**lèih**
comfortable	**syūfuhk**
comparatively	**béigaau**
completely	**saai, sèhng**
concert	**yāmngohkwúi [go]**
congee with beef	**ngàuhyuhkjūk**
congee with mixed meat	**gahpdáijūk**
continent	**jāu [go]**
convenient	**fōngbihn**
cook, to	**jyú(-yéhsihk)**
cook a meal, to	**jyú-faahn**
cool	**(chīng)lèuhng**
cost, to	**yiu**
could, might	**hóyíh**
country	**gwokgā [go]**
cuisine	**choi**
Cultural Centre	**Màhnfa-Jūngsām**
cup	**būi, chàhbūi [go, jek]**
custard tart	**daahntāat [go]**
cycle, to	**cháai-dāanchē**
dance, to	**tiu-móu**
daughter	**néui [go]**
day	**yaht**
day before yesterday	**chìhnyaht**
December	**sahp-yih-yuht**
decent	**hóu**
delicious	**hóusihk**
diagonally across	**chèhdeuimihn**
dining chair	**chāangdang, chāanyí [jēung]**
dining room	**faahntēng [gāan]**
dining table	**chāantói [jēung]**
dinner	**máahnfaahn**
dinner, to have	**sihk-máahnfaahn**
dirty	**wūjōu**
do, to	**jouh**
doctor	**yīsāng [go]**
documentary	**géiluhkpín [chēut]**
dollar	**mān**
dozen	**dā**
dress	**kwàhn [tìuh]**
dress shop	**fuhkjōngdim [gāan]**
drink, to	**yám**
drive (a vehicle), to	**jā-chē**
drizzle	**mèihyúh**
drugstore	**yeuhkfòhng [gāan]**
dry	**gōn(chou)**
early morning	**jiujóu**
east	**dūng**
easy chair	**ōnlohkyí [jēung]**
eat, to	**sihk**
eat-in	**hái douh sihk**
eight	**baat**
eighty	**baat-sahp, baat'ah**
elder brother	**daaihlóu, gòh-gō [go]**
elder sister	**jèhjē, gājē [go]**
electrical appliance store	**dihnheipóu [gāan]**
empty the rubbish bin, to	**dóu-laahpsaap**
England	**Yīnggwok**
English (language)	**Yīngmán**
entrance	**mùhnháu [go]**
environment	**wàahngíng**
Europe	**Aujāu**

evening	yehmáahn	(language)	
evening, this	gāmmáahn	French fries,	syùhtíu
every (Sunday,	fùhng (sīngkèih-	chips	
Monday . . .)	yaht, sīngkèih-	fresh (of fruit)	leng
	yāt . . .)	Friday	sīngkèih-ńgh,
everyone	daaihgā		láihbaai-ńgh
expensive	gwai	friend	pàhngyáuh [go]
extension,	noihsin	from (a place)	lèih, yàuh
telephone		front of, in	chìhnmihn
fall, to (of rain,	lohk	fruit	sāanggwó [go]
snow)		fruit-stall	sāanggwódong
family member	ngūkkéiyàhn [go]		[go]
far	yúhn	fully	sèhng
fat	fèih	fun, having	hóuwáan
father	bàh-bā [go]	furniture	gāsī
February	yih-yuht	garage	chēfòhng [go]
feel, to	gokdāk	garden	fāyún [go]
ferry	syùhn [jek]	generally	tūngsèuhng,
ferry pier	máhtàuh [go]		pìhngsìh
fifty	ńgh-sahp, ńgh'ah	German	Dākmán
film, movie	dihnyíng, hei	(language)	
	[chēut]	Germany	Dākgwok
finally	jeui hauh	get up, to	héi-sān
fine, sunny	hóutīn, tīnchìhng	girl	néuihjái [go]
(weather)		give, to	béi
first (of all)	sáusīn	give (as	jáau
fish-ball noodles	yùhdángmihn	change), to	
fishburger	yùhláuhbāau [go]	glass, drinking	séuibūi [go, jek]
five	ńgh	glasses	ngáahngéng [go,
floor	deihhá [go]		fu]
flower shop	fādim [gāan]	glove	sáumaht [jek]
fog	mouh	go, to	heui
food (cuisine)	choi	go for a beer, to	yám-bējáu
food (for	sung	go for a drink,	yám-yéh, yám-jáu
cooking)		to	
football, soccer	jūkkàuh	gone out	hàahnghōi-jó
for	tùhng	go out, to	chēut-gāai, heui-
forty	sei-sahp, sei'ah		gāai
four	sei	go shopping, to	máaih-yéh
France	Faatgwok	go to school, to	fāan-hohk
free, not busy	dākhàahn	go to work, to	fāan-gūng
French	Faatmán	go traveling, to	heui-léuihhàhng

good	hóu	horse-racing	choimáh
good (of a film	hóutái	hot	(yìhm)yiht
or television		hot-dog	yihtgáu [jek, go]
program)		hour	jūngtàuh [go]
good value	dái	house	ngūk [gāan]
grape	tàihjí [lāp]	how	dím(yéung)
gray	fūisīk	How are you?	néih hóu
green	luhksīk	how long (a	géinoih
Guangzhou/	Gwóngjāu	period of time)?	
Canton		how much, how	géidō
guest room	haakfóng [gāan]	many?	
hair	tàuhfaat	how old?	géidō seui/yáuh
half	bun		géi daaih
hamburger	honbóubāau [go]	humid	(chìuh)sāp
handbag	sáudói [go]	hundred	baak
handsome	lengjái	hundred	sahp-maahn
hang clothes	lohng-sāam	thousand	
out to dry, to		husband	sīnsāang
Happy birthday!	sāangyaht faailohk	I	ngóh
Happy New	sānnìhn faailohk	in (a place)	hái
Year!		(to be)	
hat	móu [déng]	India	Yandouh
have, to	yáuh	Indian	Yandouhwá
Have a good	yātlouh seuhnfūng	language(s)	
flight!		inside	léuihmihn
have to, to	yiu	interest	hingcheui
Hawaii	Hahwāiyìh	introduce, to	gaaisiuh
he	kéuih	invite, to	chéng
Hello! (on the	wái	iron clothes, to	tong-sāam
phone)		it	kéuih
help, to	bōng(sáu)	Italian	Yidaaihleihmán
her	kéuih	(language)	
here	nīdouh	Italy	Yidaaihleih
herself	kéuih jihgéi	jacket	ngoihtou [gihn]
high	gōu	January	yāt-yuht
him	kéuih	Japan	Yahtbún
himself	kéuih jihgéi	Japanese	Yahtmán
hit, to	dá	(language)	
hobby	sihou	jasmine tea	hēungpín
holiday	gakèih	jeans	ngàuhjáifu [tìuh]
home	ngūkkéi [go]	July	chāt-yuht
Hong Kong	Hēunggóng	jumper, sweater	lāahngsāam [gihn]

June	luhk-yuht	local (in Hong Kong)	búngóng
just, a short while ago	ngāam-ngāam	London	Lèuhndēun
kangaroo	doihsyú [jek]	long	chèuhng
Keep the change!	msái jáau lak	long (time)	noih
		look at, to	tái
kind, sort	yeuhng	look for, to	wán
kitchen	chyùhfóng [gāan]	Los Angeles	Lohkchaamgēi
kiwifruit	kèihyihgwó [go]	lost	mgin-jó
know, to	jī(dou)	low	dāi
know how to, to	sīk	lunch, to have	sihk-ngaan
Korea	Hòhngwok	Lung-ching tea	lùhngjéng
Korean (language)	Hòhnmán	lychee	laihjī [lāp]
		mail, to	gei
language	wá [júng], -mán	man	nàahmyán [go]
large	daaih	Mandarin (language)	Póutūngwá
last night	chàhmmáahn, kàhmmáahn	mango	mōnggwó [go]
last year	gauhnín	Manila	Máhnèihlāai
later on	yìhnhauh	manners, good	láihmaauh
lawyer	leuhtsī [go]	many	dō
leave, to	jáu	March	sāam-yuht
leave (behind) (e.g. a message), to	làuh	market	gāaisíh [go]
		May	nģh-yuht
		may I ask	chíng mahn
leave home, to	chēut-mùhnháu	me	ngóh
leave work, to	fong-gūng	meeting, to be at/have a	hōi-wúi
left, on the	jóbīn		
letter	seun [fūng]	Merry Christmas!	singdaan faailohk
library	tòuhsyūgún [go]	message	háuseun [go]
like, to	jūngyi, héifūn	middle, in the	jūnggāan
like this	gámyéung	midnight, after midnight	bunyeh
line engaged (on the phone)	góng-gán	million	baak-maahn
listen (to), to	tēng	minibus	síubā [ga]
listen to music, to	tēng-yāmngohk	minute	fān(jūng)
		Miss	síujé
listen to the radio, to	tēng-sāuyāmgēi	missing	mgin-jó
		Monday	sīngkèih-yāt, láihbaai-yāt
little, a	síusíu		
live, to	jyuh	money	chín

month	**yuht [go]**	not in	**hàahnghōi-jó**
month before last	**chìhn go yuht**	not that much	**màh-má-déi,**
more	**-dī; juhng**		**mhaih géi**
morning	**seuhngjau**	not yet	**meih**
morning, early	**jīujóu**	November	**sahp-yāt-yuht**
most	**jeui**	now	**yìhgā**
mostly	**dōsou**	number	**houh(máh) [go]**
mother	**màh-mā [go]**	o'clock	**dím(jūng)**
moustache	**wùhsōu [pit]**	October	**sahp-yuht**
Mr	**sīnsāang**	office	**gūngsī [gāan]**
Mrs	**(taai-)táai**	OK	**dāk**
much	**dō**	old	**lóuh**
music	**yāmngohk**	on	**seuhng(mihn)**
must, to have to	**yiu**	one	**yāt**
myself	**ngóh jihgéi**	opposite, across	**deuimihn**
name	**méng**	the road	
named, to be	**giujouh**	or (in questions	**dihng**
near	**káhn**	with two	
nearby	**fuhgahn**	alternatives)	
neat	**jíngchàih**	orange	**cháang [go]**
neck-tie	**tāai [tìuh]**	orange (color)	**cháangsīk**
need, to	**yiu**	orange juice	**cháangjāp**
need not	**msái**	ourselves	**ngóhdeih jihgéi**
New York	**Náuyeuk**	outlying island	**lèihdóu [go]**
New Zealand	**Náusāilàahn**	outside	**chēutmihn**
news	**sānmán**	overcast	**yāmtīn, tīnyām**
newspaper	**boují [jēung]**	overcoat	**daaihlāu [gihn]**
next month	**hah go yuht**	over here	**nībīn**
next week	**hah go**	over there	**góbīn**
	láihbaai/sīngkèih	packet	**bāau**
next year	**hah (yāt) nín**	pair	**deui**
night	**(yeh)máahn**	Pakistan	**Bāgēisītáan**
nine	**gáu**	pantyhose	**sīmaht [deui]**
ninety	**gáu-sahp, gáu'ah**	papaya	**muhkgwā [go]**
No problem!	**móuh mahntàih**	Paris	**Bālàih**
north	**bāk**	pay, to	**béi-chín**
not	**m-, -mh-**	pear	**léi [go]**
Not at all!	**msái mgōi**	Peking	**Bākgīng**
(polite re-		pen	**bāt [jī]**
sponse to		person, people	**yàhn [go]**
mgōi)		Philippine	**Fēileuhtbānwá**
not here	**mhái douh**	language(s)	

Philippines, the **Fēileuhtbān**
photocopies, to **yíngyan**
  make
pictures, to take **yíng-séung**
pier **máhtàuh [go]**
pineapple **bōlòh [go]**
plate (measure) **dihp**
plate (object) **díp [jek]**
play a ballgame, **dá-bō**
  to
play basketball, **dá-làahmkàuh**
  to
play electronic **wáan-yàuhheigēi**
  games, to
play football, **tek-jùkkàuh**
  soccer, to
play sports, to **jouh-wahnduhng**
play tennis, to **dá-móhngkàuh**
Please . . . **mgōi . . .**
plum **boulām [go]**
pork dumpling **sīumáai [go, jek]**
post, to **gei**
postcard **mìhngseunpín**
  [jēung]
pot (for tea) **wùh**
pound (weight) **bohng**
predict, to **yuhchāak**
pretty **leng**
previous (week, **seuhng**
  month, year)
Pu-erh tea **bóuléi**
purple **jísīk**
purse **ngàhnbāau [go]**
put on (a scarf), **laahm**
  to
put on (spec- **daai**
  tacles, cap
  or hat), to
put on a tie, to **dá-tāai**
Putonghua **Póutūngwá**
quick **faai**
quite **géi, hóu**

radio **sāuyāmgēi [ga, go]**
railway station **fóchējaahm [go]**
rain **yúh**
rain, to **lohk-yúh**
read, to **tái(-syū)**
really **jān haih**
red **hùhngsīk**
relative **sēungdeui-**
  humidity **sāpdouh**
remember, to **geidāk**
report **bougou [go]**
return, to **fāan**
ride a bicycle, to **cháai-dānchē**
right, on the **yauhbīn**
room **fóng [gāan, go],**
  tēng [go]
roughly, **daaihyeuk**
  approximately
rubbish **laahpsaap**
run, to (for **páau-bouh**
  exercise)
running shoe **páaubouhhàaih**
  [jek]
same, the **yāt yeuhng**
San Francisco **Sāamfàahnsíh**
sandal **lèuhnghàaih [jek]**
Saturday **sīngkèih-luhk,**
  láihbaai-luhk
scarf **génggān [tìuh]**
scenery **fūnggíng**
school **hohkhaauh [gāan]**
school, primary **síuhohk [gāan]**
school, **jūnghohk [gāan]**
  secondary
schoolmate **tùhnghohk [go]**
see, to **tái, gin**
see a film, to **tái-dihnyíng, tái-**
  hei
See you **tīngyaht gin lā**
  tomorrow!
self **jihgéi**
sell, to **maaih**

send something by post, to	gei(-seun)	six	luhk
September	gáu-yuht	sixty	luhk-sahp, luhk'ah
servant's room	gūngyàhnfóng [gāan]	skirt	(bunjiht)kwàhn [tìuh]
seven	chāt	slacks	(sāijōng)fu [tìuh]
seventy	chāt-sahp, chāt'ah	sleep, to	fan-gaau
several	géi	slipper	tōháai [jek]
shall (in predictions)	wúih	slowly	maahn-máan
Shanghai	Seuhnghói	small	sai
Shanghainese (language)	Seuhnghóiwá	small (in body build)	ngáisai
shark	sāyùh [tìuh]	smart (in dress)	sīmàhn
she	kéuih	snow	syut
shirt	sēutsāam [gihn]	snow, to	lohk-syut
shoe	hàaih [jek]	so	gám; gam
shoe, high-heeled	gōujāanghàaih	soccer, football	jūkkàuh
shoe, leather	pèihhàaih	sock	maht [jek]
shoe, sports	bōhàaih	sofa	sōfá [jēung]
shoe shop	hàaihpóu [gāan]	some	dī
shop	dim, pou [gāan]	son	jái [go]
shopping, to go	máaih-yéh	Sorry!	deui mjyuh
short	dyún	south	nàahm
short (in body build)	ngái	Spain	Sāibāanngàh
shorts	dyúnfu [tìuh]	Spanish (language)	Sāibāanngàhmán
should	yīnggōi	speak, to	góng
shower (of rain)	jaauhyúh [chèuhng]	spectacles	ngáahngéng [fu, go]
shower, to (have/take a)	chūng-lèuhng	sports	táiyuhk, wahnduhng
shrimp and bamboo-shoot dumpling	fángwó [jek]	sports shoe	bōhàaih [jek, deui]
shrimp dumpling	hāgáau [jek]	spring roll	chēungyún [tìuh]
		stationery shop	màhngeuihdim [gāan]
sing, to	cheung-gō	stay, to	làuh
sister, elder	jèhjē, gājē [go]	still	dōu, juhng
sister, younger	(mùih-)múi [go]	store	dim, -póu [gāan]
sitting room	haaktēng [go]	street	gāai [tìuh]
		strong	kèuhnggihng
		student	hohksāang [go]
		study	syūfóng [gāan]

study, to	**duhk-syū**
such	**gam**
suit (ladies')	**toujōng [tou]**
suit (men's)	**sāijōng [tou]**
summer	**hahtīn**
Sunday	**sīngkèih-yaht, láihbaai-yaht**
supermarket	**chīukāp-síhchèuhng [gāan]**
sure(ly)	**yātdihng**
surface mail	**pìhngyàuh**
surname, to have the	**sing**
surroundings	**jāuwàih**
sweater, jumper	**lāangsāam [gihn]**
sweep the floor, to	**sou-deih**
sweets	**tòhnggwó**
sweet shop	**tòhnggwódim [gāan]**
swim, to	**yàuh-séui**
swimming pool	**wihngchìh [go]**
Sydney	**Sīknèih**
table, coffee	**chàhgēi [jēung]**
table, dining	**chāantói [jēung]**
Taiwan	**Tòihwāan**
take, to	**daai**
take (a means of transport), to	**daap**
take-away	**līk-jáu**
take pictures, to	**yíng-séung**
tall	**gōu**
tall and thin	**gōu-gōu-sau-sau**
taxi	**dīksí [ga]**
taxi rank	**dīksíjaahm [go]**
tea	**chàh**
teach (in school or university), to	**gaau-syū**
teacher	**sīnsāang, lóuhsī [go]**

telephone	**dihnwá [go]**
telephone, to	**dá-dihnwá**
telephone extension	**noihsin**
television	**dihnsih**
television drama	**dihnsihkehk [chēut]**
television set	**dihnsihgēi [go, ga]**
tell, to	**wah ... tēng**
temperature	**heiwān**
ten	**sahp**
tennis	**móhngkàuh**
tennis racket	**móhngkàuhpáak**
ten thousand	**maahn**
thank you (very much) (for a favor)	**mgōi (saai)**
thank you (very much) (for a gift)	**dōjeh (saai)**
that	**gó**
them	**kéuihdeih**
themselves	**kéuihdeih jihgéi**
then	**gānjyuh, yìhn-hauh, jauh**
then, only then	**sīnji**
there, over there	**gódouh**
there is/are	**yáuh**
they	**kéuihdeih**
thin	**sau**
thing	**yéh [yeuhng]**
thirty	**sāam-sahp, sā'ah**
this	**nī**
this evening	**gāmmáahn**
this year	**gāmnín**
thousand	**chīn**
three	**sāam**
thunderstorm	**lèuihbouh [go]**
Thursday	**sīngkèih-sei, láihbaai-sei**
ticket	**fēi [jēung]**
tidy up, to	**jāp**

tie	tāai [tìuh]	vacuum-clean, to	kāp-chàhn
time	sìhgaan	Vancouver	Wāngōwàh
time, a	chi	vegetables with oyster sauce	yàuhchoi
today	gāmyaht		
toilet	chisó [go]	very	hóu
Tokyo	Dūnggīng	video-recorder	luhkyínggēi [go, ga]
tomorrow	tīngyaht		
tomorrow evening/night	tīngmáahn	video-tape	luhkyíngdáai [béng]
tonight	gāmmáahn	violet	jísīk
Toronto	Dōlèuhndō	visit friends, to	taam-pàhngyáuh
total, in	júngguhng	wait, to	dáng
train	fóchē [ga]	wait a minute, to	dáng yāt jahn/dáng
tram	dihnchē [ga]		
tram stop	dihnchējaahm [go]	waiter	fógei [go]
transport	gāautūng	walk, to	hàahng(-louh)
troublesome	màhfàahn	want, to	yiu
trousers	(sāijōng)fu [tìuh]	want to, to	séung
T-shirt	tīsēut [gihn]	warm	(wān)nyúhn
Tuesday	sīngkèih-yih, láihbaai-yih	wash, to	sái
		wash clothes, to	sái-sāam
twenty	yih-sahp, y'ah	wash the dishes, to	sái-díp
two	yih, léuhng		
type, to	dá(-jih)	wash up (bowls), to	sái-wún
typhoon	tòihfūng [go]		
UK, the	Yīnggwok	watch, to	tái
umbrella	jē [bá]	watch a film, to	tái-dihnyíng, tái-hei
under, beneath	hah(mihn)		
underground railway (in Hong Kong, MTR or Mass Transit Railway)	deihtit	watch football, to	tái-jūkkàuh
		watch television, to	tái-dihnsih
		water	séui
underground (MTR) station	deihtitjaahm [go]	water-melon	sāigwā [go]
		we	ngóhdeih
university	daaihhohk [gāan]	wear, to	jeuk
us	ngóhdeih	weather	tīnhei
USA, the	Méihgwok	Wednesday	sīngkèih-sāam, láihbaai-sāam
usually	tūngsèuhng, pìhngsìh		
		week	sīngkèih, láihbaai [go]

week before last	chìhn go láihbaai/ sīngkèih	winter	dūngtīn
Welcome!	fūnyìhng (gwōnglàhm)	wish to, to	séung
		with	tùhng
west	sāi	woman	néuihyán [go]
what?	mātyéh, dímyéung	wonder, to	mjī
what is the price?	dím maaih a	won-ton noodles	wàhntānmihn
what time?	géidímjūng	wrong number (on the	daap cho sin
when?	géisìh	phone)	
where?	bīndouh	year	nìhn
which?	bīn(+ *classifier/ demonstrative,* e.g. bīn jek, bīndī)	year, last	gauhnín
		year, this	gāmnín
		year before last	chìhnnín
		years of age	seui
white	baahksīk	yellow	wòhngsīk
who?	bīngo, bīnwái	yesterday	chàhmyaht, kàhmyaht
why don't we . . .?	bātyùh		
		yesterday evening	chàhmmáahn, kàhmmáahn
wife	taai-táai [go]		
will (in predictions)	wúih	you (singular)	néih
		you (plural)	néihdeih
wind	fūng [jahng]	young	hauhsāang
window	chēung [jek]	younger brother	dàih-dái, sailóu [go]
window-shopping, to go	hàahng-gāai	younger sister	(mùih-)múi [go]
		yourself	néih jihgéi
windy	daaihfūng, fūngsái kèuhnggihng	yourselves	néihdeih jihgéi
		zero	lìhng

Further reading

Dictionaries

Chiang Ker Chiu (n.d.) *A Practical English–Cantonese Dictionary*. Singapore: Chin Fen Book Store.

Chik Hon Man and Ng Lam Sim Yuk (1989) *Chinese–English Dictionary: Cantonese in Yale Romanization, Mandarin in Pinyin*. Hong Kong: New Asia: – Yale-in-China Language Centre, Chinese University of Hong Kong.

Cowles, Roy T. (1965) *The Cantonese Speaker's Dictionary*. Hong Kong: Hong Kong University Press.

Cowles, Roy T. (1986) *A Pocket Dictionary of Cantonese*. 3rd edn. Hong Kong: Hong Kong University Press.

English–Cantonese Dictionary: Cantonese in Yale Romanization (1991) Hong Kong: New Asia: – Yale-in-China Chinese Language Centre, Chinese University of Hong Kong.

Huang, Parker Po-fei (1970) *Cantonese Dictionary: Cantonese–English, English–Cantonese*. New Haven and London: Yale University Press.

Kwan Choi Wah (1989) *The Right Word in Cantonese*. Hong Kong: Commercial Press.

Lau, Sidney (1973a) *A Cantonese–English and English–Cantonese Glossary to Accompany 'Elementary Cantonese' (Lessons 1–20)*. Hong Kong: Government Printer.

Lau, Sidney (1973b) *A Cantonese–English and English–Cantonese Glossary to Accompany 'Intermediate Cantonese' (Lessons 21–40)*. Hong Kong: Government Printer.

Lau, Sidney (1977) *A Practical Cantonese–English Dictionary*. Hong Kong: Government Printer.

Matthews, Stephen and Virginia Yip (forthcoming) *Cantonese: A Comprehensive Reference Grammar*.

Meyer, Bernard F. and Theodore F. Wempe (1978) *The Student's Cantonese–English Dictionary*. 4th edn. Hong Kong: Catholic Truth Society.

Appendix

Here are two graphic representations of the contours of the six tones of Cantonese, made using *VisiPitch*®, a system which displays pitch traces of spoken language.

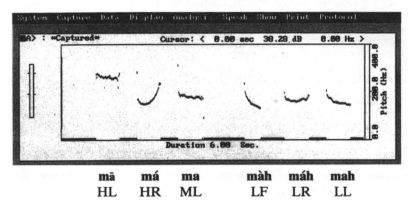

| mā | má | ma | màh | máh | mah |
| HL | HR | ML | LF | LR | LL |

Figure 1 Reproduced by courtesy of Kay Elemetrics Corp.

In Figure 1, the black lines represent the syllable **ma**, pronounced on each of the six tones, in the traditional Chinese sequence. If you have the cassette tapes, you may want to listen to the recorded demonstration.

The first tone (**mā**) is the high level tone, on a consistent high pitch.

The second tone (**má**) is the high rising tone. Notice the curve, which rises from a fairly low pitch almost to the pitch of the first tone.

The third tone (**ma**) is the mid level tone, the tone of one's normal voice.

The fourth tone (**màh**) is the falling tone, falling from a medium pitch to a lower pitch.

The fifth tone (**máh**) is the low rising tone, but the rise is far less obvious compared with that of the second tone.

The sixth tone (**mah**) is the low level tone, which stays more or less at the same pitch. But notice that the difference in pitch between this tone and the third (mid level) tone is smaller than that between the first (high level) tone and the third (mid level).

Note that each of these tones is relative to the other. There is no absolute pitch as, of course, no two people's voices are identical. The important thing to remember is to differentiate the relative levels and contours of the tones, with particular respect to the 'benchmark' third tone, your normal, or neutral, voice level. Provided that each tone is appropriately distinguished in this way, your Cantonese speech will be readily understood.

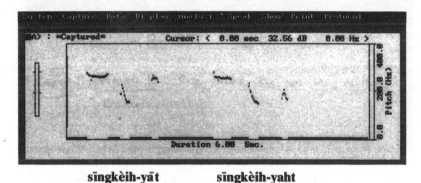

sīngkèih-yāt   **sīngkèih-yaht**

Figure 2 Reproduced by courtesy of Kay Elemetrics Corp.

Figure 2 displays a representation of the words **sīngkèih-yāt** (*Monday*) and **sīngkèih-yaht** (*Sunday*). In both, the first syllable, **sīng**, is pronounced on the first, high level, tone. The second syllable, **kèih**, is pronounced on the fourth, low falling, tone. The words **sīngkèih-yāt** and **sīngkèih-yaht** are distinguished only by the tone of the third syllable. In **sīngkèih-yāt**, the **yāt** is pronounced on the first tone (on the same tone as **sīng**, but note that it is much shorter because of the unexploded final consonant **-t**). In **sīngkèih-yaht**, the **yaht** is pronounced on the sixth, low level, tone. Again, notice how short the word is. However, despite its shortness, its tone is still significant.

Index of grammatical structures (by lesson)